ASEGI STORIES

QWO-LI DRISKILL

ASEGI STORIES

Cherokee Queer and Two-Spirit Memory

THE UNIVERSITY OF
ARIZONA PRESS
TUCSON

The University of Arizona Press
www.uapress.arizona.edu

Printed in the United States of America

21 20 19 18 17 16   6 5 4 3 2 1

ISBN-13: 978-0-8165-3048-9 (paper)

Cover design by Leigh McDonald

Publication of this book is made possible in part by a subsidy from the School of Language, Culture, and Society at Oregon State University.

Library of Congress Cataloging-in-Publication Data
Names: Driskill, Qwo-Li, author.
Title: Asegi stories : Cherokee queer and two-spirit memory / Qwo-Li Driskill.
Description: Tucson : The University of Arizona Press, 2016. | Includes bibliographical references and index.
Identifiers: LCCN 2015033001 | ISBN 9780816530489 (pbk. : alk. paper)
Subjects: LCSH: Cherokee Indians—Sexual behavior. | Sexual minorities—Identity. | Indian sexual minorities—Social conditions. | Gender identity.
Classification: LCC E99.C5 D795 2016 | DDC 975.004/97557—dc23 LC record available at http://lccn.loc.gov/2015033001

♾ This paper meets the requirements of ANSI/NISO Z39.48–1992 (Permanence of Paper).

The root of oppression is loss of memory.
PAULA GUNN ALLEN

I know there is something larger than the memory of a dispossessed people. We have seen it.
JOY HARJO, FROM "GRACE"

CONTENTS

ILLUSTRATIONS

ACKNOWLEDGMENTS

WADO TO MY FAMILY: partner Michael Floyd for his love and support. I couldn't have finished this book without you. *Gvgeyu, Usdi.* *Wado* to my father Paul Driskill, who passed away before he could see this book. I miss you terribly. *Wado* to my mother Jeannie Driskill for always supporting me in being happy. *Wado* to my sister Rebecca Fuller for her love and support. There are few folks who are lucky enough to have a friendship that spans most of their life: *wado* to Colin Kennedy Donovan for gifting me with being one of those lucky few.

Wado to all of my colleagues at Oregon State University, particularly Patti Duncan, who talked me through both ideas and stress and gave feedback early on in the writing of this book. *Wado* to our Oregon State University writing group, Kryn Freeling-Burton, Ron Mize, and Patti Sakurai, for creating a space for me to work and for being willing to read and comment on drafts.

Wado to the other scholars who have been both an emotional and intellectual support during this work, providing feedback and helping me talk through ideas, particularly Chris Finley, Daniel Heath Justice, Scott Lauria Morgensen, Lisa Tatonetti, and Jim Ridolfo.

Some of this work and research started while I was a PhD student in Cultural Rhetorics at Michigan State University. A particular *wado* to Malea Powell, who served as my dissertation director and continues to mentor me and support my work. There is no way to say how grateful I am for all of your love, support, and friendship. *Wado*, as well, Kimberli Lee, my friend and mentor, as well as Jeff Grabill and Terese Guinsatao Monberg for your mentorship.

Wado to my friend and mentor Susan Applegate Krouse, who was a constant support of my work and a close friend while I was at Michigan State University. I miss you, Susan. I'll finish the tear dress.

Wado to my Cherokee wonder twin Angela Haas, for being a dear friend and co-conspirator. *Gvgeyu, Oganali.*

Wado to The Clamecac Collective: Catalina Bartlett, Casie C. Cobos, Gabriela Ríos, Marcos Del Hierro, Victor Del Hierro, Aydé Enríquez-Loya, Garrett Nichols, Stephanie Wheeler, and Alma Villanueva.

Wado to my colleagues at Texas A&M University, particularly Shona Jackson and Vanita Reddy, whose friendships were lifelines to me while living in College Station. *Wado*, as well, to Valerie Balester, Angie Cruz, Amy Earhart, Robert Griffin, Angela Pulley Hudson, and Mikko Tukhanen.

Wado to Kristen Buckles at the University of Arizona Press for believing in this project.

Wado to the research sites and people that allowed me to do archival work for this project: the City of Camden Archives & Museum, Bo Taylor and the Museum of the Cherokee Indian, the Newberry Library, the Mulberry Plantation (James and Mary Boykin Chestnut House), the Peabody Museum of Archaeology and Ethnology at Harvard University. *Wado* to Joe Floyd, who helped facilitate my research in Camden, South Carolina.

Earlier versions of chapter 1 and chapter 5 were published in *GLQ: A Journal of Lesbian and Gay Studies* 16, no. 1–2 (2010): 69–92, and in *Queer Indigenous Studies: Critical Interventions in Theory, Politics, and Literature* (Tucson: University of Arizona Press, 2011), respectively.

Some of the research for this book was supported by grants from Texas A&M University's Glasscock Center for Humanities Research and the Program to Enhance Scholarly and Creative Activities.

Wado to all of the Cherokee Two-Spirit and queer folks who share their words, stories, and memories.

ASEGI STORIES

INTRODUCTION

ASEGI STORIES

Memories Between the Basket Walls

You have to be able to look that far in the future and know. Because if you can see that far into the past, you can see that far into the future. If you look at how our people used to live, you know what was important to them. You can tell. . . . [T]hat's what we try to keep going.

COREY TABER, CHEROKEE TWO-SPIRIT ACTIVIST

SPLINT ꮬꮻ/*SOQUO*/ONE: ꮸꮹꮪ/*TALUTSA*/BASKET

WEAVE BASKETS. Mostly, I weave the double-wall baskets that are closely associated with Cherokees in Oklahoma, but I also weave our old Southeastern style of doublewoven rivercane baskets and coiled baskets.[1] I'm not an expert weaver and still have a lot to learn: how to gather materials for weaving, how to process cane, how to weave other styles of baskets that are now a part of Cherokee weaving traditions. I share this because weaving deeply informs my theorizing about Cherokee Two-Spirit and queer memories and histories and has become my guiding metaphor for thinking about the ways in which Cherokee Two-Spirit and queer people are reimagining our pasts and futures through a practice of re-storying in the present.

By "re-storying," I mean a retelling and imagining of stories that restores and continues cultural memories. Chicana scholar Casie C. Cobos theorizes "embodied storying," the ways in which Chicanas continue Indigenous identities through embodied practices, and writes that embodied storying "requires interrogating ways that History and the archive have acted upon Indigenous bodies and looking for ways that this can be countered by (re)telling stories."[2] *Asegi Stories* centralizes such an interrogation of dominant histories in order to listen to the Other stories and what they do as a tactic to transform our collective futures.

Asegi Stories is a weaving, drawing material from interviews and historical documents in order to articulate Cherokee-centered Two-Spirit critiques that can contribute to larger intertribal movements for social justice. The theoretical and methodological underpinnings of this research draw from numerous activist, artistic, and intellectual genealogies, what Maori scholar Linda Tuhiwai Smith calls "dissent lines."[3] These dissent lines include Cherokee traditions, other Indigenous traditions, women of color feminisms, grassroots activisms, queer and trans studies and politics, rhetoric, Native studies, and decolonial politics. I conceive these dissent lines as splints of cane that are doublewoven with my personal reflections and relationship with these materials in order to create a basket that looks like a book to carry these stories.

Like a rivercane basket, at times a particular splint emerges in the pattern before going back into the larger weaving. An "over/under" weaving pattern that alternates the strands of personal reflections and academic analysis as an intentional part of the design for this book takes inspiration from Marilou Awiakta's use of doubleweaving as a Cherokee-centered writing structure in *Selu: Seeking the Corn-Mother's Wisdom.*[4] In Cherokee "tradition," baskets are usually (though not exclusively) woven by women. This weaving, then, is also intentionally an expression of my identity as *asegi aquadanto*, or "strange hearted" person.

Miami scholar Malea Powell begins her scholarship with the phrase, "This is a story," reminding us that theory and scholarship are always "stories about how the world works."[5] As she points out elsewhere, they are part of a "much larger, more complicated accumulation of stories."[6] This book is also an accumulation of stories, and a reimagining of stories, in order to create new stories for Cherokee Two-Spirit people and larger Two-Spirit movements and communities. A re-storying.

And this reminds me of a story.

I am in Peterborough, Ontario, studying at the summer workshop for the Centre for Indigenous Theatre. All day long we work intensely on an original performance. At night, I spend a lot of time weaving baskets that I want to give to the ensemble and directors at the end of our three weeks together. As I weave, I think about the performance work we are doing together as well as the scholarship I'm pursuing on Cherokee Two-Spirit people and Cherokee performance rhetorics for my dissertation. And, as I weave these small double-wall baskets, I realize that I can press cedar against the inner wall of the basket and weave over the fresh green sprigs with the outer wall so that the cedar can't be seen. But, as the person weaving the basket, I know it's present.

This story is a brief moment, but one that is central to my theorizing about Cherokee Two-Spirit memory. It was through the physical process of weaving baskets that I realized that double-wall and doublewoven baskets create a *third space* between the basket walls. In *The Decolonial Imaginary: Writing Chicanas into History*, Emma Pérez writes, "I believe that the time lag between the colonial and the postcolonial can be conceptualized as the decolonial imaginary." She theorizes the decolonial as "a rupturing space, the alternative to that which is written history" and "that interstitial space where differential politics and social dilemmas are negotiated." She continues, "If the colonial imaginary hides something, then the decolonial imaginary teetering in a third space recognizes what is left out."[7] Chicana theories have done major work in theorizing decolonial politics and the complex relationship between gender, sexuality, colonialism, and nation and are therefore fruitful places from which to think deeply about Indigenous Two-Spirit decolonization. The "dissent lines" I theorize from, then, are meant to contribute to broader political and intellectual alliances, as called for by scholars such as Maylei Blackwell, Casie C. Cobos, Aydé Enríquez-Loya, Gabriela Ríos, Malea Powell, and Andrea Smith.[8]

Cherokee Two-Spirit and queer people have been largely hidden or ignored in the colonial past and present and the "postcolonial," and through the re-storying of Cherokee histories, Cherokee Two-Spirit people are performing a politics of decolonial imagination.[9] There are other memories and stories hidden between the basket walls that rupture the dominant stories told about Cherokees, both by U.S. culture and by particular forms of Cherokee nationalist hegemonies.

The term "Two-Spirit" is a contemporary term being used in Native communities to describe someone whose gender exists outside of colonial logic. It is an umbrella term that references Indigenous traditions for people who don't fit into rigid gender categories. It also, depending on the context, refers to Native people who identify as Gay, Lesbian, Bisexual, Transgender, and Queer.[10]

There are several ways to describe "Two-Spirit" people in Cherokee, and their diversity reflects the limits of any umbrella term in English: *asgayusd' udant[i/a]* (s/he feels/thinks like a man), *ageyusd udant[i/a]* (s/he feels/thinks like a woman), *nudale ageyha udantedi* (different-spirited woman), *nudale asgaya udantedi* (different-spirited man), *sgigi* ("that way"), *uligisdidegi* ("flirt"), *taliqwo didantvn* (s/he has two hearts), *utselidv* (special), *nudale udanto/udantedi* (different heart/spirit), *atsoine* (s/he is third, as in gender), and *asegi udanto/udant[i/a]/udantedi* (strange heart/spirit[ed]). It is this final term that I would like to look to as a critical apparatus from which to both launch a critique of colonial heteropatriarchy as well as to begin to reimagine the histories of Cherokee gender and sexuality. *Asegi udanto* refers, specifically, to people who either fall outside of men's and women's roles or who mix men's and women's roles.[11] *Asegi*, which translates as "strange," is also being used by some Cherokees as a term similar to "queer." *Asegi* provides a means by which to reread Cherokee history in order to listen for those stories rendered "strange" by colonial heteropatriarchy.

My rereading of particular moments in Cherokee history centralizes stories as a critical tool of (re)membering, while (re)telling intentionally challenges the colonial imaginary and colonial renderings of "history." Malea Powell argues for stories as a "rhetoric of survivance" rooted in imagination: "Scholarship is an act of imagination and of telling the stories of that imagining, stories about how the world works."[12] Christopher B. Teuton explains that in the Cherokee language, the word for a storyteller is *gagoga*, which translates as "he/she is lying."[13] He contextualizes this within a Cherokee-centered framework:

> What first may appear as a derogatory name for bearers of tribal oral tradition has its roots in the grammar of the Cherokee language. Cherokee puns allow for a sometimes necessary slippage of meaning in language. . . . As an open-ended term for a culturally central Cherokee art, "lying" has multiple meanings that change with particular cultural contexts. Among Cherokees, telling "lies" refers to storytelling generally, but in particular to telling stories that stretch the imagination and belief.[14]

Cherokee storytelling traditions are a "cultural process of interpreting contemporary experience in relation to the cultural truths traditional stories express."[15] Rather than rooting itself in traditional historiography, *Asegi Stories* retells moments from the past through an understanding that dominant histories are stories that do particular work in the world, and telling *asegi* stories can disrupt these dominant histories through retelling the past through a critical Cherokee queer center.

I don't, then, approach archival documents as a "traditional" historian looking for "evidence" of the past, but rather as a rhetorician, poet, and activist employing what Patti Duncan calls "critical remembering" as a way to (re)tell stories to push against dominant histories: "It is by small acts and insights that change occurs, through a process of critical remembering. By broadening the parameters, pushing the boundaries to their extremes, we reach logical and often illogical conclusions. We begin to alter history."[16] Such "altering" of history reflects Aurora Levins Morales's argument that "[h]istory is the story we tell ourselves about how the past explains our present, and how the ways in which we tell it are shaped by contemporary needs," and that a "medicinal" approach to history disrupts "imperial histories" created as a "substitute for the memories of the colonized."[17] This dynamic process of memory as a story does not attempt to hide my own relationship with these materials or perpetuate the colonial idea that scholars are "objective" observers. This book does not attempt to argue for cultural "truths," but, rather, argues for radical disruption of master narratives through the telling and retelling of stories that disrupt dominant formations of Cherokee history and culture that would erase the presence of same-sex desire and nonbinary gender systems, and, by doing so, erase the sexualized and gendered nature of European and Euro-American colonization of Cherokee land and life. This is a political and activist project.

Asegi stories are the "Other" stories, the "strange" and "queer" stories that are told in the absent presence of Two-Spirit and same-gender-loving people in both archival and embodied memories. They are the stories that Cherokee Two-Spirit people tell each other in order to revise cultural memories. They are "stories that stretch the imagination and belief" as an act of resistance to the erasures of *asegi* memories in imaginations of both colonizers and the colonized. They are the stories hidden between the basket walls. And it is through the (re)telling and (re)imagining of these *asegi* stories that we—as Cherokees—can work to place gender and sexuality at the center of radical decolonial work.

SPLINT ᏪᎵ/TAL/TWO: ᏏᏱᎢ/GANVNV/PATH

My scholarship emerges from personal and political commitments and experiences as a noncitizen, diasporic Cherokee Two-Spirit person and comes from a journey I've been on for several years. In 1994, during my first year as an undergraduate student at the University of Northern Colorado, I read Chrystos's poem, "I Walk in the History of My People." Reading a poem by a woman who was both Menominee and a Lesbian helped me realize that I didn't have to compromise any part of my identity. I was hungry for other reflections of queer Native identities. I started to "come out" in 1994, and shortly thereafter purchased a copy of *Gay and Lesbian Poetry in Our Time*, edited by Joan Larkin and Carl Morse (1988).[18] That collection included the work of several queer Native poets, including Paula Gunn Allen, Beth Brant, Chrystos, Maurice Kenny, and Vickie Sears. Just as importantly, it included an extensive bibliography that listed Brant's *A Gathering of Spirit: A Collection by North American Indian Women* and Gay American Indians (San Francisco)/Will Roscoe's *Living the Spirit: A Gay American Indian Anthology* as resources.

As I searched for other representations of Cherokee queerness, both present and past, I became very interested in trying to find out information about Cherokee "Two-Spirit" traditions, knowing that other tribes had particular "roles" for Two-Spirit people. Frustratingly, representations of Cherokee Two-Spirit people were few and far between. As mentioned, Larkin and Morse included work by Sears. *Living the Spirit* included some Cherokee contributors (Nola M. Hadley, Joe Lawrence Lembo, and Anne Waters). However, there was no historical information available about Cherokee understandings of gender "variance" or sexuality before invasion, and Cherokees were not listed in the list of "North American Tribes with Berdache and Alternative Gender Roles" at the end of the collection.[19]

In 1997, two scholarly collections were published with similar titles: *Two Spirit People: American Indian Lesbian Women and Gay Men*, and *Two-Spirit People: Native American Gender Identity, Sexuality, and Spirituality*.[20] The first collection, while containing some strong essays, included little information about Cherokees. The second—while valuable—also had hardly any historical or social information about Cherokee Two-Spirit people. Scholars were simply not focusing on Cherokee Two-Spirit folks, and there were few Cherokee Two-Spirit creative writers publishing at that time. I couldn't find any reference in books on Cherokee history that mentioned same-sex relationships or nonbinary gender expressions.

I moved from Colorado to Seattle in 1998 to begin work on my master's degree, and there I continued to focus my activist and artistic work on queer and trans communities of color and Two-Spirit issues. In Seattle, I met other Indigenous and Cherokee queer and Two-Spirit–identified people who were involved in similar personal, political, and scholarly projects to articulate Two-Spirit politics and practices in our lives and as part of larger decolonial struggles. Like many other Cherokee Two-Spirit folks, we yearned for information about how Cherokees understood gender and sexuality before colonization in order to find ways to understand ourselves in the present. Mostly we couldn't find this information, and so we imagined with each other what it meant to be Cherokee Two-Spirit people in the present through reimagining stories, bearing witness to each other's lives, and envisioning a radical decolonial future—a process José Esteban Muñoz might say is a tactic of "queer utopian memory, that is, a utopia that understands its time as reaching beyond some nostalgic past that perhaps never was or some future whose arrival is continuously belated—a utopia in the present."[21] Even as our reimagining and retelling of stories revises the past and the future (and refuses Eurocentric notions of linear time), the telling of *asegi* stories is an act of Indigenous queer and Two-Spirit "utopia" in the present, one that resists the ongoing dystopian reality of heteropatriarchal terror through genocidal settler occupation of our homelands.

In the fall of 2004, just after I had left Seattle to begin my PhD coursework at Michigan State University, Kathy Reynolds and Dawn McKinley put a call out to the Two-Spirit community to aid them in a battle against the Cherokee Nation. After these two women had been issued a marriage certificate by the tribe in May of that year, a moratorium on all marriages was placed, and the day before the moratorium was lifted, an objection was filed against the marriage by Todd Hembree, an attorney for the tribe. Reynolds and McKinley's call came shortly before a court date in which they were being asked to demonstrate the historical existence of Two-Spirit people within Cherokee "tradition" in order to justify their attempt at a legal recognition of their marriage.[22] This call— and the encouragement of other Cherokee Two-Spirit and queer friends— prompted me to begin research with Cherokee Two-Spirit people that could revise what performance studies scholar Diana Taylor calls "the rift" between *the archive*, "supposedly enduring materials (i.e., texts, documents, buildings, bones)," and *the repertoire*, "embodied practice/knowledge (i.e., spoken language, dance, sports, ritual)," by creating a record of our experiences through oral histories that will eventually move into an ensemble performance.[23] This project, "On the Wings of *Wadaduga*: Cherokee Two-Spirit Lives," is still in development, but I weave excerpts from these oral histories throughout the text not only to disrupt this rift between archive and repertoire, but also to centralize the stories Cherokee Two-Spirit/LGBTQ people are telling about the past, present, and future. I approach these excerpts not as some kind of ethnographic evidence of cultural truths, but instead as part of what Audra Simpson calls an "ethnographic refusal." She writes, "I refuse to practice the type of ethnography that claims to tell the whole story and have all the answers."[24] These oral histories aren't ethnography at all, in fact, but *asegi* stories that inform my own thinking about Cherokee Two-Spirit memory as well as my understanding about how critical remembering can function to de-normalize dominant tellings of history, what Blackwell calls "retrofitted memory" as a "radical act of re-membering, becoming whole in ways that honor alternative or non-normative ways of being."[25]

When I started this journey as an eighteen-year-old, I felt very much alone. I didn't know any other Native folks who identified as queer or Two-Spirit, so my politics and identity were deeply informed by the work of queer Indigenous feminist writers such as Paula Gunn Allen, Gloria Anzaldúa, Cherríe Moraga, Beth Brant, and Chrystos, as well as the creative work and activism of other queer writers of color such as Audre Lorde and Essex Hemphill. These writer-activists continue to inform my work as a writer and scholar. Toward the end of my time at the University of Northern Colorado, Maidu Two-Spirit poet Janice Gould joined the faculty, and she—along with a few other radical scholars—became a lifeline in an otherwise dangerously conservative atmosphere.

Thankfully, the path to queer and Two-Spirit Indigenous work was cleared by grassroots activists and artists who started this work decades ago (if not more). In 1999, Craig S. Womack (Creek/Cherokee) published *Red on Red: Native American Literary Separatism*, which included his essay, "Lynn Riggs as Code Talker: Toward a Queer Oklahomo Theory and the Radicalization of Native American Studies." Not only did this essay address creative work by a queer Cherokee writer, Womack provided a critical, Indigenous-centered framework with which to look at this work. In 2001, Womack's novel *Drowning in Fire* contributed further to tribally specific queer work.[26]

The ongoing work of creative writers, activists, and scholars has contributed to an emergence of a critical mass of Indigenous queer and Two-Spirit scholarship, including special issues of *GLQ, Studies in American Indian Literatures*, and *Yellow Medicine Review*, the publication of two edited collections (*Queer Indigenous Studies* and *Sovereign Erotics*), and publications by scholars such as Daniel Heath Justice, Deborah Miranda, Scott Lauria Morgensen, Mark Rifkin, Lisa Tatonetti, and Andrea Smith. This scholarship intervenes into colonial ways scholarship is "done," by insisting on centralizing the analysis of *ongoing* settler-colonialism and heteropatriarchy as an entwined project of oppression and control. It also extends an analysis of resistance to such oppression and control. What scholars, activists, and artists are arguing is that homophobia, heterosexism, misogyny, and gender binaries are central to the invasion and occupation

of Indigenous lands and the marginalization, genocide, and oppression of Indigenous people. Resistance, then, must centralize gender and sexuality as a
central site of radical social transformation. My hope for this work isn't, however, that it grows into a "new" area of academic inquiry. Rather, the purpose of
this work is to encourage decolonial activisms through shifting our forms of
analysis across disciplines—and across the perceived divide between grassroots
activism and academic spaces—in order to centralize a critique of the ways heteropatriarchy is used as a form of settler-colonial violence.

The path to *Asegi Stories*, then, is as personal as it is scholarly and activist: I
started this work as a personal journey, and that journey continues to lead me
toward scholarship and activism to re-story Cherokee Two-Spirit people and
is informed by my work as a creative writer and activist participating in scholarly conversations focused on developing Indigenous queer and Two-Spirit
critiques.

As such, this book continues the refusal of Indigenous and other women of
color feminists to separate history, theory, and creative work. Deborah A. Miranda's *Bad Indians: A Tribal Memoir* demonstrates that personal story, familial
experiences, and Indigenous histories are never separate, and that a refusal to
separate the personal from the historical is an act of resistance that takes place
through stories. She writes, "Culture is ultimately lost when we stop telling
stories of who we are, where we have been, how we arrived here, what we once
knew, what we wish we knew; when we stop our retelling of the past, our imagining of our future, and the long, long task of inventing an identity every single
second of our lives."[27] *Asegi Stories* is only one part of a larger, multifaceted storytelling project.

SPLINT KT/*TSO'*/THREE:
RE-STORYING ᎦᏥᏍ (*WADADUGA*)

As I bring these strands together, the *asegi* story of ᎦᏥᏍ (*Wadaduga*, Dragonfly) emerges as a powerful metaphor for Cherokee Two-Spirit people.
ᎦᏥᏍ enters only peripherally in recorded Cherokee stories. Similarly, while
contemporary scholarship has addressed the roles of Two-Spirit/LGBTQ
people within many Native traditions and histories, discussions of Cherokee
Two-Spirits have largely been left out of the discourse. As pointed to earlier,
an absence of such scholarship and the lack of recovered archival documents

regarding identities we might now call "Two-Spirit" has been used by some Cherokees—as in the same-sex marriage case mentioned earlier and, as of this writing, a same-sex marriage ban also passed by the Eastern Band of Cherokee Indians—to argue that Two-Spirit/LGBTQ people are, in fact, not a part of Cherokee "traditions."[28]

There is an old Cherokee story about how Water Spider brought fire to the world on her back. Like all stories, it's a story nested within other stories. James Mooney, an Irish American ethnographer, published a version in 1902. This and similar versions are the most well-known: "In the beginning there was no fire, and the world was cold, until the Thunders . . . who lived up in Gălûñ'lătĭ, sent their lightning and put fire into the bottom of a hollow sycamore tree which grew on an island. The animals knew it was there, because they could see the smoke coming out at the top, but they could not get to it on account of the water, so they held a council to decide what to do."[29] Raven, Screech-owl, Hooting Owl, Horned Owl, the black racer snake, and the great black snake all attempted to get the fire, but each failed. The smoke, fire, and ash gave each of these animals their distinct physical characteristics.

> Now they held another council, for still there was no fire, and the world was cold, but birds, snakes, and four-footed animals, all had some excuse for not going, because they were all afraid to venture near the burning sycamore, until at last . . . the Water Spider said she would go. . . . She can run on top of the water or dive to the bottom, so there would be no trouble to get over to the island, but the question was, How could she bring back the fire? "I'll manage that," said the Water Spider; so she spun a thread from her body and wove it into a *tusti* bowl, which she fastened on her back. Then she crossed over to the island and through the grass to where the fire was still burning. She put one little coal of fire into her bowl, and came back with it, and ever since we have had fire, and the Water Spider still keeps her tusti bowl.[30]

In a footnote, Mooney mentions other versions of this story: "In the version given in the Wahnenauhi manuscript the Possum and the Buzzard first make the trial, but come back unsuccessful, one losing the hair from his tail, while the other has the feathers scorched from his head and neck. In another version the Dragon-fly assists the Water-spider by pushing the tusti from behind."[31]

Mooney's brief mention of ᎦᎸᏍᏍ (*Wadaduga*) opens up an alternate, and often untold, version of the origin of fire. Mooney briefly mentions ᎦᎸᏍᏍ

(*Wadaduga*) again, this time in relation to a story about a stickball game between birds and four-footed animals.[32] This story, like the story of the origin of fire, is also about characters that dwell in liminal spaces and cross boundaries, what both Craig Womack and Daniel Heath Justice might point out as "anomalies."[33] These ways of being—while initially met with derision or skepticism—prove to be valuable assets to community:

> The birds had the Eagle for their captain. . . . The dance was over and they were all pruning their feathers up in the trees and waiting for the captain to give the word when here came two little things hardly larger than field mice climbing up the tree in which sat perched the bird captain. At last they reached the top, and . . . asked to be allowed to join in the game. The captain looked at them, and seeing that they were four-footed, he asked why they did not go to the animals, where they belonged. The little things said that they had, but the animals had made fun of them and driven them off because they were so small. Then the bird captain pitied them and wanted to take them. But how could they join the birds when they had no wings? The Eagle, the Hawk, and the others consulted, and at last it was decided to make some wings for the little fellows.[34]

Wings for ꭹꮆꭵꮗ (*Tlameha*, Bat) were made from the groundhog skin from the head of a drum, and wings for ꮏꭷ (*Tewa*, Flying Squirrel) were made by two other birds by stretching the animal's skin into wings. These two animals helped the birds win the ball game against the larger animals.[35] In a brief explanation of a ceremonial ball game formula in which ꭶꮈꭷꮞ (*Wadaduga*) appears, Mooney writes, "The Watatuga, a small species of dragon-fly, is also invoked, together with the bat, which, according to a Cherokee myth, once took sides with the birds in a great ball contest with the four-footed animals, and won the victory for the birds by reason of his superior skill in dodging."[36]

Because of the way both ꭶꮈꭷꮞ and Cherokee Two-Spirit people have remained marginal in both published work and cultural memories, ꭶꮈꭷꮞ emerges for me as a powerful metaphor for contemporary Cherokee Two-Spirit experiences. And reading into that liminal space—into the *asegi* stories—becomes a guiding principle in order to reimagine and re-story Cherokee histories.

When I began the process of gathering interviews for the oral history performance project mentioned earlier, I was contacted by a Cherokee woman, Cat, who wanted to tell me a version of the origin of fire she had learned.[37] Cat's version of this story helps to re-story ꭶꮈꭷꮞ into our consciousness, much in the same way as the stories that Cherokee Two-Spirit people are telling are re-storying our place within Cherokee communities and futures. Because of the significance of this story to my own theorizing, I include Cat's oral history here in its entirety:

I was really little, I was probably about four or five, it was right before my grandma died. And, we went down to the creek in the morning. And I think we were either looking for crawdads, or we were gonna go get papaws from under the trees down there. And, we were watching the water spiders on the surface of the creek, and the dragonflies. And I was talking about how pretty the dragonflies were, and I always loved the water spiders. So my grandma started telling me the story about how we got fire, and how the Water Spider brought fire in a little bubble on her back. But her story was a little different from what I've heard since, because what she said was along with all the other animals who went and tried and failed and came back different, Water Spider tried and didn't make it because it was just too far. So, Dragonfly offered up her back. And Water Spider got up on the Dragonfly's back and flew to get the fire, and Water Spider got the fire, got back up on the Dragonfly's back, and when the Dragonfly got tired she sat down on the surface of the water and the Water Spider got the rest of the way.

So, the story's a little different from how I've heard it told since. And it's very different from what I've read. And I don't know if my grandmother was doing that because she wanted me to appreciate the dragonflies for what they were, or simply because that was the way she'd heard it. But the other thing she said about the dragonflies after she told the story was, we were watching them and I was admiring their color, how beautiful they were, and she said that I always had to appreciate them because no matter how frail and delicate they looked, that they were very strong. And that they were very fierce hunters and fighters and lovers. And I was a very little girl when she told me that story, and ever since I've never forgotten that, and I've always admired the dragonflies because of that story. And I've always thought of myself that way sometimes. When I get a little afraid or a little . . . you know . . . about the way the world is around me, I think back to that time that was a little more innocent and the power of that moment. And I think of that Dragonfly and I think I need to be like that. Because that was my grandmother's lesson for me, was to tell me that that's what I needed to understand, that was no matter how fragile things seem, that they're stronger than we think. So I think that was about it of the story, that I can really tell you. I mean, I could go through the whole story about the different animals who went to the tree to get the fire, but somehow that doesn't seem right to tell you that right now. But that's my story.[38]

Cat's telling of this story does very different theoretical work than the version of the story that most of us are accustomed to hearing and reading.[39] Rather than a story about Water Spider's individual victory, it is a story of cooperative labor (ᏍᏆ, *gadugi*), of two small animals collaborating in order to ensure the continuance of the world. This version of the story reminds us that there are many stories in Cherokee communities that counter established stories.

It's important to remember that the nature of stories is that they have infinite meanings, that there are "turtles all the way down."[40] A story's significance is constructed through our relationships to and understandings of it. I don't think that "The Origin of Fire" is a "Two-Spirit" story, but, rather, that it is one story of many that can help Cherokee Two-Spirits understand our place within Cherokee cosmology and give us strength in our present revitalization movements. By *doubleweaving* stories of ᏩᏓᏚᎦ (*Wadaduga*) with Two-Spirit stories, additional ways of seeing Cherokee Two-Spirit lives and struggles are able to emerge.

SPLINT ᎤᏯ/*NVG'*/FOUR: DOUBLEWEAVING ᏚᏳᎪ (*DUYUK'TA*) AND ᏍᏆ (*GADUGI*)

Within Cherokee traditions there exist two concepts that are central to my own methodologies, traditions that reflect concerns of critical, decolonial analysis: ᏚᏳᎪ (*duyuk'ta*) and ᏍᏆ (*gadugi*). These concepts demand a balancing of power relationships through collaborative, cooperative scholarship that builds reciprocal relationships.

ᏚᏳᎪ/*DUYUK'TA*

ᏚᏳᎪ is central to Cherokee values and community. In addition to "truth" and "justice," ᏚᏳᎪ is used to translate the following English words: honest, outright, and right. It is also connected with the concept of being pious, *duyugidv asdawadegi*.[41] ᏚᏳᎪ is often referred to as "the White Path," likely because the concept of ᏚᏳᎪ is told through the use of wampum belts, one of which depicts a white path against a field of purple beads. In Oklahoma, the Keetoowah Society—a traditionalist organization—keeps seven wampum belts that are used to teach the concept of **SGAⱺ'** (*duyuk'ta*) as a core religious teaching. The story of the belts is performed annually for Cherokee ceremonial communities in Oklahoma.[42]

SSY/GADUGI

Like **SGAⱺ'** (*duyuk'ta*), **SSY** (*gadugi*) is a concept and practice that serves the continuation and survival of Cherokee communities. Raymond D. Fogelson and Paul Kutsche's 1959 essay "Cherokee Economic Cooperatives: The Gadugi" describes the **SSY** as "a group of men who join together to form a company, with rules and officers, for continued economic and social reciprocity."[43] It is important to point out that, despite the patriarchal language used in this description, women and children are both clearly part of the **SSY** structure. Wilma Dunaway reports, "Men and women alike formed the gadugi, a labor gang that tended the fields and garden lots of elderly or infirm members of the village."[44]

Fogelson and Kutsche trace the **SSY** to town structures, red (war) and white (peace) organizations, as well as agricultural and hunting parties.[45] Looking to the work of James Mooney and Cherokee language speakers in the Qualla Boundary, Fogelson and Kutsche posit that the word *gadugi* is related to *sgatugi* (township) and *gatutiyi* ("town-building place"), and suggests that all of these words have an etymological relationship with *gadu* (bread): "Gadu anigi, according to one informant, means 'to eat bread.' According to the same informant Gadugi means not only the cooperative work organization, but also, 'Where all the group meets and eats bread together.' . . . Our informant told us, 'If a Cherokee asks, 'When are we going to have Gadugi?' he means, 'When are we going to have the bread eating and the working?'"[46] **SSY**, then, is entwined with concepts of community, continuance, and sustenance. It is labor that emerges out of community needs and is carried out to sustain survival. Robert K. Thomas's 1953 thesis, *The Origin and Development of the Redbird Smith Movement*, points out that in the 1890s, "Although the families lived in individual homesteads, much of the work was done communally. The Cherokee of this time were a very compact and united people. Most of the large efforts in their economy were accomplished by community work."[47]

Along with the concept of SGAℰ (*duyuk'ta*), my research seeks to utilize ᏑᏑᏯ as one of its central methodologies. Approaching my work with Cherokee Two-Spirit people with SGAℰ (*duyuk'ta*) as a central methodology helps ensure research that collaborates with and contributes to work happening in Cherokee Two-Spirit communities.

As mentioned earlier, ᏑᏑᏯ (*gadugi*) has a specific relationship with stomp dance communities. Jason Baird Jackson points out that stomp dance grounds are seen "as the present-day manifestations of town organizations," a basic unit of traditional civic organizations for Southeastern Native people.[48] Robert Thomas discusses the fact that when the Keetoowah Society was formed in Indian Territory in 1859, it was "a partial return to some type of town organization. . . . The Keetoowah Society provided for a little captain for each community and for committee members chosen from the community."[49] As the descendants of townships, stomp grounds are sometimes referred to as *sgadugi*. Charlotte Heth's 1975 dissertation on the Cherokee stomp dance music and communities says that the Stokes Smith ceremonial ground is called *ajiskvnvgesdi skadugi* or *ajiskv nagehesda skadugi*.[50] In an analysis of a stomp dance song she translates the phrase *heye gedugi* as "this stomp dance."[51] ᏑᏑᏯ (*gadugi*), like SGAℰ (*duyuk'ta*), has a critical relationship with performance as a means of survival and cultural continuance and locates performance within cooperative communities. ᏑᏑᏯ (*gadugi*) provides an understanding for a methodology that is collaborative, reciprocal, and surfaces out of community needs.

As part of the doubleweaving of ᏑᏑᏯ (*gadugi*) and SGAℰ (*duyuk'ta*), my scholarship responds to calls in Native studies for both tribally/nationally specific and alliance-building approaches. Work by scholars such as Craig Womack, Daniel Heath Justice, and Robert Warrior that calls for nationally centered approaches has been deeply influential on Native studies, particularly Native literary studies. These approaches are deeply important, particularly because of colonial discourse that minimizes and erases issues of sovereignty, nationhood, and cultural specificity in order to create the idea of "the Indian."

Just as importantly, scholars in Native studies have called for radical political and scholarly alliances both within and outside of the field of Native studies. Womack's Creek-centered work, in fact, also argues for alliances in which "tribal specificity and pan-tribalism might corroborate each other."[52]

Andrea Smith has argued that alliances can take place on both theoretical and political levels:

Centering Native American studies as a starting point to articulate method-ological approaches . . . does not suggest that these approaches can be found only within the field. On the contrary, it provides us with an opportunity to see how the concerns of Native American studies intersect, overlap, and/or contra-dict other frameworks, demonstrating that Native American studies is part of a larger world that can inform and be informed by other intellectual approaches and methods. . . . [I]f we really want to challenge our marginalization we must build our own power by building stronger alliances with those who benefit from our work, both inside and outside the academy. When we become more directly tied to larger movements for social justice, we have a stronger base and greater political power through which to resist marginalization. When we build our own power, we can engage and negotiate with others from a position of strength rather than weakness.[53]

A methodological approach rooted in the concepts of ᏍᏏᎩ (*gadugi*) and SᏩᎪᎤᎤ (*duyuk'ta*), then, seeks balance between tribally specific and alliance-building work through drawing on broader conversations and theories (both inside and outside of Native studies) as part of the cooperative labor of schol-arly activism. This book, then, draws not only on scholarship in Native studies, but also from numerous other discourses including feminisms of color, queer theories, and grassroots activisms. As Malea Powell argues, "Maybe, as allies, we can spur one another on to even more disruptive tactics. Maybe we can learn to take hold of one another and emerge at the beginning of a new story about ourselves, not a 'prime' narrative held together by the sameness of our beliefs, but a gathering of narratives designed to help us adapt and change as is neces-sary for our survival."[54]

SPLINT ᎪᎤᎩ/*HISG'*/FIVE: CHEROKEE TWO-SPIRITS IN THE ARCHIVE

One of the goals of this project, and my larger work, is to revise historical mem-ory through both the *archive* and the *repertoire*. Certainly, all Two-Spirit people are currently in a process of uncovering this history, but I think that for some Native people—including Cherokees—this process is more challenging than it is for others. Like the near absence of ᎦᏚᏍ (*Wadaduga*) in recorded stories,

I've encountered very little reference to Cherokee Two-Spirit people in historical accounts, though such references do exist. I am certainly not the only Cherokee Two-Spirit person involved with uncovering these histories, and I am sure that there is more documentation, published and not, than these brief mentions that I am pointing to here. And—as expressed through interviews with Cherokee Two-Spirit people—much of this knowledge is held in the repertoire. In an interview with Daniel Heath Justice, Daniel insists:

> A lot of families have this evidence, as they have Gay and Lesbian and Queer kids, parents, cousins, aunts, uncles, friends, and so on. And they don't necessarily talk about it a lot, but we've all heard stories of very public admissions from high-level people in the community. But these acknowledgments haven't gotten written down . . . there's power in the words. And there are very important traditionalists who have been very vocal about it, some of whom are Queer. So, yeah, we have the evidence.[55]

In addition to the fact that few records about Cherokee Two-Spirit people have been recovered, documentation that has been recovered is often based on European colonists' reactions to Cherokee gender, who thought that *all* of our genders were "variant." Colonists likely saw female warriors or women in positions of leadership as living as men, even though these were acceptable—and important—roles for women in Cherokee gender systems. Trying to glean from colonial accounts which of these female-embodied people might now be called "Two-Spirit" and which were simply acting in accordance with Cherokee traditions for women is very difficult. We must remember these kinds of complexities as we continue to uncover our past and re-story our present.

SPLINT ᏌᏗ/*SUDAL'*/SIX: THE RIBS OF THE BASKET

The chapters of this book are imagined as the ribs of a basket around and through which stories—through rereading history, through interviews, and through personal story—are woven. Chapter 1, "Doubleweaving Two-Spirit Critiques: Building Alliances Between Native and Queer Studies," extends the metaphor of doubleweaving to articulate the importance of deepening conversations about the relationship between colonization, heteropatriarchy, and decolonization and provides a discussion of what I'm calling "Two-Spirit critiques," Indigenous-centered critiques of colonial heteropatriarchy and gender regimes, as central to decolonization.

Chapter 2, "The Queer Lady of Cofitachequi and Other *Asegi* Routes," employs a Cherokee-centered Two-Spirit critique, *asegi* stories, to reread accounts of European invasion in ways that can enable us to understand the colonization of Cherokee genders and sexualities—not only those that we might now refer to as "Two-Spirit" or "queer," but, rather, a colonization that defined all Cherokee sexualities and genders as aberrant, mapping colonial desires onto Indigenous bodies and land.

Continuing an examination of the colonization of Cherokee genders and sexuality, chapter 3, "Unweaving the Basket: Missionaries, Slavery, and the Regulation of Gender and Sexuality," examines missionization and Cherokee adoption of chattel slavery before Removal, as two influences that gave rise to heteropatriarchy and anti-Black racism in Cherokee law and governance, in order to understand the relationship between colonization and heteropatriarchy.

Chapter 4, "Beautiful as the Red Rainbow: Cherokee Two-Spirits Rebeautifying Erotic Memory," continues my work arguing for the erotic as a central location of decolonial resistance by employing the Cherokee concept of "rebeautification" in order to recover histories of Cherokee relationships to love and the erotic.

Drawing on these commitments to both cultural memory and the future, chapter 5, "D4Ᏽ DᏏC (*Asegi Ayetl*): Cherokee Two-Spirit People Reimagining Nation," examines how Cherokee Two-Spirit activists reimagine Cherokee nationhood beyond what Andrea Smith and other scholars call "a nation-state model" through re-storying a Cherokee national past that centralizes Two-Spirit people.

The epilogue, "Doubleweave: An *Asegi* Manifesto," asserts the importance of radical, multi-issue, decolonial activism and calls on activists and scholars to continue to work to re-story the possibilities for future social justice movements.

In my interview with Corey Taber, he asserts: "I've heard our medicine people say that everybody deserves a place at the fire. There's room for everybody at the fire."[56] This book emerges from a similar yearning for a reflection of Cherokee Two-Spirit histories and experiences. It is a weaving that I hope can be used to further both resistance and imagination of—to translate Dr. Martin Luther King, Jr.'s, words into Cherokee—a ᏆᏙᏍᎩ ᏟᎨᎤ (*skadugi tsigeyu*): a "beloved community" in which there is room for "everybody at the fire."

1

DOUBLEWEAVING
TWO-SPIRIT CRITIQUES

Building Alliances Between Native and Queer Studies

THE BEGINNING OF THE TWENTY-FIRST CENTURY is a time in which Indigenous Two-Spirit/LGBTQ people are asserting uniquely Native-centered understandings of gender and sexuality as a means of critiquing colonialism, queerphobia, and misogyny within larger decolonial struggles, as well as the racism and colonialism of non-Native LGBTQ movements. The radical Two-Spirit cultural work from the late twentieth century has cleared a path for Two-Spirit people to form our own modes of critique and creativity that are suited for Native-focused decolonial struggles. Necessary in this process are critiques of both the colonial nature of many LGBTQ movements in the United States, Canada, and other settler-colonial states, as well as the queer/transphobia internalized by Native nations.

Within queer studies, emergent critiques examining the intersections of race, sexuality, and empire—what Martin F. Manalansan IV has called "the new queer studies"—have at once held promise to, and then disappointed, those of us concerned with bringing Native studies and queer studies into critical conversations, or what Malea Powell calls "alliance as a practice of survivance."[1] Our hope for these emergent critiques lies in the thought that a turn in queer studies to more carefully articulate issues of race and nation could open up spaces for a conversation about ongoing decolonial struggles and the relationships between sexuality, gender, colonization, and decolonization in the United States and Canada. Our disappointment lies in the recognition of an old story within "the new queer studies:" Native people, Native histories, and the ongoing colonial project are included only marginally, when included at all. Even while major and hopeful contributions to queer Indigenous studies have emerged—including work by Scott Lauria Morgensen, Mark Rifkin, and Lisa Tatonetti, as well as special issues of *GLQ, Transgender Studies Quarterly, Yellow Medicine Review,* and *Settler Colonial Studies,* and the co-edited collections *Queer Indigenous Studies* and *Sovereign Erotics*—critiques of ongoing settler-colonialism's relationship to heteropatriarchy largely remain contained within work that focuses on Indigenous peoples, and fail to analyze (or even acknowledge) that within settler-states such as the United States, Canada, Australia, and Aotearoa/New Zealand, inseparable racial, sexual, and gendered constructions all take place on occupied Indigenous lands and both over and through Indigenous bodies and peoples.

This disturbs me. It disturbs me because I think that the radical potential of queer of color critiques actually becomes dissipated through all but ignoring Native people. It disturbs me because I think that this erasure colludes with, rather than disrupts, colonial projects in the Americas and Hawai'i, as well as other landbases still engaged in decolonial struggles. It disturbs me because I think that this work is brilliant scholarship that it is deeply necessary, and I *want* it to do better in its relationship with Native people and Native struggles than other intellectual movements in the academy. Sadly, I think it presently falls short of my own impossible desires.

A story.

I am at the Homonationalism and Pinkwashing Conference in New York City. It is an exciting conference that includes radical scholars in queer studies coming together to discuss challenges to (mostly) U.S. imperialism. The conference title comes through Jasbir Puar's important book, Terrorist Assemblages: Homonationalism in Queer Times, *and the work of scholars and activists to disrupt Israel's use of LGBTQ rights to both justify and erase the colonization of Palestine and ongoing human rights abuses against Palestinians. This work is vitally disruptive and provides scholars and activists with further modes of analysis and understanding of how LGBTQ identities are deployed as parts of imperial projects. For the first time outside of a specifically Indigenous studies space, I hear the term "settler colonialism" used often, partially because of Morgensen's important interventions and intellectual alliances, put forth in* Spaces Between Us. *However, I never hear anyone except for Indigenous scholars and scholars in Indigenous Studies ever acknowledge that New York City is built on Lenape land—Lenapehoking—or use "settler colonialism" to discuss the United States or Canada.*

Whose land are you on, dear reader? What are the specific names of the Native nation(s) who have historical claim to the territory on which you currently read this book? What are their histories before European invasion? What are their historical and present acts of resistance to colonial occupation? If you are like most people in the United States and Canada, you cannot answer this question. And this disturbs me. This chapter is meant to challenge queer studies not only to pay attention to Native people and Native histories, but to shift its critiques, in order to include a consciousness about the ongoing colonial reality in which all of us living in settler-colonial states are entrenched.

One of my goals is to challenge queer studies to include an understanding of Native queer/Two-Spirit resistance movements and critiques in its imagining of the future of queer studies itself. Finally, it is my hope that this essay articulates specific Two-Spirit critiques that are simultaneously connected to and very separate from other queer critiques. In short, I am asking all of us engaged in queer studies to remember exactly on whose land it is built.

DOUBLEWEAVE

In order to contribute to decolonial and tribally specific theories, I would like to doubleweave queer and Native concerns into a specifically Indigenous creation.[2] For my purposes here, I imagine the conversation between queer studies and Native studies as a *doubleweaving*. As discussed earlier, doubleweave is a form of weaving in Cherokee (and other Native Southeastern) craft traditions that has its origins in rivercane weaving. Sarah H. Hill writes: "One of the oldest and most difficult traditions in basketry is a technique called doubleweave. A doubleweave basket is actually two complete baskets, one woven inside the other, with a common rim."[3] Doublewoven baskets can have two independent designs, as a result of the weave, one on the outside and one on the inside. Doubling is likewise employed as a Cherokee rhetorical strategy, in which two seemingly disparate rhetorical approaches exist concurrently.

I draw the concept of doubleweave as a feature of Cherokee rhetorical theory and practice through Marilou Awiakta's book, *Selu: Seeking the Corn-Mother's Wisdom*, which is deliberately constructed after doublewoven baskets. She explains, "As I worked with the poems, essays and stories, I saw they shared a common base. . . . From there they wove around four themes, gradually assuming a double-sided pattern—one outer, one inner—distinct, yet interconnected in a whole."[4] Cherokee scholar and creative writer Daniel Heath Justice utilizes the term *doubleweave* as an interpretive device in his essay, "Beloved Woman Returns: The Doubleweaving of Homeland and Identity in the Poetry of Marilou Awiakta," focusing on the balance created between homeland and identity in her work. He writes, "The Cherokee philosophy of balance . . . is the basic foundation upon which Awiakta crafts her work. Intimately connected with the concept of balance is that of *respect*—one cannot exist without the other."[5]

Doubleweave can also be seen as a rhetorical feature of Justice's scholarship as well as of his fantasy fiction series, *The Way of Thorn and Thunder*. In *Our Fire Survives the Storm*, Justice draws on the scholarship of Mary C. Churchill to look to red and white town structures to build a Cherokee methodology that interprets literature. Justice calls these a red "Chickamauga consciousness" and a white "Beloved Path" reading of Cherokee literature.[6] This approach doubleweaves these modco. "Neither exists independently; there is a necessary tension that brings the war and peace perspectives together into constant movement. . . . This interdependence and relationship provides an interpretive guidepost to much of the Cherokee literary tradition."[7] Similarly, *The Way of Thorn and Thunder* uses the structure of fantasy fiction as a way to critique colonialism, racism, queer/transphobia, and misogyny. On the outside of the series is the fantasy genre apparatus, while on the inside is woven a story that deals with historical and contemporary Indigenous politics.[8]

By looking to doubleweave as a Cherokee theory and practice, we can theorize a *third space* that materializes through the process of doubling. Doubleweaving privileges the voices and stories that colonial projects have attempted to destroy but that, hidden in a third space forgotten about by colonial cultures, survive. Concepts of doubleweaving and *third space* lend themselves to critical understandings of Native-centered Two-Spirit/queer critiques. Such critiques, when conceptualized as intertwined walls of a doublewoven basket, enable us to see the numerous splints from which these critiques are (and can be) woven. Such a weaving, then, both utilizes and moves outside the metaphor of "intersectional" politics.

Kimberlé Crenshaw has, now famously, contributed the vocabulary of "intersectional" critiques to radical scholarship and activism. Her work helped to bring conversations already taking place in the work of women of color activists and writers to conceptualize the multiple, interlocking forms of oppression experienced by women of color, and by Black women in particular. Her critiques were meant to specifically elucidate how the logic of antidiscrimination law fails to account for the specific forms of power deployed against Black women. She explains:

> The point is that Black women can experience discrimination in any number of ways and that the contradiction arises from our assumptions that their claims of exclusion must be unidirectional. Consider an analogy to traffic in an intersection, coming and going in all four directions. Discrimination, like traffic through an intersection, may flow in one direction, and it may flow in another. If an accident happens in an intersection, it can be caused by cars traveling from any number of directions and, sometimes, from all of them. Similarly, if a Black woman is harmed because she is in the intersection, her injury could result from sex discrimination or race discrimination.[9]

Since Crenshaw's pivotal essay, "intersectionality" has been taken up as a buzzword in feminist and queer scholarship, too often while retaining racist forms of analysis and practice. Increasingly, "intersectionality" has come under critique by activists as a term emerging from the academy and outside of grassroots movements. The problem with the concept of intersectionality is not Crenshaw's contribution, but the way the word "intersectionality" is misused by activists and academics. I don't reject the metaphor of "intersections" here— Crenshaw's work and the work of other women of color feminist activists and writers are central to my critiques. Doubleweaving utilizes these critiques to understand the multiple ways power functions, while placing Indigenous Two-Spirit critiques at the center.

Though intersections do take place in the process of doubleweaving, the weaving process also creates something else: a story that is much more complex and durable than its original and isolated splints; a story that is simultaneously unique while also rooted in an ancient and enduring form. An *asegi* story. It is from this stance that I wish to look a bit at "the new queer studies" in order to put these analyses in dialogue with Native studies, in order to help build an alliance between queer studies and what I am calling Two-Spirit critiques.

DISIDENTIFYING WITH THE NEW QUEER STUDIES

In his book *Disidentifications: Queers of Color and the Performance of Politics*, José Esteban Muñoz writes, "Disidentification can be understood as a way of

[M]y analysis of "race" in this study is limited to constructions of "blackness" and "whiteness," primarily because prevailing discourses of race and racial segregation in late-nineteenth- and early-twentieth-century American culture deployed this bifurcation more pervasively than other models of racial diversity. . . . I do not specifically interrogate the cultural constructions of Asian, Jewish, or Native American bodies, for instance, but recent work by scholars such as Lisa Lowe, Sander Gilman, and others suggests that this line of inquiry deserves further research.[20]

While Somerville at least addresses the limitation of her analysis, what remains troubling is the question of whether or not constructions of "blackness" and "whiteness" can actually be meaningfully analyzed without an attention to constructions of "Indianness." I would argue that, in fact, they cannot. And while dominant discourses of race that focus on a black/white dichotomy may indeed be those that consciously prevail, this is certainly not because of a lack of discourse around Native people and politics from the late nineteenth and early twentieth centuries. "The Indian problem" was (and continues to be) a central dilemma of an expanding United States. Race cannot be understood in this country if Native people, Native nations, and Native bodies are un-seen.

Does this mean that I expect the writers I mention above—or those in the new queer studies that are not mentioned—to focus their work on Native people? Of course not. It is perfectly understandable to me that Gopinath's work focuses on diasporic South Asian communities, that Manalansan's work focuses on diasporic Filipino Gay men, or that Somerville's work focuses on black/white constructions of race. What is troubling, however, is the way that an analysis of an ongoing colonialism and a Native presence are nearly absent from the building of these critiques, bringing into question whether or not Native people, histories, and decolonial struggles are actually part of their scholarly and political consciousness and imagination.

Native people are not only another group of color that "new" queer critiques should include. The experiences of Native people differ substantially from other people of color in North America, and these differences give rise to very particular forms of critique and resistance. Chrystos writes, "It is not a 'simple' (I use this term sarcastically) war of racism, which is the struggle of other Peoples of Color living here, although we also fight racism. This continent is morally and legally our land, since no treaty has been observed. . . . Logically, then, we remain at war in a unique way—not for a piece of the 'white pie,' but because we do not agree that there is a pie at all."[21]

While I do not necessarily agree that non-Native people of color are fighting for inclusion in an already existing system, Chrystos brings up a major paradigm shift that must take place for solidarity work to happen with Native people: the realization that *the United States and Canada are not postcolonial*. I am among the suspicious ones that Linda Tuhiwai Smith mentions when she writes, "[T]here is, amongst indigenous academics, the sneaking suspicion that the fashion of post-colonialism has become a strategy for reinscribing or reauthorizing the privileges of non-indigenous academics because the field of 'postcolonial' discourse has been defined in ways which can still leave out indigenous peoples, our ways of knowing and our current concerns."[22]

I am similarly suspicious with emergent queer critiques, as valuable as they might be. Native people must *disidentify* with the very critiques that claim to be decolonial and counterhegemonic interventions for queer people of color in order to make them viable for our communities. Through the process of disidentification, other critiques emerge that centralize Native peoples, nations, identities, landbases, and survival tactics, which can be called Two-Spirit critiques. These critiques not only serve to disidentify with queer of color and queer diasporic critique, I believe they create more robust and effective interventions in systems of oppression from which both Native studies and queer studies can benefit.

Through the process of doubleweaving Two-Spirit critiques with queer critiques, I would like to invite an alliance between queer studies and Native studies that can intervene in this un-seeing of Native people, an un-seeing that serves to bolster the colonial project. Powell writes:

> We cannot separate scholarship in the United States from the "American tale." We cannot separate the material exterminations of first-wave genocide in North America (beginning in 1492) from the intellectual and cultural exterminations of second-wave genocide, a process that has been ongoing since the Indian Removal Act of 1830. But we can begin, by consciously and explicitly positioning our work within this distasteful collection of narratives, to open space for the existing stories that might run counter to the imperial desires of traditional scholarship, stories that have been silenced by its hegemonic drone.[23]

In the process of doubleweaving this critique, I am choosing the term *Two-Spirit*, rather than other terms I could use such as Native queer or Native trans people, for several reasons. The term *Two-Spirit* is intentionally complex. It is meant to be an umbrella term for Native LGBTQ people as well as an umbrella term for people who use words and concepts from their national traditions in order to describe themselves.

Like other umbrella terms— including *queer*—it risks erasing difference. But also like *queer*, it is meant to be inclusive, ambiguous, and fluid. Some Native LGBTQ folks have rejected the term *Two-Spirit*, while others have rejected terms such as *Gay*, *Lesbian*, *Bi*, *Trans*, and *Queer* in favor of *Two-Spirit* or tribally specific terms. Still others move between terms depending on the specific rhetorical context. The choice to use the term *Two-Spirit*, as well as the numerous tribally specific terms for those who fall outside of dominant Eurocentric constructions of gender and sexuality, employs what Scott Richard Lyons calls *rhetorical sovereignty*: "Rhetorical sovereignty is the inherent right of *peoples* to determine their own communicative needs and desires in this pursuit, to decide for themselves the goals, modes, styles, and languages of public discourse."[24] Further, contemporary Two-Spirit politics, arts, and movements are part of what Robert Warrior terms *intellectual sovereignty*, "a decision—a decision we make in our minds, in our hearts, and in our bodies—to be sovereign and to find out what that means in the process."[25]

Two-Spirit is a word that itself is a critique. It's a challenge to the field of anthropology's use of the word *berdache* as well as to the white-dominated LGBTQ community's labels and taxonomies. It claims Native traditions as precedent to understand gender and sexuality, and asserts that Two-Spirit people are vital to our tribal communities. Further, *Two-Spirit* asserts ceremonial and spiritual communities and traditions and relationships with medicine as central in constituting various identities, marking itself as distinct from dominant constructions of LGBTQ identities. This is not an essentialist move, but rather an assertion that Indigenous gender and sexual identities are intimately connected to land, community, and history.[26]

Two-Spirit is also useful because it recenters a discussion on gendered constructions, both from within and outside of Native traditions. While important work is being done around Transgender, Genderqueer, and other "gender nonconforming" people and communities, *queer* too often refers to sexualized practices and identities. *Two-Spirit*, on the other hand, places gendered identities and experiences at the center of discussion. Indeed, many of the traditions that scholars and activists have identified in Native communities as "Two-Spirit" are not necessarily about sexuality, they are about gendered experiences and identities that fall outside of dominant European gender constructions. No understanding of sexual and gender constructions on colonized and occupied land can take place without an understanding of the ways colonial projects continually police sexual and gender lines. Two-Spirit critiques, then, are necessary to an understanding of homophobia, misogyny, and transphobia in the Americas just as an analysis of queerphobia and sexism is necessary to understand colonial projects.

Part and parcel of the colonial experience for Native people in the United States is that we are constantly disappeared and un-seen through the stories that non-Native people tell, or don't tell, about us. Too often, other people of color are as complicit in acts of un-seeing Native people as Euro-Americans. Native studies poses a challenge to queer studies, including its most recent waves of scholarship, because it problematizes many of the theories that queer of color critique draws from.

Native people often have an uneasy relationship with other struggles for social justice because the specificity of our struggles—rooted in sovereignty and a claim to this land—is too often ignored, contributing further to our erasure. This includes many of the radical theories which queer of color critique draws from. While women of color feminisms, for instance, certainly have an important place in the struggles of Native people, they have not necessarily included Native concerns in their formations. Native feminist analyses often see patriarchy as a tool of colonization. Chrystos writes, "What we experience is not patriarchy, but the process of colonization, which immigrant women have profited from right along with the greedy boys. Patriarchy is only one of the many tools of colonizer mentality & is often used by women against other women."[27] Similarly, Andrea Smith addresses the ways in which patriarchal violence is used in genocidal projects launched against Native people: "The extent to which Native peoples are not seen as 'real' people in the large colonial discourse indicates the success of sexual violence, among other racist and colonialist forces, in destroying the perceived humanity of Native peoples."[28] Native feminisms, while allied with other women of color and radical feminisms, have very clear decolonial analyses and agendas, see patriarchal violence as a tool of colonialism, and see themselves as part of struggles for tribal sovereignty and land redress.

If queer of color critique claims intellectual genealogies with traditions that have un-seen Native people, what can it offer to Two-Spirit communities? I am not saying it has nothing to offer us. On the contrary, it offers an immense amount of possibility for Two-Spirit scholars and activists. Doubleweaving Two-Spirit critiques substantially challenges queer studies and can push emergent queer theories to more fully realized decolonial possibilities.

in spaces cleared by Two-Spirit activists and artists that work in numerous communities, including their tribal communities, Native urban spaces, non-Native LGBTQ communities, feminist movements, and non-Native communities of color. Warrior argues that Native poets provide a model of the practice of intellectual sovereignty, and should be used as a model for Native critical studies.[33] Many of our most important poets have been, and are, Two-Spirit and/or LGBTQ identified, including Beth Brant, Paula Gunn Allen, and Chrystos. Through collections such as Brant's *A Gathering of Spirit* and Gay American Indians and Will Roscoe's *Living the Spirit*, Two-Spirit people have used artistic spaces as part of Two-Spirit critiques.[34] Two-Spirit critiques within academic writing, then, should not only look to these artists as models but also remain accountable and accessible to Two-Spirit communities outside of the academy. Native studies insists on methodologies and theories that are rooted in, responsible to, and in service of Native communities. Like women of color feminisms, Native studies positions itself as activist scholarship that centralizes the relationship between theory and practice. Queer and feminist theories in the academy have a history of "theorizing" themselves away from grassroots communities. Not only do Two-Spirit critiques remain accountable to both academic and nonacademic audiences, they are informed by Two-Spirit artist and activist movements. Being Two-Spirit is a tactic of resistance to white supremacist colonialism. Two-Spirit critiques see theory practiced through poetry, memoir, fiction, story, song, dance, theater, visual art, film, and other genres. Theory is not just *about* interpreting genres, these genres *do* theoretical work. Two-Spirit critiques remember that "the only difference between a history, a theory, a poem, an essay, is the one that we have ourselves imposed."[35]

3. TWO-SPIRIT CRITIQUES ENGAGE IN BOTH INTERTRIBAL AND TRIBALLY SPECIFIC CONCERNS.

A growing number of Two-Spirit organizations and gatherings in the United States and Canada have focused on creating Two-Spirit communities across tribal nations, using the common goal of (re)claiming Two-Spirit identities as a way of bringing Native people together.[36] While intertribal, Two-Spirit critiques also insist on tribally specific approaches as a way to create intertribal alliances and coalitions. Just as there is no such thing as a generalized "Native" person, there is no such thing as a general "Two-Spirit"identity. As pointed out in the introduction, there are several words and ways to talk about "Two-Spirit" people in Cherokee, not one umbrella term. Two-Spirit identities and tactics are "rooted in a solid national center."[37] Kathy Reynolds and Dawn McKinley's legal battle against the Cherokee Nation of Oklahoma, for instance, was very specifically a Cherokee struggle, not only to validate a same-sex union under the Cherokee Nation's law, but also to reestablish specific Cherokee cultural memory of same-sex relationships and unions and challenge the notion that community recognition of same-sex relationships is outside of Cherokee cultural precedent.

4. TWO-SPIRIT CRITIQUES ARE WOVEN INTO NATIVE FEMINISMS BY SEEING SEXISM, HOMOPHOBIA, AND TRANSPHOBIA AS COLONIAL TOOLS.

As queer of color critique draws on and expands women of color feminisms, Two-Spirit critiques draw on Native feminisms specifically to understand heterosexism and gender regimes as manifestations and tools of colonialism and genocide. As Andrea Smith argues, "U.S. empire has always been reified by enforced heterosexuality and binary gender systems. By contrast, Native societies were not necessarily structured through binary gender systems. Rather, some of these societies had multiple genders and people did not fit rigidly into particular gender categories. Thus, it is not surprising that the first peoples targeted for destruction in Native communities were those who did not fit into Western gender categories."[38] Homophobia, transphobia, and misogyny, then, are part of colonial projects intent on murdering, removing, and marginalizing Native bodies and nations.

5. TWO-SPIRIT CRITIQUES ARE INFORMED BY AND MAKE USE OF OTHER NATIVE ACTIVISMS, ARTS, AND SCHOLARSHIPS.

Two-Spirit critiques use the materials available to weave radical and transformational critiques. Indigenous critical theories, decolonial activism, and radical artistic traditions—even if not "Two-Spirit"—are useful in the doubleweaving of critical Two-Spirit resistance. Gerald Vizenor's concept of trickster hermeneutics, for instance, could lend itself to Two-Spirit critiques: "The trickster is reason and mediation in stories, the original translator of tribal encounters; the name is an intimation of transformation, men to women, animals to birds, and more than mere causal representation in names. . . . Trickster stories are the translation of liberation, and the shimmer of imagination is the liberation of the last trickster stories."[39]

Drawing on Vizenor's work, Powell has noted that "the androgyny of the trickster offers compelling possibilities for unpacking gender binaries in feminist rhetorics. In stories, the trickster is often assigned gender, but frequently cross-dresses and mutates as well."[40] As Powell also notes, trickster figures have played an important role in work by several Native women, including Two-Spirit women such as Beth Brant, Janice Gould, and Chrystos.[41] Vizenor's concept of trickster hermeneutics, then, lends itself to Two-Spirit critiques.

Womack has likewise pointed to tricksters in relation to Two-Spirit people: "[T]he thinking behind the term 'queer,' which seems to celebrate deviance rather than apologize for it, seems embodied with trickster's energy to push social boundaries."[42] He goes on to look at the term Two-Spirit as itself a trickster tactic.[43] Similar, perhaps, to disidentification, trickster hermeneutics critique, transform, and create new possibilities in the ruptures of discourse.

6. TWO-SPIRIT CRITIQUES SEE THE EROTIC AS A TOOL IN DECOLONIAL STRUGGLES.

Two-Spirit critiques see the erotic as a power that can aid in the healing of historical trauma, disrupt colonization, and reclaim our bodies, lands, lives, and languages. Elsewhere I have suggested that a *sovereign erotic* can be utilized as a Two-Spirit tactic for healing.[44] Other Two-Spirit writers and artists, such as Clint Alberta, Beth Brant, Chrystos, Daniel Heath Justice, Deborah Miranda, and Gregory Scofield have likewise formulated the erotic as central to Indigenous resistance.

7. TWO-SPIRIT CRITIQUES SEE TWO-SPIRIT IDENTITIES IN RELATIONSHIP WITH SPIRITUALITY AND MEDICINE.

This, I think, is an important difference between Two-Spirit critiques and (other) queer critiques. Two-Spirit critiques position Two-Spirit identities as part of responsible spiritual relationships with Native communities, landbases, and historical memory. Anguksuar (Richard LaFortune) explains:

The term *two-spirit* . . . originated in Northern Algonquin dialect and gained first currency at the third annual spiritual gathering of gay and lesbian Native people that took place near Winnipeg in 1990. What we who chose this designation understood is that *niizh manitoag* (two-spirits) indicates the presence of both a feminine and a masculine spirit in one person.

More essentially, it may refer to the fact that each human is born because a man and a woman have joined in creating each new life; all humans bear imprints of both, although some individuals may manifest both qualities more completely than others. In no way does the term determine genital activity. It does determine the qualities that define a person's social role and spiritual gifts.[45]

The stance that Two-Spirit people carry very particular medicine is one rooted within Native world views and landbases, and separates itself from non-Native belief systems as part of larger practices of maintaining and continuing Native cultural practices.

Taking these splints of Two-Spirit critiques and doubleweaving them into a conversation with queer studies pushes queer studies in the United States and Canada toward decolonial work that is responsible to the land it lives and builds itself on. Two-Spirit critiques simultaneously challenge and bolster work in queer studies that seeks to decentralize white, male, middle-class formulations of queerness. Through Native disidentifications with queer studies, Two-Spirit critiques and queer critiques can be complicated and more fully realized.

David Eng, Judith Halberstam, and Jose Esteban Muñoz have asked, "What does queer studies have to say about empire, globalization, neoliberalism, sovereignty, and terrorism? What do queer studies tell us about immigration, citizenship, prisons, welfare, mourning, and human rights?"[46] In an attempt to answer such questions, Two-Spirit critiques point to queer studies' responsibility to examine ongoing colonialism, genocide, survival, and resistance of Native nations and peoples as well as radically engage with issues of gender and sexuality. Two-Spirit critiques are part of ongoing weavings to resist colonialism, queer and gender oppressions, and the un-seeing of Native peoples and histories. "On our separate, yet communal journeys," Beth Brant tells us, "we have learned that a hegemonic gay and lesbian movement cannot encompass our complicated history—history that involves so much loss. Nor can a hegemonic gay and lesbian movement give us tools to heal our broken Nations. But our strength as a family not only gives tools, it helps *make* tools."[47] Two-Spirit critiques are a *making* that asks all of our disciplines to formulate analyses that pay attention to the current colonial occupation of Native lands and nations and the way Two-Spirit bodies and identities work to disrupt colonial projects.[48] By doubleweaving and paying attention to Two-Spirit critiques, our scholarship can aid in the resistance and struggles of Native communities and help create theories and movements that are inclusive and responsive to Indigenous Two-Spirit people.

2

THE QUEER LADY OF COFITACHEQUI AND OTHER *ASEGI* ROUTES

MULBERRY PLANTATION: CAMDEN, SOUTH CAROLINA, OCTOBER 2014

I STAND ON THE EDGE OF AN OVERLOOK *at a river that moves slowly below us. "Don't get too close to the edge," the woman who owns the plantation tells me, "the ground there is eroding." What stories are in this eroding ground? What memories does the river hold? I remember the enslavement of generations of African and Indigenous peoples. The moment when the people of Cofitachequi looked down and across the river to see De Soto's army waiting on the other side. The major disruptions to Indigenous life after De Soto's army left smallpox, swine, and the spaces of stolen bodies in its wake.*

As the plantation owner shows me the plantation grounds, she points out the Catawba Path that runs through this landbase. She tells me of how she used to find artifacts as a child playing on these grounds. I am excited to see river cane still growing on the edge of the woods as we drive across the grounds, and she stops her truck so I can take a picture. I wonder what patterns were woven into mats and baskets here, imagine this place before colonization, genocide, and chattel slavery. Colonists found river cane throughout the Southeast a barrier to plantations and farming and tried to eradicate it. They didn't understand that the complex rhizomatic system of roots held the land together.[1]

FIGURE 1. Rivercane, Mulberry Plantation. Photograph by Qwo-Li Driskill.

I am here because the Mulberry Plantation is thought to be the sight of Cofit-achequi, a city written about by De Soto's chroniclers that was governed by a woman called "the Lady of Cofitachequi." It was not a Cherokee city, but the moment of De Soto's army invading this area—and "the Lady of Cofitachequi's" resistance while traveling as a prisoner through Cherokee territory—opens up an asegi *rereading of history that helps us understand the relationship between colonialism and heteropatriarchy, particularly for Southeastern Indigenous peoples, and recognize larger mappings of colonial heteropatriarchal desire onto Indigenous bodies and lands.*

THE QUEERING OF CHEROKEE BODIES

In order to begin to listen for the narrative wisps of Cherokee Two-Spirit people and Cherokees who had relationships with members of the same gender, we must understand that within dominant European worldviews *all* Cherokees were characterized as gender-nonconforming and sexually deviant. Early records from European men make this characterization numerous times, emphasizing and Otherizing Cherokee women's sexual and social power and autonomy. Cherokee culture became characterized as one in which all Cherokees behaved in ways Europeans thought only men should behave, and, because of this, Cherokee men feminized. While same-sex sexualities and people we would now call Two-Spirit are rarely mentioned, I think this is in part because such people are rendered invisible within a larger characterization of all Cherokees as always-already gender-nonconforming and sexually deviant. The specificities of Cherokee understandings of same-gender-loving people and people outside of European gender binaries, then, often become indiscernible because all Cherokees, and other Southeastern Indigenous people, were characterized as having disruptive, and strange, genders and sexualities.

This chapter is doublewoven. Two stories created from numerous strands converge here into one weaving. One story is the analysis of colonial representation of Southeastern Indigenous genders and sexualities in the Southeast. The other story is my own "theory in the flesh"² —my imaginings and grappling with this information. These colonial stories have everything to do with our bodies as asegi *people. They're personal and intimate.*

One of the problems with some contemporary scholarship on "gender" and "sexuality" among Native people is often an assumption—unconscious or not—of the existence of these things we now call "gender" and "sexuality" in the first place. Within our contemporary, colonized frameworks, we project contemporary constructions of these ideas onto the past.

As an activist and rhetorician, I know that my own "passionate attachments," as Jacqueline Jones Royster says, are present in this project.[3] Walter Mignolo writes, "The past is a set of possible worlds that cannot be changed and voices that cannot be restored, but we could certainly change our current perception of the past by constructing new images of how things might have been if they were not what missionaries and men of letters told us they were."[4] I want to claim, then, an *asegi* approach to these histories as an *intentional* and *named* troubling that might critically interrogate the ways in which such histories are often approached and how we choose to remember.

In her history of Choctaw women, Michelene E. Pesantubbee asserts that because of colonial erasures and bias around Southeastern Indigenous women, "we must look to innovative ways to theorize about women's roles."[5] Pesantubbee, then, draws on numerous disciplines as well as broader Southeastern women's histories to reconstruct Choctaw women's history. Drawing on Pesantubbee's stance, my reimagining of Cherokee *asegi* presence looks to broader histories and memories of colonial gender violence in the Southeast. We may only be able to locate limited "evidence" of Two-Spirit Cherokees in the archives, but we can imagine *asegi* spaces within the dominant record in order to understand those erasures and in order to create *asegi* memories.

Something keeps pulling me back to these moments in history when everything in our world changed. I don't think that our world before colonization was some kind of fantasy free of power or pain. But there is something here that feels hidden, a larger story. Because the De Soto expedition only briefly passed through Cherokee territory, and there are no descriptions of mass violence, the violence of the entire De Soto expedition through Cherokee territory is erased.

We had wars before European invasions. We had a revolution to end the misuse of power by a ruling class. We had a history of resistance long before European invasion. And we have a memory that spans to the beginning of the universe. European invasions are just a small moment in our history.

But there is a memory in that moment when De Soto's army and Cherokees first set eyes on each other. It burns. A hot ember I don't notice at first and then I see it burning through my shirt, burning into my heart. It makes me hold my breath. I keep trying to imagine what that moment was like, and then stop myself. There's some-

thing about that imagining that feels like betrayal. I don't know that world, or what was to follow. There's something about that imagining that feels absolutely necessary. And dangerous.

As asegi yvwi *we often imagine who we were before. Before invasion and Removal. We ask questions. We find each other and tell each other stories. Stories we're told by elders, by our tradition bearers who are brave enough to speak. Stories from our own experiences. These stories are nothing like the stories colonists told and tell about us.*

There are stories colonists told to each other in these first moments, and they unleashed the stories that followed. Over and over again. One expedition after another. Looking for land for plantations and treasure. Looking for human bodies to use as slaves. Rape. Cut into pieces. To use for dogs to hunt.

There are some stories that get passed down in our families. They haunt me. Bloody footprints left in snow eaten by starving dogs. Steamboats. The terror some of the people had at seeing and hearing a train for the first time, thinking it was Uktena.

There are some stories that don't get passed down in our families. They haunt me more.

This chapter is a story, too. A story that uses our knowledge as *asegi aniyvwiya* to reexamine and undo the colonial narratives mapped onto our bodies. A story that attempts to understand a gap in cultural memories that begins with the De Soto expedition.

One of the reasons the De Soto expedition and the stories it told and tells is important is that the accounts of this expedition created literal and figurative maps across the Southeast that were used by colonists afterward. Mishuana Goeman contends that "these early events have set up gendered colonial structures that continue to dominate and enact violence on both the interpersonal and state level on Native peoples," and that they created "spacial violence asserted through . . . geographical imaginings and subsequent mappings."[6] Juan Pardo and others attempted to retrace De Soto's route through the Southeast through the stories chroniclers told. But these routes are not just literal—the chronicles of De Soto's expedition also mapped gendered colonial violence onto our lands and bodies, told stories about who Indigenous people were in the Southeast that created a paradigm and precedent for the colonists that were to follow. As colonists after De Soto attempted to retrace his army's steps through descriptions of people and places, the reinscription of heteropatriarchal violence took place as well. My interest here is specifically in the tropes about Southeastern Indigenous genders and sexualities that emerged through these colonial accounts as colonists attempted to claim land and bodies for use in European empire building.

People we now call "Two-Spirit" are not entirely absent from these chronicles, but when we do appear it is against a larger backdrop in which colonists use the presence of people they recognized as outside of a gender binary system as evidence of the need for colonization. More broadly, though, all Indigenous people became characterized through dominant European gendered frameworks that constantly placed Indigenous people in positions to be colonized: we are characterized either as desiring colonization and subservient to male colonial power, or as rebellious and a threat to male colonial power. Either way, the final argument from colonists is that Indigenous lands and bodies should be colonized.

Because of the absence—or perceived absence—of *asegi* people in colonial records, we need to imagine *asegi* stories that revise and revive cultural memories of nonbinary gender systems and same-sex love and erotics. As Jodi Byrd writes, "To read mnemonically . . . understands indigeneity as radical alterity and uses remembrance as a means through which to read counter to the stories empire tells itself."[7] While such a revision of cultural memories entails pointing to *asegi* presence in the archive, historical records written by colonists present versions of Indigenous cultures in the Southeast that best serve colonial interests. However, we can center *asegi* stories in the way we approach these records to understand the spaces and moments rendered strange and queer by colonists. We can use *asegi* stories as a tool in a Two-Spirit—rather than heteropatriarchal and colonial—imaginary. *Asegi* stories are moments of rupture and chaos in heteropatriarchal colonial narratives.

Heterosexuality within written Cherokee histories is often assumed as a natural given, and the presence of men and women in "marriages" or who have children with each other seen as evidence of heterosexuality. The problem, of course, is that the concepts of "heterosexuality" and "homosexuality" did not exist until they were coined by Károly Mária Kertbeny in 1868 and later brought into Western discourse through the emerging field of psychology in the late nineteenth century. Foucault argues that "sexuality" is a "steady proliferation of discourses," and Eve Sedgwick argues that these discourses create binaries through which dominant Western society creates knowledge through a "language of sexuality [that] not only intersects with but transforms the other languages and relations by which we know."[8]

Human behavior, desire, love, relationships, and sex are much more fluid and complex than these easy cleavages between "heterosexual" and "homosexual," and—as queer theory has long pointed out—only recently tied to identity. Not only does this binary—a Western and colonial one—erase the fact that most humans do not fit into such a binary, it also structures ways of seeing and knowing. This means that, within our current colonial context and through acts of memory—both in our communities and through academic discourse—the past (and present, and even future) are often understood through what Judith Butler calls *the heterosexual matrix*, "that assumes that for bodies to cohere and make sense there must be a stable sex expressed through a stable gender (masculine expresses male, feminine expresses female) that is oppositionally and hierarchically defined through the compulsory practice of heterosexuality."[9]

What happens, then, when we look at past documents, or listen to stories of the past, or try to make sense of history, is that we often assume "heterosexuality" as "natural" and "normal," and as the identity and behavior of most humans. We assume male/female sexual relationships and reproduction as evidence of "straightness" and project contemporary heterosexist bias (and, for that matter, contemporary LGBT identities) onto our readings, memories, and conceptions of the past. However, understanding that the concepts of "heterosexual" and "homosexual" are recent European and colonial inventions and that most humans experience love, desire, and sex outside of such binaries enables us to understand the absence and presence of same-gendered love and erotics and genders outside of a colonial binary.

Why, then, the use of the term "heteropatriarchy" to describe a system of power and control that employs an understanding of "heterosexuality" as a concept? To explain that "heterosexual" and "homosexual" are recent social constructions is not to erase the fact that within dominant Western logics and systems of power the binary opposition "man/woman" is central, or that discourses of sin, sodomy, lust, etc., did not exist. These, of course, predate the creation of the "heterosexual/homosexual" binary. "Proper" gender and sexual behavior were still violently enforced, systems of what Foucault calls "bio-power" deployed through invasion and colonization—via attempts to ensure Christian male power through the control of women's reproduction—that were taking place in Spain at the time of the first Columbus invasion in 1492. Ideas of sin, sodomy, correct behaviors for "men" and "women"—which included a patriarchal family structure as well as a governmental structure—already carried with them the enforcement of particular kinds of highly racialized/classed opposite-gendered relationships and behavior in order to control women's reproduction and ensure the continuation of "pure" bloodlines. Roxanne Dunbar-Ortiz and Peter Rachleff explain how ideas of race were developed and deployed through the Inquisition: "Before this time the concept of biological race based on 'blood' is not known to have existed as law or taboo in Christian Europe or anywhere else in the world. As scapegoating and suspicion of *conversos* and *moriscos* intensified in Christian Spain, the doctrine of *limpieza de sangre*, 'purity of blood,' was popularized and had the effect of granting psychological, and increasingly legal, privileges to 'Old Christians' thereby obscuring the class differences between the poor and the rich."[10]

Similarly, Gregory S. Hutcheson and Josiah Blackmore assert that *limpieza de sangre* and control of women's reproduction and "*honra* (the integrity of the female body) . . . are ultimately manifestations of the same master discourse, the conflation of notions of purity and orthodoxy into a reflexive impulse against the threat of racial, cultural, and sexual queerness (and the desires invoked by each)."[11]

These regulations over bodies, behaviors, and desires were not considered somehow evidence of separate sexualities. In fact, these enforcements show that Spain (and other colonial powers) saw these as *acts* that all people were vulnerable to committing without the disciplining powers of the church and state.

ASEGI SPACES

Within Cherokee cosmologies, humans must help maintain a system of balance and justice—*duyuktv*—within all relationships with both the human and the more than human world. *Duyuktv* is necessary in order to ensure the continuance of the world as well as Cherokee peoplehood. *Duyuktv* is reflected in all "traditional" systems of governance and cultural practices. Rowena McClinton explains: "The Cherokees tried to keep things associated with opposing sections of the cosmic order separate to avoid dire consequences. . . . The Cherokees' categorization of the cosmos and their desire to keep their classifications pure produced an elaborate ritual and ceremonial system. The Cherokees valued order and believed things should stay in their place; therefore, they attached special meanings to anomalies because these occurred along the interstices of their categorical systems."[12]

"Anomalies" in Cherokee and other Southeastern systems are often seen as powerful in ways that hold potentially generative and destructive qualities simultaneously. While all things must be kept in order, throughout Southeastern cosmologies anomalies appear that are sometimes generative and sometimes destructive (or both). Craig S. Womack theorizes anomalies through Tie-Snake, as a "queer" figure "who is part of the underworld realm in Creek cosmology, is part of the balance of oppositions, that fragile tension wherein Upper World, Lower World, and This World cohere."[13] Daniel Heath Justice takes a "theory of anomaly" further, as a way of understanding queer identities within Southeastern Indigenous contexts. His approach helps to render *asegi* spaces legible in cultural memories: "I propose . . . the Mississippian category of *anomaly* . . . to understand queerness and tribal belonging in ways that affirm the most inclusive ideals of our shared dignity and kinship while also explicitly addressing the lived realities of queer Native people."[14]

Southeastern Indigenous conceptions of the universe often focus on balance between dualities, but this is not necessarily a strict binary opposition between two separate poles. Mary C. Churchill challenges the notion of an "oppositional model" often used in academia to discuss Cherokee cosmologies. She writes, "There is evidence to the contrary that Cherokee traditions could be more accurately interpreted in terms of an indigenous-based model of complementarity rather than opposition."[15] Within traditional Cherokee township governance structures of Red (war) and White (peace) towns, "all Cherokee towns were capable of assuming either a Red or White stance as needed."[16] Similarly, the status of "Beloved" for elder men and women was a status one obtained after war, childbirth, or menstruation—the shedding of blood—was over. Even the concept of *duyuktv* suggests a third space that mediates these dualities—the Middle world between Upper and Lower, the stickball game as a mediation of war and peace, the status of "Beloved" men and women as peacemakers who had been warriors, and *ani asegi didantvn*, "strange hearted people" outside of men's and women's roles.

Duyuktv, then, is not just a balance between two binaries, but balance in a multidimensional, spherical cosmology constantly in motion and constantly at risk of imbalance. While dominant European traditions, for instance, conceive of four directions (north, south, east, and west), Cherokee cosmologies understand three more (above us, below us, center). The center is mobile. Each of us is the directional center of wherever we are. The sacred fires in ceremonial communities—that once existed in all townships—are likewise multiple, even while they're representative of a larger whole. *Duyuktv* suggests balance in *ay-etl*—the middle/center, the seventh direction and the place of the sacred fire. It might be more appropriate to understand Cherokee cosmologies—including gender—more like a spinning jack that must be kept in motion through constant human action than a static space between two unmoving poles.

An *asegi* retelling of history, then, looks to these anomalous spaces between worlds as productive both in a balancing of different worlds as well as in throwing the structured world of colonial accounts and interpretations of history into generative chaos. *Asegi* stories assume the following: (1) That opposite-sex relationships, constructions of labor, households, and reproduction are not heterosexual and that opposite-sex relationships do not, in fact, mean that people were not also in same-sex relationships. (2) That heterosexuality is a colonial construction and that a "reading" of Cherokee (or other Indigenous) family structures as always in relationship with dominant Western heteropatriarchy is a settler-colonial act. (3) That colonial powers saw all bodies—not only Indigenous bodies—as needing the disciplinary powers of the state and the church to ensure "correct" gender and sexual behavior. (4) That the queering of Cherokee/Indigenous bodies and nations in colonial discourse was (and is) a project to justify invasion and colonization (but that doesn't mean that same-gender sex/relationships didn't exist). In short, we can employ an *asegi* imaginary as a tactic in a "decolonial imaginary" to examine the strange, queer, and anomalous spaces that exist between the colonial and the postcolonial in order to rupture colonial narratives.[17]

An *asegi* remembering of the past assumes that, regardless of how it was (or was not) defined, most people had same-gender intimacies, sometimes recognized by colonists as "sodomy" or otherwise "uncivilized" gendered/sexual behavior, and sometimes not seen at all. What *was* seen and commented on by colonists was how Cherokee and other Indigenous people's gender roles and expressions (labor, family structure, clothing, sexual practices, and body adornment) did or did not conform to European concepts of correct gendered hierarchies and behaviors.

COLONIZATION AND HETEROPATRIARCHY

Since the first waves of invasion into Cherokee territory, European men were shocked, threatened, and titillated by Cherokee—and other Southeastern

Indigenous—gender and sexuality. Throughout numerous European invasions, Indigenous nations and bodies are written of always in relationship to heteropatriarchal colonization as either complicit with, or hostile toward, colonial goals. The gendered and sexualized process of colonization is now well established by the work of Indigenous queer and feminist scholars, artists, and activists. And the brutal actions of Spain throughout the Americas are well documented. The relationship between Cherokees and Spanish colonialism, however, is often neglected, partially, no doubt, because Spain was not successful in establishing a permanent settlement in Cherokee territory and other Indigenous nations in the "interior" of Southeastern North America.

But if we neglect to look in greater depth at these invasions—both in Cherokee territory and in neighboring nations—we also neglect to have an understanding of histories of colonization in our territories. Each attempt at colonization in the Southeast created routes for later colonists, not only by providing details of geographic features and Indigenous nations—and reporting resources and treasures that would make further colonization worthwhile—but also by mapping European gender and sexuality onto Indigenous nations and bodies, which would be repeated over and over again in later European "explorations" of Indigenous lands. Casie C. Cobos contends that "[c]artography, rather than only the study of maps and their productions, works within and through bodies."[18] Colonial invasions and explorations of Indigenous territories, then, work through the gendering and sexualization of Indigenous bodies and lands in order to place both Indigenous peoples and landbases into colonial legibility in order to facilitate European expansion, settlement, and claim of resources (including human bodies). These gendered and sexual mappings precede De Soto—they can be traced all the way to the Columbus invasions, and even earlier. There are many places we can start this story, but in this telling it begins with the interactions between De Soto and his army and "The Lady of Cofitachequi," who is rendered in colonial accounts as "queer," not because of a contemporary understanding of gender or sexuality, but because her status as a female leader who resisted European Christendom's gendered and sexual norms positions her as strange, troublesome, and chaotic in colonial accounts. It emerges on the ground of what is now the Mulberry Plantation near Camden, South Carolina, where a queer story begins as the Lady of Cofitachequi sees De Soto's army waiting for her on the other side of the river—on the edge of memory where my feet back away from the eroding cliff. Where river cane still grows despite attempts by colonists, plantation owners, and farmers to eradicate it. This is an *asegi* story.

FIGURE 2. Looking across the river from the Mulberry Plantation, the site of the city of Cofitachequi. Photograph by Qwo-Li Driskill.

Columbus. De Soto. De Vaca. Balboa. Cortez. Pardo. Luna. Names of invaders haunt our history as Indigenous people. They're not unconnected—all of them were part of establishing Spanish power in the Americas.

There are other paths, other stories. Old trade routes that have nothing to do with European invasion. Robert Warrior reminds us, "Trade routes . . . have existed in the Americas since the first pathways linking people emerged in a time that no one can remember. Those pathways became trails and then networks of trails that crisscrossed the single landmass that is the Americas."[19] As I sit with these texts, maps are always present. Maps of our lands. Maps through our lands. Charting and documenting resources. Routes to enable trade and settlement. Not all invaders created literal maps, but instead described travels and interactions with Indigenous peoples that were later used to make maps. Gender and sexuality, and colonial desires for their regulation, are a constant presence in these descriptions, mapping colonial desires onto Indigenous bodies. Walter Mignolo contends that maps, "once they are accepted . . .

become a powerful tool for controlling territories, colonizing the mind and imposing themselves on members of the community using the map as the real territory."[20] In the process of exploration and mapping, colonial gender and sexuality likewise were imposed on Indigenous people, not only through violent representation, but also through very real violence and genocide. In this story, the maps appear alongside the writing to remind readers of the descriptions of colonial routes that take place through gendered and sexualized colonial accounts. What the maps don't show—but are a constant presence in colonial accounts—are the routes through and over our bodies.[21] Routes cleared by our bodies. Bodies left in the wake of invasions. Bodies stolen. Bodies that resisted and escaped.

What the maps don't show is our bodies.

ROUTE I: THE DE SOTO EXPEDITION

Hernando De Soto's first encounter with Cherokees was in 1540. Lucas Vázquez de Ayllón had already brought African slaves to build a settlement called San Miguel de Guadalupe (thought to have been at the mouth of the Pee Dee River in what is currently being called South Carolina). San Miguel de Guadalupe was the first European settlement in what is now called the United States, the first place a group of enslaved Africans was brought to in what is now the United States, and, soon after it was built, the site of the first slave rebellion (which included both African and Native slaves).

In order to understand the context of imperial violence of De Soto's brief travels through Cherokee territory, it's important to provide a sketch of De Soto and his army's expedition in the Southeast. De Soto was a Spanish *hidalgo*, a member of the Spanish nobility with "pure Christian blood." He traveled to the Americas with Pedraris Dávila, the first Spanish governor of Panama. He was inspired by Juan Ponce de León and Núñez de Balboa and participated with Balboa in acts of colonial violence. He became a *regidor* of León, Nicaragua, in 1530, and, later, a captain in Francisco Pizarro's invasion and colonization of the Inca, returning to Spain and receiving a share in stolen riches from the King of Spain. He wanted to become the governor of Guatemala because he hoped to find a route to the Pacific Ocean, but was "given" Cuba instead and was told to colonize North America within four years in exchange for land, wealth, and power.

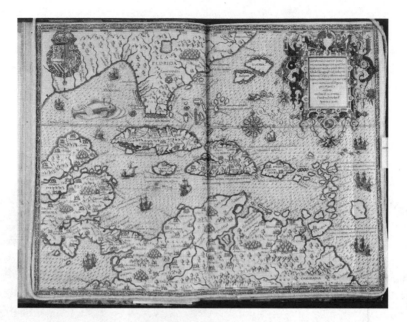

FIGURE 3. Map by Theodor de Bry, 1594. Theodor de Bry, "Occidentalis Americae Partis, vel earum Regionum Quas Christophorus Columbus," Yale University Library, Beinecke Rare Book & Manuscript Library, Digital Collections, http://brbl-dl.library.yale.edu/vufind/Record/3518998.

De Soto was actively participating in genocide even before coming to the Southeast. He was trained by Balboa, who, notoriously now, had Two-Spirit folks ripped to pieces by dogs. In Paul E. Hoffman's biography of De Soto, he writes that "De Soto's first known participation in a raid was with Vasco Núñez de Balboa's expedition of August 1515 into the Cueva Indian province of 'Dabaiba,' up the Rio Grande River in Panama."[22] Only two years earlier in what is now called Panama, Balboa slaughtered six hundred (according to colonial accounts) Indigenous people. "Unable to face the arrows of our archers, they turned and fled, and the Spaniards cut off the arm of one, the leg or hip of another, and from some their heads at one stroke, like butchers cutting up beef and mutton for market."[23] After this butchering of Indigenous people, Balboa led a slaughter of people we would now call Two-Spirit:

Vasco discovered that the village of Quarequa was stained by the foulest vice. The king's brother and a number of other courtiers were dressed as women, and according to the accounts of the neighbours shared the same passion. Vasco ordered forty of them to be torn to pieces by dogs. The Spaniards commonly used their dogs in fighting against these naked people, and the dogs threw themselves upon them as though they were wild boars or timid deer. . . .

When the natives learned how severely Vasco had treated those shameless men, they pressed about him as though he were Hercules, and spitting upon those whom they suspected to be guilty of this vice, they begged him to exterminate them, for the contagion was confined to the courtiers and had not yet spread to

FIGURE 4. Theodor de Bry, "Valboa throws some Indians, who had committed the terrible sin of sodomy, to the dogs to be torn apart," 1594. "Theodor de Bry's America," Special Collections, University of Houston Libraries, http://digital.lib.uh.edu/collection/p15195coll39/item/87.

the people. Raising their eyes and their hands to heaven, they gave it to be understood that God held this sin in horror, punishing it by sending lightning and thunder, and frequent inundations which destroyed the crops. It was like wise the cause of famine and sickness.[24]

Deborah A. Miranda uses Maureen S. Hiebert's term *gendercide* to describe this specific attack on Indigenous people, and, more broadly, to describe Spanish atrocities against Indigenous peoples of California. Miranda argues, "This is not homophobia. . . . What the local Indigenous people had been taught was gendercide, the killing of a particular people *because of their gender*." Gendercide is employed as a particular tool of larger genocidal projects, a system that becomes internalized through brutal—and often performative—violence. Miranda asserts, "Now that the Spaniards had made it clear that to tolerate, harbor, or associate with the third gender meant death . . . the indigenous community knew that demonstrations of acquiescence to this force were essential for the survival of the remaining community," a process that "continues to fester in many contemporary Native communities."[25]

This particular incident is often cited and remembered as an example of the deployment of gendered/sexualized violence against people we now call "Two-Spirit." It is important to understand the larger context of this attack—one that comes after the "butchering" of hundreds of Indigenous people. Such acts of violence are meant to not only destroy Indigenous people and squelch resistance, but to terrorize Indigenous people through horrifying attacks on systems of gender and sexuality. Heteropatriarchal gender regimes become a central means to physically, psychologically, and spiritually control Indigenous people.

It is within this context of gendercide that De Soto launched his attempt to conquer what is now the Southeastern United States. Hoffman makes this context of violence clear:

That he was happy to engage in the "hunting of Indians" is well attested by events in Nicaragua, Peru, and La Florida. . . . Trained in Indian warfare in the schools of Balboa, Espinosa, and Pedrárias, he approached all Indians with the Central American tradition, which was one of brutal oppression directed at rulers, first of all. On at least two occasions, he was party to, and probably led, the burning of Indians as a method of torture. He had no qualms about the Indian slave trade either in Central America, where slaves were branded on their foreheads, or in La Florida.[26]

Without these larger, intertwined narratives, the context of gendercide in Cherokee territory is rendered invisible. While De Soto's path through Cherokee towns is only mentioned briefly, these brief mentions are part of gendered, sexualized, and colonial violence that would be continually repeated in other waves of encroachment. *Asegi* memories of these moments revise our understandings of colonization by centralizing a critique of heteropatriarchy in order to make explicit the gendered and sexualized violence of colonization and examine the numerous routes of gendered/sexualized violence across our lands and bodies.

THE QUEER LADY OF COFITACHEQUI

De Soto's expedition provides the first mention in colonial records of Cherokee people. His expedition through Cherokee territory was made possible through the kidnapping and forced guidance of the "*cacica*" of Cofitachequi ("The Lady of Cofitachequi").[27] Cofitachequi was a large and powerful nation thought now to be Catawban, and the city of Cofitachequi was near what is now Camden, South Carolina.[28] The Lady of Cofitachequi can be imagined as occupying an *asegi* space through her perceived anomalous authority, through her mediating of different worlds in an attempt to maintain balance, and through her disruption of heteropatriarchal colonial control. Within colonial accounts, Cofitachequi only becomes legible through rendering her as first within a male/female binary and, then, as resistant to colonial patriarchal authority as an Indigenous, non-Christian woman.

While there may not be any archival evidence that she was Two-Spirit, there is also no archival evidence that she was not. Nor could there be. Because even while gender and sexual norms were highly policed by the Spanish, they were policed inside a worldview that assumed a gender binary. Even those outside the binary would only be recognized by the Spanish as being outside the binary if they also seemed somehow to be *crossing* a dual-gender system. A male living as a woman and a female living as a man, for instance, would be recognized by the Spanish as outside of gender norms and, thus, recognizable in colonial records. People might be recognized (and often were) as "sodomites" or "hermaphrodites." But people living within genders outside of a binary system—let's say, who saw "gender" as a sphere rather than a binary—wouldn't have been legible. And, because "sodomites" were very specifically males, women who had sexual or romantic relationships with other women would also not have been legible. We have no evidence that Cofitachequi was someone who would be now considered Two-Spirit. But it's colonial, heterosexist, and gender-binary thinking that would assume she is someone who would now be considered heterosexual and gender normative.

However, whether or not she was someone we would now call "Two-Spirit" is not my central concern. Rather, I'm interested in looking at how Cofitachequi is rendered *queer* by the accounts of De Soto's invasion, and how this might enable us to critically remember Cofitachequi through *asegi* stories in order to create a space in which, in the words of David L. Eng, "history as the way-it-really-was gives over to alternative modes of knowing and being, through which forgotten histories and subjects might come to inhabit the world in a different manner."[29] Such an approach enables us to more deeply interrogate heteropatriarchy as a tool of colonization and reimagine our past and future.

Cofitachequi is referred to as a "*cacica*" with enormous power and (most importantly to De Soto) access to an abundance of riches and knowledge of how to get to other nations throughout the Southeast. Her body becomes central to enabling De Soto to find a route through the Southeast that can enable Spanish access to wealth and resources. A chronicler called the "Gentleman of Elvas"[30] writes that, before meeting Cofitachequi, her sister (or niece—the accounts are unclear on this point) is sent to speak with De Soto beforehand. She delivers the following speech: "Excellent Lord: My sister orders me to kiss your Lordship's hands and say to you that the reason why she has not come in person is that she thought she could better serve you by remaining as she is doing to give orders that all her canoes should be made ready quickly so that your Lordship might cross and so that you might rest, for you will be served immediately."[31] Rodrigo Rangel, another of the chroniclers, recorded the following:

> Friday, the last day of April, the Governor took some on horseback, the most rested, and the Indian woman Baltasar de Gallegos brought as guide and went toward Cofitachequi and spent the night hard by a large and deep river, and he sent Juan de Añasco with some on horseback to try to have some interpreters and canoes ready in order to cross the river. . . . The next day the Governor arrived . . . and principal Indians came with gifts, and the cacica, ruler of that land, came, whom the principal [Indians] brought with much prestige on a litter covered in white (with thin linen) and on their shoulders, and they crossed in the canoes,

and she spoke to the Governor with much grace and self-assurance. She was young and of fine appearance, and she removed a string of pearls that she wore about the neck and put it on the Governor's neck, in order to ingratiate herself and win his good will.[32]

The context of gendered violence and enslavement might be subtle in this brief excerpt, but it is important to know that "the Indian woman Baltasar de Gallegos brought as guide" was a slave. Cofitachequi's sister's address to De Soto sets a tone of service and compliance to De Soto's army. The characterization of the *cacica* as "young and of fine appearance" followed by a scene of her giving De Soto a string of pearls "to ingratiate herself and win his good will" reflects a context of Spanish gendered and colonial violence, particularly because we know—as does this chronicler—that she was soon to be captured and forced to guide the expedition to find further treasures and protect the soldiers from attack. This powerful woman, then, is characterized as bowing to Spanish patriarchal power. It was likely unknown to the Spanish, and misinterpreted as evidence of Spanish power, that gift exchanges of wampum and other shell beads were part of larger systems of Indigenous diplomacy and protocols throughout the East.[33] Far from "ingratiating" herself, the leader of Cofitachequi likely saw herself as in a position of power over De Soto and his expedition, though certainly under threat, and entering into a diplomatic negotiation.

In another account, which attempts to contain Cofitachequi and frame her within a Spanish understanding of gender and power, Cofitachequi is characterized as supportive of the Spanish. She is described not only as sending ambassadors to the Cherokee town of Guaxule, but also as warning Cherokees that they must serve De Soto and his army or she would declare war on them:

When the governor and his captains learned of this it caused them wonder and new gratification to see that that Indian lady had not been content with the service and entertainment she had given them in her own house and country with such affection and good will, but had also provided it in other [provinces]. From this they came to understand more clearly the will and desire that this lady always had to serve the governor and his Castilians, for thus it was that though she did everything she could to please them, and they saw it, she always asked the general's pardon for being unable to do as much as she wished for them, which so afflicted and depressed her that the Spaniards themselves had to console her.

By these manifestations of a generous spirit and others that she showed toward her vassals, according to what they themselves said publicly, she showed herself to be a woman truly worthy of the states she possessed and of other greater ones, and undeserving of being left in her heathenism. The Castilians did not offer her baptism because . . . they had the intention of preaching the faith after having made settlements and an establishment in that country, and marching continually as they did from one province to another, without stopping, they had little opportunity for preaching.[34]

Cofitachequi's power is only spoken of as in service to her "will and desire . . . to serve the governor and his Castilians" and she is characterized as so wanting to help De Soto's army invade, enslave, rape, and steal throughout the area that she is inconsolable. While her power as a woman is characterized as unusual to the Spanish, it would not have been unheard of. The monarchies of Spain and the rest of Europe certainly included queens and noblewomen. However, Cofitachequi is contained within Spanish narratives of feminine nobility, who obtained power through relationships with powerful men in order to continue patrilineal royal lines. De Soto certainly understood her as a leader, but only to the extent that she would provide him with protection, food, slaves, treasure, and a safe route into neighboring nations. De Soto, as Spanish male nobility and the governor of Spanish-occupied Cuba leading an army planning to conquer the continent, certainly wouldn't have characterized Cofitachequi as having more power than him, even if she did. In order to argue for Spanish settlement and demonstrate to the crown that the Southeast was conquerable, De Soto's chroniclers would need to characterize Indigenous nations in the Southeast as either savage—and thus needing to be contained by Spanish imperialism—or noble, and thus willing to concede power to the Spanish and aid them in their colonial project.

This particular narrative's departure from other accounts of the *cacica* of Cofitachequi enables us to understand more critically the *asegi* space Cofitachequi presented to the Spanish as well as the development of colonial tropes of Native people: the savage, the heathen, the noble savage, and the Indian princess. Cofitachequi is characterized as submissive to Spanish heteropatriarchy through the formation of sexualized/gendered hierarchies between her and Spanish powers. She is praised here not only for her generous hospitality, but also for "the will and desire that this lady always had to serve the governor and his Castilians," so distraught by not being able to give more that the Spanish console her. She is characterized as a powerful but benevolent queen within a European framework through the "generous spirit" she "showed toward her vassals," exemplifying characteristics of European Christian noble femininity in order both to argue for conversion but also to provide an explanation as to why she wasn't converted and brought under the control of the church. Characterizing Cofitachequi within gendered colonial frameworks makes her "worthy of the states she possessed," and "worthy," as well, of being converted to Christianity and having Spanish settlements built in the boundaries of her nation. It is the absence of baptism that is characterized as tragic, since Cofitachequi's desire to aid Spanish male powers demonstrates that she is "undeserving of being left in her heathenism."

Interestingly, this is a radically different description of Cofitachequi—and De Soto's army—from that offered by other accounts. This rupture between narratives allows us to imagine an *asegi* telling of history that centralizes how colonial gender and sexual violence were central to invading powers, and, further, how Indigenous resistance can be imagined as an *asegi* space that throws colonial power into chaos while rebalancing Indigenous communities.

Other chroniclers of De Soto's invasion discuss Cofitachequi's power, but do not represent her as a willing accomplice to Spanish invasion. Also absent from the account above are reports of De Soto and his soldiers looting burial sites in the city of Cofitachequi. Rather than a willing accomplice to De Soto, other accounts say that Cofitachequi is forced to accompany his army to Cherokee territory, where she escapes De Soto along with three slaves. Even some of the chroniclers are critical of De Soto's treatment of Cofitachequi. Elvas writes:

> On May 3, the governor set out from Cutifachiqui, and because the Indians had already risen, and it was learned that the cacica was minded to go away if she could without giving guides or tamemes for carrying because of offenses committed against the Indians by the Christians—for among many men there is never lacking some person of little quality who for very little advantage to himself places the others in danger of losing their lives—the governor ordered a guard to be placed over her and took her along with him; not giving her such good treatment as she deserved for the good will she had shown him and the welcome she had given him.[35]

Rangel's account states, "from there where it is stated they crossed the river in water up to their shins, the cacica of Cofitachequi, whom they took with them in payment of the good treatment that they had received from her, turned back."[36] Elvas continues:

> The governor set out from Xualla for Guaxule, crossing over very rough and lofty mountains. Along that way, the cacica of Cutifachiqui, whom the governor brought as above said for the purpose of taking her to Guaxule—for her lands reached that far—going one day with her slave women who were carrying her, stepped aside from the road and went into a wood saying that she had to attend to her necessities. Thus she deceived them and hid herself in the woods. . . . She took with her a box of canes made like a coffer . . . filled with unbored pearls. Some who had most knowledge of them said they were very valuable. An Indian woman was carrying them for her whom she took with her. . . . She took it and went to stop at Xualla with three slaves who had escaped from the camp and with a horseman who remained behind, for being sick with fever he wandered from the road and was lost. This man, named Alimamos tried to have the slaves abandon their evil intention and go with him to the Christians—which two of them did. . . . They related how the cacica had remained in Xualla with a slave of André de Vasconcellos who refused to come with them, and it was very certain that they held communication as husband and wife, and that both had made up their minds to go to Cutifachiqui.[37]

According to Rangel's account, "In that [province] of Xalaque a comrade deserted who was named Rodríguez . . . and also a shrewd young Indian slave from Cuba, who belonged to a gentleman called Villegas, and a very shrewd slave of Don Carlos, a native of Barbary, and Gómez, a very shrewd black man of Vasco González."[38] "Xalaque" is Rangel's transliteration of "Tsalagi"—and we see from his account that the beginning of De Soto's journey into Cherokee territory is one which is characterized as a major disruption of Spanish power.

Cofitachequi's escape is a moment of *asegi* possibilities for memory and resistance. She escapes with others brutalized by the Spanish, in Cherokee territory, in a moment that can be seen as rebellion and alliance between her and other diasporic Indigenous people. This moment can be remembered as resistance against colonization, European enslavement, gender oppression, and the constant threat of sexual violence. These descriptions starkly contrast with descriptions of Cofitachequi as prostrating herself to colonial power. No longer a generous and benevolent feminine figure, she is characterized as a deceitful thief who throws De Soto's army into a state of crisis, aiding others in a "shrewd" and "evil" escape. In Rangel's account, Rodríguez's (and other soldiers') desertion and Cofitachequi's escape enrages De Soto: "[B]ecause that day Alonso Romo led the rear guard and left them, the Governor made him return for them, and they awaited them one day; and when they arrived, the Governor wanted to hang them."[39]

Cofitachequi becomes an *asegi* figure not only through the way her power is characterized as simultaneously extraordinary and vulnerable to colonial men in these accounts, but also through aiding Gómez's escape as well as through a real or assumed sexual relationship with him. The Spanish racial caste system was very specific, and Spanish nobility very concerned with "pure" Christian bloodlines. The assumption that Cofitachequi and Gómez "held communication as husband and wife" signifies two unruly, racialized bodies in defiance of colonization through an alliance that threatens normative colonial gendered, raced, and sexualized deployments of power.

Further, Gómez isn't the only slave who escapes with Cofitachequi. According to Rangel's account above, a member of the De Soto party, an unnamed Indigenous Cuban (Taíno, Guanajatabey, or Ciboney) slave, an unnamed slave from North Africa, Gómez, and the women carrying her (who may or may not have been her slaves) all escape and join Cofitachequi. In Elvas's account, she also escapes with another Native woman carrying a basket of pearls, taking the pearls with her. While Elvas writes that the horseman Alimamos persuaded two of the slaves to return (if this account is correct, there is no doubt that it could have only taken place under violence or threats of violence), Rangel's account makes no mention of anyone returning. The next day, or within a few days (accounts differ in this regard), the De Soto party arrives in the Cherokee town of Guaxule and, a few days after that, in the Cherokee town of Canasoga.

Cofitachequi's leadership as a woman, her resistance through escape, and her "communication" with Gómez are rendered as "queer." Earlier character-izations of Cofitachequi as willing to help De Soto become understood as using her femininity as an intentional deceit and as a tool to trick De Soto and lure his slaves to freedom through sexual transgression. While the *cacica* of Cofitachequi was not Cherokee, it is during these moments that the De Soto expedition first invaded Cherokee territory. The De Soto expedition was brutally violent, regularly took Native people as slaves, and viewed Indig-enous women as sexual commodities who were, as Andrea Smith describes, inherently "rapeable."[40] The interactions between De Soto and Cofitachequi become part of a larger gendered and sexualized mapping of Indigenous bodies in the Southeast. Just a short time after Cofitachequi's escape and after passing through the Cherokee towns, De Soto invaded the Koasati town of Chiaha:

> Saturday, the fifth of June, was the day that they entered in Chiaha. . . . The Indians were with the Christians fifteen days in peace; they played with them, and also among themselves; they swam in the company of the Christians, and in all they served them very well. They went away afterward one Saturday, the nineteenth of the month, because of a certain thing which the Governor asked them for; and in short, it was that he asked them for women. The next day in the morning, the Governor sent for the cacique, and he came then, and the next day the Governor carried him with him ⌊as a hostage⌋ to make the people return, and indeed they came. In the land of this Chiaha was where these Spaniards first found the towns palisaded. . . . Chiaha gave them five hundred tamemes, and they consented to leave off collars and chains.[41]

Sexual violence is employed as a tool of colonization as De Soto demands women to be given as sexual slaves. He then takes the leader of Chiaha as a hostage and five hundred Native people are handed over to De Soto to be used as slaves. The first waves of invasion of the Cherokee and other Southeastern nations by the Spanish take place in a context of sexual violence, theft, war, and enslavement, set against a backdrop of a female leader creating gendered, sexual, and racial chaos that challenges colonial control.

This *asegi* account of the "Lady of Cofitachequi" enables us to critically interrogate the context of heteropatriarchal colonial violence in which the Spanish invaded Cherokee territory. Not only does much of this story take place within Cherokee territory, the characterization of Cherokee people parallels some accounts of Cofitachequi's feminized, complicit generosity. While, at first glance, the accounts of interactions between De Soto's army and Cherokees appear to be relatively peaceful, an *asegi* reading of these accounts enables us to more clearly perceive the context of gendered and sexual colonial violence.

Cofitachequi had not yet escaped De Soto by the time De Soto's army reached Cherokee territory. Unlike the city of Cofitachequi and other towns within the Lady of Cofitachequi's jurisdiction—which the Spanish mark as rich in resources (including people) and easily cultivated—Cherokee lands aren't seen as useful in colonial expansion. Lawrence A. Clayton, Edward C. Moore, and Vernon James Knight, Jr., write that De Soto's "experiences at Cofitachequi . . . served to create a new piece of knowledge . . . about the Southeast: that these interior places would be good for Spanish settlement and might, because of dense Indian populations, allow the establishment of *encomiendas*, whose members would cultivate the soil for their new lords."[42]

The chronicles, then, serve as a record of places that would be most useful to Spanish imperialism. Elvas's description of Cherokee territory doesn't describe the kinds of resources that the Spanish hope for: "In seven days, the governor reached a province, by name Chalaque, the poorest land in maize seen in Florida. The Indians live on roots of herbs which they seek in the open field and on game killed with their arrows. The people are very domestic, go quite naked, and are very weak."[43]

De Soto was concerned with the resources the Spanish could extract—and also utilize in the expedition, as food had become a major concern during this part of their exploration. The perceived absence of food is not only a concern for the survival of De Soto's army, but a marking of a lack of resources the Spanish could take. The mention of Cherokees living off of roots and herbs and hunting game is a way of marking both the Cherokees as unthreatening savages and the land as not hospitable to Spanish settlement. Further, language such as "very domestic," "quite naked," and "very weak," signals to Spanish powers that Cherokees might be easily conquerable. The nakedness of Cherokee bodies is not only perceived as evidence of savagery and lack of resources, but when fused together with being "domestic" (as in the distinction between domestic and wild animals) and "very weak," it signals vulnerability to Spanish male military power. Within a gendered framework of Spanish colonialism, the naked Cherokee body, and the description of Cherokees as "domestic" and "quite weak," frame Cherokees as feminine in relation to Spanish patriarchy, and as easily "domesticated." While the possibilities of Spanish agriculture and an *encomienda* system are signaled as infeasible, the vulnerability and possibility of Cherokee people being conquered and enslaved is simultaneously signaled. Cherokees in this area might not have the agricultural or monetary resources the Spanish hoped for, but their "domestic" and "weak" state signifies that they could easily be brought under Spanish control.

While Elvas describes Cherokees as people susceptible to Spanish violence, in Rangel's account De Soto's first interactions with Cherokees are characterized by what is perceived as resistance. Rangel writes, "[H]e arrived at the province of Chalaque; but he could not find the town of the lord, nor was there an Indian who would disclose it."[44] There are two possible interpretations of this passage. One is that of resistance: Cherokees refused to disclose the location of the nearest leader. Seeing that De Soto held Cofitachequi captive would have been enough to lead them to not disclose the location of any leader. However, De Soto enters into Cherokee territory assuming that there is a single leader and a central seat of power. Knowing, however, that Cherokee governance structure by the eighteenth century was not centralized, but instead a system of autonomous townships in which a men's and a women's council each made decisions, representing the seven matrilineal Cherokee clans, another possibility is that the kind of centralized leadership that De Soto was looking for simply didn't exist. Instead, it's quite possible that a decentralized representative government that included balance between genders was already being practiced by Cherokees, and such a structure would have been illegible to De Soto.

Either possibility, however, creates an *asegi* story in this brief passage. If Cherokees refused to disclose the location or identity of a central leader, this was an act of resistance to protect Cherokee people from what would have been a very visible threat of violence. It's clear that Rangel, at least, interpreted this as resistance to De Soto and his army. If, on the other hand, Cherokee township governance was illegible to De Soto—who expected there to be a central leader—the gap caused by this illegibility can be understood as an *asegi* space. Just as Spanish invaders would have always interpreted Cherokee genders as somehow paralleling European gender structures, they would have also interpreted Cherokee leadership and governance within a system of European monarchies and nobility. The possible absence of a central leader might mark, in fact, the presence of a Cherokee governance system based on *duyuktv* that is rendered invisible by colonial accounts.

Elsewhere in their travel through Cherokee territories, Cherokees' generosity is seen as support of the Spanish, rather than as expressions of a system of reciprocity or attempts at *duyuktv* employed by Cherokees in order to mitigate the possible violence that De Soto's army might inflict. Just as Cofitachequi is characterized as bowing to Spanish male power, Cherokee generosity is interpreted as subservience to De Soto's army. Rangel's account of De Soto's arrival into Cherokee territory likewise characterizes Cherokees as welcoming Spanish invaders:

And they slept in a pine forest, where many Indian men and women began to come in peace with presents and gifts. . . . And on Monday, the seventeenth of that month, they departed from there and spent the night in a forest; and on Tuesday they went to Guaquili, and the Indians came forth in peace and gave them corn, although little, and many hens roasted on barbacoa, and a few little dogs, which are good food. . . . They also gave them tamemes, which are Indians who carry burdens.[45]

While it is understood that "many Indian men and women" came " in peace with presents and gifts," it isn't understood that they were likely participating in a gift exchange and expected reciprocity. Likewise, the Cherokees presenting the Spanish with food is seen as supplication. Even while the Spanish understood these as signs of peace, "peace" would have only been understood as consent to Spanish settlement. The "gift" of *tamemes* points to this—what the Cherokees might have lacked in treasure and resources, they didn't lack in human labor and servitude. While it is certainly possible that "they" (and there is no clear indication who "they" are, as a central leader is still not mentioned) "gave" the Spanish slaves, it is likely that this was under the threat of violence. Cherokees during this time did have slaves—prisoners of war, not a system of chattel slavery that was adopted under American pressure—and so it may have been seen as part of an alliance to "give" enemies over to De Soto to "carry burdens."

In Rangel's account, De Soto arrives in Guasili shortly after Cofitachequi and Gómez escape: "The next day they spent the night in an oak grove, and the following day, alongside a large creek . . . and the next day messengers came in peace, and they arrived early at Guasili, and they gave them many tamemes, many little dogs, and corn; and because this was a good resting place, the soldiers afterward called it, while throwing the dice, the House of Guasili, or a good encounter."[46]

Within Spanish heteropatriarchal colonization and imperialism all of these actions are gendered. Indigenous people who are seen as generous are considered submissive, and thus feminized, in relation to De Soto's patriarchal invasion. Indigenous people who resist are masculine threats to Spanish patriarchal power. A "good encounter" for the Spanish was one in which Indigenous people were seen as helping Spanish in heteropatriarchal colonial schemes.

Elvas has a similar account, which takes place in his narrative immediately after he writes of Cofitachequi and Gómez "in communication as husband and wife":

> In five days, the governor arrived at Guaxulle. The Indians there made him service of three hundred dogs, for they observed that the Christians liked them and sought them to eat; but they are not eaten among them [the Indians]. In Guaxulle and along that road there was very little maize. . . . The governor left Guaxulle and after a march of two days reached a town called Canasagua. Twenty Indians came out to meet him each carrying his basket of mulberries which grow in abundance.[47]

After leaving Canasoga, De Soto arrives in Chiaha, the Kosati town spoken of above in which women are demanded from the "cacique." None of these descriptions, of course, take place outside of the context of invasion, and further, outside of these chroniclers making arguments to the Spanish crown about the feasibility of invasion and settlement of the Southeast. Like Cofitachequi, Native people of all genders are characterized as either grateful and submissive to Spanish invasion or rebellious and unruly bodies that threaten Spanish power. The motivation on the part of chroniclers to make an argument to the crown that not only is Spanish settlement feasible but *desired* by Indigenous people becomes central to these narratives. This "desire" becomes a colonial narrative tool to argue for Spanish heteropatriarchal superiority and gives rise to moments such as this monologue from a Muskogee leader called Patofa, speaking to De Soto:

> Powerful Lord: Now with reason I will beg fortune to pay me some slight adversity for so great happiness; and I call myself happy for I have obtained what I desired in this life—that of seeing your Lordship and being able to render you some service. Although speech is the image of what is in the heart and what my heart feels with this happiness it cannot conceal, yet my tongue is not sufficient to enable me to express that happiness entirely. From whence did this your land, which I am governing, merit the visit of so sovereign and so excellent a prince to whom all people in the world owe service and obedience? And from whence has come so great a good fortune to those who inhabit this land, they being so insignificant, unless to recall to their memory some great misfortune which might happen in accordance with the arrangement of fortune? There, now and forever,

if we are worthy of your Lordship holding us as yours, we can not cease to be favored and maintained in true justice and reason and called men; for those who lack reason and justice can be compared to brute beasts. In my heart with the respect due to such a prince as your Lordship, I offer myself, and beg you that in payment of this true good will, you may wish to be served by my person, land, and vassals.[48]

In perfect Castilian, I'm sure. Elvas's entire chronicle is written with a particularly romantic flourish characteristic of "knight errant" narratives popular in Western Europe during this period. This particular excerpt portrays Patofa as feminine within Spanish logics through his supplication to Spanish power and his expressions of love and desire for Spanish Christian colonization through what David Spurr describes as "that strain of discourse which represents the colonized world as the feminine and which assigns to subject nations those qualities conventionally assigned to the female body."[49] This discourse happens after, and through, dichotomous descriptions of Cofitachequi as having a deep desire to aid De Soto (feminine), on the one hand, or as a wily disruptor of colonial control unwilling to concede to Spanish power (masculine), on the other. Patofa's speech is constructed through concepts of proper femininity in a Spanish Catholic framework, and femininity becomes a domesticating and civilizing force of the Church through the Spanish monarchy and the Inquisition. This power redeems Native people from being "brute beasts" and a masculine threat, and, through baptism and conversion, not only redeemed but also under the jurisdiction of the Inquisition and Spain.

The accounts of De Soto's expedition into the Southeast illustrate how gendering Indigenous peoples becomes a necessary tactic for colonization. It is through tropes of colonial patriarchal gender that Indigenous bodies and nations are constructed as either feminine (even in male bodies) and thus willing to accede power to colonial control, or masculine (even in female bodies) and thus a danger to colonial desires and in need of colonial conquest. In this light, Cofitachequi becomes a very queer lady, indeed—she refuses colonial patriarchal authority through her disruptive gender and sexuality and thus becomes illegible to colonial desires. Through De Soto, the gendering of Indigenous bodies—and gendered and sexualized violence against Indigenous peoples—becomes embedded into a mapped imaginary for future colonial invasions and explorations of Southeastern Indigenous lands.

ROUTE II: TRISTÁN DE LUNA Y ARELLANO

In 1559, twenty years after the De Soto invasion, Tristán de Luna y Arellano used De Soto's records—and a few of De Soto's soldiers—to launch his own attempt to conquer the Southeast. Luna's expedition traveled into Coosa, a Muskogeean "chiefdom" that would later become the Cherokee town of Coosawattee in the eighteenth century. Luna also brought with him "at least one woman from Coosa who had been enslaved by De Soto and taken to Mexico by the survivors of the invasion. This woman was to serve as a translator when they reached Coosa."[50] In a letter to Luna, Luis de Velasco writes, "You say that the Indian whom my niece, Doña Beatrice, has would be useful as an interpreter, as would the other married woman of Tlaxcala whom my sister-in-law has. This is the simplest thing in the world; she is badly crippled, but if she recovers I will send her. The Tlaxcala woman has hidden, but if she can be found I will send her too."[51]

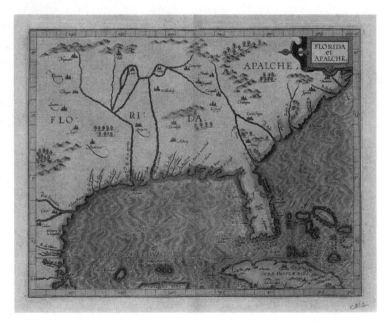

FIGURE 5. Map of the Southeast by Cornelius Wytfliet, 1597. "Florida et Apalche Map" (#MC0027), East Carolina Manuscript Collection, J. Y. Joyner Library, East Carolina University, Greenville, North Carolina. http://digital.lib.ecu.edu/special/ead/findingaids/MC0027.

I'm haunted by the memory of this Muskogee woman taken as a slave twenty years earlier, forced from her homeland, now brought back in another attempt to colonize her people. She wasn't the only person from Coosa enslaved by De Soto. What were her thoughts on learning she would be returning to her homeland? What had happened to her during her twenty years as a slave in Mexico? Did she and other Southeastern slaves continue to speak their languages with each other? Did this unnamed woman convert to Christianity, or say she did? What did she endure? Was she sick? Injured? How was she "badly crippled"? And what of the other unnamed Nahua woman from Tlaxcala, the woman who escaped? How did she resist? Did she survive?

I have to stop here. There is something about all of this imagining that is too close to the bone. There is something violent in it—an imagining I don't want to imagine. An imagining I need to make sense of the last five hundred years. These moments of untold stories. Or, if told, seldom remembered. Southeastern Indigenous slaves in Mexico are not something I ever considered until encountering these texts. Nahua and Muskogee and Choctaw and Chickasaw and Catawba and Cherokee people captured by De Soto. De Soto died along the Mississippi River, but his expedition continued into Mexico. What became of those "tamemes" that were captured along the way? Who survived? Did they survive the journey to Mexico only to be sold into the slave trade back to other parts of the Spanish empire? What connections to each other as Indigenous people do we forget when these histories are erased? What histories of shared resistance are possible when we begin to uncover the asegi stories outside of the "normal" tellings of history? Not a romanticized and sometimes colonial fantasy of a people returning to and claiming Aztlán, but a literal kinship. Shared ancestors, histories, and struggles. Shared memories, if we choose to remember.

The Luna expedition was disappointed by Coosa when they arrived. The records of De Soto's expedition had described the area in ways that were much more favorable to Spanish colonization. In a letter written in Coosa by Fray Domingo to Francisco Navarro, who stayed behind in the town—which Luna had turned into the Spanish settlement of Nanipacana—Domingo reports of the disappointing situation:

> There has not been found in all that we have seen any place where Spaniards could settle even though we should take the Indians' own lands away from them. These Indians of Coosa are of very good disposition; they give us what we need and do what we command them very willingly and with joy. It gives me great

pain to see that people of such good will are not in a place where they might be taught, although the secrets of God are so great that affairs are directed whither man least expects. . . . They all go as naked as they were born except the women, who dress according to the custom of those there.[52]

Domingo's report may express frustration at the resources Coosa had available to the Spanish, but the bodies and souls of Indigenous people themselves become commodities that could be useful as both sources of labor and possibilities of conversion. The tropes of Indigenous submission and vulnerability deployed by the De Soto expedition reemerge in the Luna expedition, including attention to naked, or mostly naked, bodies and a lack of significant gendered distinction between them. In another letter—from Domingo and others in Luna's party—written a month later to Don Luis de Velasco (the viceroy of New Spain), this trope is reinforced yet again. This letter, meant to be a detailed account of the expedition, also illustrates Indigenous resistance to Spanish invasion. Domingo et al. write, "[W]e went on for another ten or twelve days' journey. . . . At the end of that time we came upon the first towns of Coosa. There the Indians received us with good will, and gave us food without our having to go and forage for it as we had done up to that time at great trouble and danger to our persons, for all the towns behind us had been deserted and the food had been hidden."[53]

Throughout Luna's expedition, Indigenous people remembered De Soto's expedition, and often abandoned towns, hid food, and fought back against the invaders. After the devastation the De Soto expedition brought upon Indigenous nations throughout the Southeast, Indigenous people were often opposed to interaction with the Spanish. Even while the people in the townships of Coosa are described as having "good will" toward the Spanish, Domingo et al. report that "[t]he people of this land of Coosa seem to us to be more peaceful and to confide in us more than all those we have left behind, though they are not so confident as to neglect to put their property and women in safety."[54]

The Spanish arrived in the townships of Coosa starving, as were their horses, and were probably not seen as quite the threat that they had been before embarking to Coosa. Additionally, the leader of Coosa had his own purposes for keeping the Spanish alive—he later asks them to enter an alliance to attack a township that was refusing to pay tribute to the city of Coosa.

So, while the Spanish interpret the generosity of Indigenous people in the townships of Coosa as compliant, the people themselves may have seen the arrival of the Spanish as an opportunity to assert their own power over a township resisting the authority of the leader of Coosa. Even the generosity of the people is limited. Domingo et al. write, "They do not give us food in as great abundance as our need requires, but we think best to preserve the peace by suffering a little want rather than to bring on war by seeking abundance."[55] The Spanish were simply not in the position to fight against the Indigenous people of Coosa.

In this same letter, Domingo and the other signatories again report on the bodies of Indigenous people, along with descriptions of available food and the feasibility of a permanent Spanish settlement: "The people in this country have good constitutions and appearance; although they live in a cool country they have as brown a color as those down there. Their dress is what nature gave them, except that the women wear kirtles made of thread from mulberry roots; they are about two palms wide and with them they cover their privy parts."[56] Again, we can see the process of a colonial gaze examining and classifying the bodies and genders of Indigenous people not only as a kind of exoticization of Indigenous bodies, but also in order to describe to Spanish powers Indigenous people as either obstacles, resources, or allies in colonization. The nakedness of Indigenous people simultaneously communicates to Spanish leadership innocence, savagery, and heathenism. Unlike Christian Spain, Indigenous people carried no shame about naked bodies, and gendered distinctions in clothing are almost nonexistent. This renders Indigenous people aberrant within a Christian Spanish worldview. The same letter states, "There are temples in some of the towns, but they are as rudely constructed and as little frequented as is uncouth the religion which they practice in them."[57]

In another letter to Velasco, Fray Pedro de Feria implores Velasco to send aid to Coosa and Santa Elena (now called Parris Island, South Carolina) in order to secure them as Spanish settlements. While de Feria is certainly and clearly invested in Spanish settlement and conversion of Indigenous people, he also hopes to intervene in what he sees as brutal mistakes—and sins— of previous Spanish colonization. Unsurprisingly, his letter reveals more about sexual and gender violence than other accounts of Spanish invasions, as he argues for colonization through winning the hearts of Indigenous people.

FIGURE 6. "La Florida," map by Geronimo Chaves, 1584. Courtesy of
the Special Collections Department, University of South Florida,
http://fcit.usf.edu/florida/maps/pages/9300/f9323/f9323.htm.

or mockery. Of course, Cherokee women could also participate as warriors,
but Pardo seems unaware of this fact. The Cherokee leader is confronted by
Pardo along with his interpreters and "many soldiers" to find out why a male is
dressed as a woman and living with women. Knowing about the brutal history
of the Spanish against many Indigenous peoples—particularly in the murders
of Two-Spirit people—the presence of "many soldiers" can clearly be seen as a
threat toward the Cherokees present.

Juan Pardo's invasions into the Southeast were a literal attempt to retrace De
Soto's steps, and drew heavily from Luna's expedition. By the time of Pardo's
"exploration" of Cherokee territory in 1567, Cherokees would have already
known about Spanish invaders through direct contact with De Soto's army or
would have heard about the Spanish through other Indigenous people they
interacted with. The later Battle of Mabila would likely have been well known
by Cherokees by the time Pardo arrived, and Spanish violence was quite likely
already notorious.[62]

ROUTE IV: JOHN LAWSON

The sexualities and gender structures of Cherokee and other Southeastern Indigenous people often fell under extreme scrutiny by colonial powers in order to make arguments for the need for colonization and how colonization could be best achieved. While John Lawson, a land surveyor for the British in the Carolinas, did not travel into Cherokee territory in the eighteenth century, his *A New Voyage to Carolina*, published in 1709, demonstrates the way British colonists viewed Indigenous people and nations in the Southeast and remaps

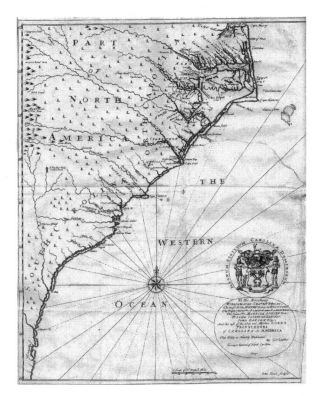

FIGURE 7. "Part of North America," map by John Lawson, 1709. *A New Voyage to Carolina; Containing the Exact Description and Natural History of That Country: Together with the Present State Thereof. And A Journal of a Thousand Miles, Travel'd Thro' Several Nations of Indians. Giving a Particular Account of Will Their Customs, Manners, &c.*, electronic edition, http://docsouth.unc.edu/nc/lawson/lawson.html.

earlier colonial accounts of Indigenous gender and sexuality onto Indigenous bodies, setting the stage for later colonial interactions with Cherokees.

Like the chronicles of the De Soto and Luna expeditions, *A New Voyage to Carolina* is a narrative of "discovery" and an argument for the feasibility of expanding empire in what is currently the Southeastern United States. As with all colonial accounts, Lawson brought his own political agenda to his "accounts" of Native cultures. The colonization of gender systems and cultural norms around sexuality are central to this project. Lawson explicitly proposes a plan for colonization that he juxtaposes against Spanish strategies of physical violence, one that focuses, instead, on assimilation. In Lawson's proposal, the intermarriage of poor white people with "civilized" Indians and the adoption of plantation life would create Indigenous children of mixed parentage who, then, could be put into indentured labor apprenticeships and gradually assimilate into British political control while simultaneously sharing information with colonists about Indigenous geographies and cultural practices that could be used to advance British empire.[63] This, he argues, would aid in the conversion of Indians to Christianity and provide an alternative to white indentured servitude (the implication of which would be that African enslavement would be further entrenched as a central logic of colonization):

> [I]t is highly necessary . . . to give Encouragement to the ordinary People, and those of a lower Rank, that they might marry with these Indians, and come into Plantations, and Houses, where so many Acres of Land and some Gratuity of Money, (out of a Publick Stock) are given to the new-married Couple; and that the Indians might have Encouragement to send their Children Apprentices to proper Masters, that would be kind to them, and make them Masters of a Trade, whereby they would be drawn to live amongst us, and become Members of the same Ecclesiastical and Civil Government we are under; then we should have great Advantages to make daily Conversions amongst them, when they saw that we were kind and just to them in all our Dealings. . . . In my opinion, it's better for Christians of a mean Fortune to marry with the Civiliz'd Indians, than to suffer the Hardships of four or five years Servitude, in which they meet with Sickness and Seasonings amidst a Crowd of other Afflictions, which the Tyranny of a bad Master lays upon such poor Souls, all which those acquainted with our Tobacco Plantations are not Strangers to.[64]

Lawson argues that such an approach "seems to be a more reasonable Method of converting the Indians, than to set up our Christian Banner in a Field of Blood, as the Spaniards have done in New Spain, and baptize one hundred with the Sword for one at the Font."[65] He worries that Spanish strategies of colonization would create enemies among Indigenous nations who would then support other colonial powers in their expansion rather than the British: "Whilst we make way for a Christian Colony through a Field of Blood, and defraud, and make away with those that one day may be wanted in this World, and in the next appear against us, we make way for a more potent Christian Enemy to invade us hereafter, of which we may repent, when too late."[66]

These plans, as discussed further in chapter 3, are exactly what happened in Southeastern Indigenous history in the nineteenth century, ultimately leading to policies of removal and allotment and eerily foreshadowing Richard Henry Pratt's unleashing of the boarding and residential school system in North America.

Lawson's vision was rooted in a gendered and sexualized control over Native women's bodies. In order to make his argument feasible, it becomes necessary to provide evidence that Indigenous nations in the Southeast have a deficient system of gender that fails to control women's sexualities, leaving a space for British men to take over jurisdiction of Indigenous women, lands, and children. While he consistently characterized Indigenous matrilineal and matrifocal systems as evidence of savagery, he also argued that these systems could be taken advantage of in order to perpetuate colonial interests. Because many Southeastern Indigenous customs are matrilineal and matrifocal, Indigenous people saw the incorporation of European men and their children into matrilineal kinship networks as a tactic of assimilating *them* into Native communities, not vice-versa. Lawson, however, does not understand these worldviews, and instead sees relationships between British men and Indigenous women as a means by which the British might gain a political advantage over other Europeans:

The Indian traders . . . have commonly their Indian wives . . . and, besides the Satisfaction of a She-Bed-Fellow, they find these Indian Girls very serviceable to them, on Account of dressing their Victuals, and instructing 'em in the Affairs and Customs of the Country. Moreover, such a man gets a great Trade with the Savages; for when a Person that lives amongst them, is reserv'd from the Conversation of their Women, 'tis impossible for him ever to accomplish his Designs amongst that People.[67]

According to this argument, the logic of "discovery" is not only about the claiming of lands and resources. It is very specifically a discovery of Indigenous practices of gender and sexuality that both queers Indigenous peoples as well as asserts British heteropatriarchal power over Indigenous bodies. Native women are particular targets for Lawson, who writes about them as exotic beauties available to serve the sexual desires of British men. Entire Indigenous nations and cultures, in fact, are constructed through the sexual availability of Indigenous women to white men's sexual desires. Matrilineal and matrifocal practices common in the Southeast, for instance, are explained by Lawson as rooted in Native women's sexual promiscuity, "the Female Issue carrying the Heritage, for fear of Imposters; the Savages well knowing, how much Frailty possesses the Indian Women, betwixt the Garters and the Girdle."[68] In this particular instance Lawson is explaining how male leaders receive authority through their mothers, which simultaneously portrays Native men as under women's control and, therefore, outside of the confines of European masculinity.

In order to make the prospect of British trade and colonization appealing to British men, he both eroticizes and exoticizes Indigenous women through detailed descriptions of women's bodies and representations of Native women's "femininity": "They are of a very hale Constitution; their Breaths are as Sweet as the Air they breathe in, and the Woman seems to be of that tender Composition, as if they were design'd rather for the Bed than Bondage."[69] David Spurr calls this "the eroticization of the colonized," which is accomplished through "a set of rhetorical instances—metaphors, seductive fantasies, expressions of sexual anxiety—in which the traditions of colonialist and phallocentric discourses coincide."[70]

Native women's bodies are portrayed as inherently sexual, and, further, as particularly desirous complements to a white masculine virility. Speaking of sexual and "marital" practices among Native people, Lawson writes, "they lie together under one Covering for several Months, and the Woman remains the same as she was when she first came to him. I doubt, our *Europeans* would be apt to break this Custom, but the *Indian* Men are not so vigorous and impatient in their Love as we are. Yet the Women are quite contrary, and those *Indian* Girls that have convers'd with the *English* and other *Europeans*, never care for the Conversation of their own Countrymen afterwards."[71]

Native women and girls here are placed outside of the discourse of proper femininity constructed by Christian Europe, and therefore their sexuality is marked as "contrary." Such a queering of Indigenous women's sexualities positions Native women as so desirous of European male sexual aggression, and Native men as so sexually deficient, that after having sex with white men they never want to have sex with Native men again. Native women, then, are described in terms of their sexual and social benefit to white men.

These are a very comely Sort of *Indians*, there being a strange Difference in the Proportion and Beauty of these Heathens. . . . The Women here being as handsome as most I have met withal, being several fine-finger'd Brounetto's amongst them. These Lasses stick not upon Hand long, for they marry when very young, as at 12 or 14 Years of Age. The *English* Traders are seldom without an *Indian* Female for his Bed-fellow, alledging these Reasons as sufficient to allow of such a Familiarity. First, They being remote from any white People, that it preserves their Friendship with the Heathens, they esteeming a white Man's Child much above one of their getting, the *Indian* Mistress ever securing her white Friend Provisions whilst he stays amongst them. And lastly, This Correspondence makes them learn the *Indian* Tongue much the sooner, they being of the *French*-man's Opinion, how that an *English* Wife teaches her Husband more *English* in one Night, than a School-master can in a Week.[72]

Native women and girls are also characterized as "whorish," and an entire system of prostitution is described that both represents Native women's sexuality as available to white men and represents Native men as financial beneficiaries to prostitution. The argument to British men in this text is that Native women and girls are not only available as prostitutes and wives for British men (and, indeed, Lawson argues that there is little distinction), but that Native men also enable such sexual behavior. British men, therefore, will find no resistance from Native men in the process of colonizing Native women's bodies and lands.

The Girls, at 12 or 13 Years of Age, as soon as Nature prompts them, freely bestow their Maidenheads on some Youth about the same Age, continuing her Favours on whom she most affects, changing her Mate very often, few or none of them being constant to one, till a greater Number of Years has made her capable of managing Domestick Affairs, and she hath try'd the Vigour of most of the Nation she belongs to; Multiplicity of Gallants never being a Stain to a Female's Reputation, or the least Hindrance of her Advancement, but the more *Whorish*, the more *Honourable*, and they of all most coveted, by those of the first Rank, to make a Wife of. The *Flos Virginis*, so much coveted by the *Europeans*, is never valued by these Savages.[73]

While Lawson's proposal of a civilizing project ultimately hopes to regulate Native women's sexuality through the domestic sphere, Native nations in the Southeast are also constructed as a sexual playground for European men. In order to make this argument, Native women are depicted as sexually promiscuous and Native men both sexually impotent and oversexed: "[S]ome of their War Captains, and great Men, very often will retain 3 or 4 Girls at a time for their own Use, when at the same time, he is so impotent and old, as to be incapable of making Use of one of them; so that he seldom misses of wearing greater Horns than the Game he kills."[74] Such passages are meant to demonstrate an uncivilized masculinity—one that claims women's bodies but does not "make use" of them. The implication here is that, within a sphere in which women's bodies are commoditized, Native men are sexually greedy and wasteful. Lawson's colonial and white supremacist misogyny characterizes, through women's bodies, Native people as outside of European gender and sexual norms. This, he argues, places white men at an advantage, since not only are Native women sexually available for white men, but Native men are characterized as "effeminate" through a lack of control and claim over Native women's bodies, and also perversely masculine through characterizations of Native men as profiting off of Native women's sexual labor.

Lawson's preoccupation with gender and sexuality queers all Native people by constructing Native systems of gender and sexuality as non-normative. Just as Native women's bodies are claimed through a colonial gaze, there is particular sexual scrutiny of Native men's bodies in ways that simultaneously queer Native men's bodies and rupture the purely "heterosexual" gaze of settler colonialism: "They have no Hairs on their Faces (except some few) and those but little, nor is there often found any Hair under their Arm-Pits. They are continually plucking it away from their Faces, by the Roots. As for their Privities, since they wore Tail-Clouts, to cover their Nakedness, several of the Men have a deal of Hair thereon. It is to be observ'd, that the Head of the *Penis* is cover'd (throughout all the Nations of the *Indians* I ever saw) both in Old and

Young."[75] All of these characterizations are created to show settler men's sexualized, gendered, and racial dominance over all Indigenous people.

Because Native men fail to control Native women's bodies, and Native cultures are sexually open and lack the kinds of sexual restrictions imposed by European marriage, British men have unrestricted access to Native women's bodies. "Marriages of these *Indians* are no farther binding, than the Man and Woman agree together. Either of them has Liberty to leave the other, upon any frivolous Excuse they can make."[76] This sexual freedom, then, leaves space for European men to encroach onto Native lands and bodies without fear of repercussions from either European men—who are few and far between—or Native men, who are characterized as having no control over women's bodies. This lack of control of women's bodies, contradictorily, creates a masculinity that becomes the center of an entire system of sexual trade. Native women are described as inherently available for use as prostitutes because women's sexuality, left untamed by men, gives rise to a culture of prostitution while women's lack of "proper" femininity fails to subdue Native men's savage masculinity. Native people's sexual freedom gives rise to entire cultures of sexual transgression that British men must simultaneously take advantage of and control. Lawson writes,

> They set apart the youngest and prettiest Faces for trading Girls; these are remarkable by their Hair, having a particular Tonsure by which they are known, and distinguish'd from those engag'd to Husbands. They are mercenary, and whoever makes Use of them, first hires them, the greatest Share of the Gain going to the King's Purse, who is the chief Bawd, exercising his Prerogative over all the Stews of his Nation, and his own Cabin (very often) being the chiefest Brothel-House.[77]

Sex itself, however, becomes a means by which to tame Native women's insatiable sexuality and, ultimately, create a proper monogamous relationship: "As they grow in Years, the hot Assaults of Love grow cooler; and then they commonly are so staid, as to engage themselves with more Constancy to each other. I have seen several Couples amongst them, that have been so reserv'd, as to live together for many Years, faithful to each other, admitting none to their Beds but such as they own'd for their Wife or Husband: So continuing to their Life's end."[78]

Later, Lawson writes that the "Trading Girls . . . at last they grow weary of so many, and betake themselves to a married State, or to the Company of one

Man; neither does their having been common to so many any wise lessen their Fortunes, but rather augment them."[79] Southeastern Indigenous territories, then, are characterized as a sexual playground that, nevertheless, would ultimately result in proper monogamous marriages between white men and Native women that would, as discussed earlier, produce white/Indigenous mixed-race children who could become loyal to the British crown.

This narrative is meant to provide evidence to Lawson's audience of the feasibility of his proposed civilizing project. The hypersexuality of Native women, and their supposed desire for European men and their children, situates white male sexuality as a tool with which to claim Native women, children, and lands and dislocate Native men's ineffectual masculinity. Sex itself is a central tool of colonization.

While women's sexual freedom is seen as an opportunity for European colonization, matrilineal systems are seen as an obstacle to this civilizing project:

> But one great Misfortune which oftentimes attends those that converse with these Savage Women, is, that they get Children by them, which are seldom educated any otherwise than in a State of Infidelity; for it is a certain Rule and Custom, amongst all the Savages of *America*, that I was ever acquainted withal, to let the Children always fall to the Woman's Lot; for it often happens, that two *Indians* that have liv'd together, as Man and Wife, in which Time they have had several Children; if they part, and another Man possesses her, all the Children go along with the Mother, and none with the Father. And therefore, on this Score, it ever seems impossible for the Christians to get their Children (which they have by these *Indian* Women) away from them; whereby they might bring them up in the Knowledge of the Christian Principles.[80]

Lawson proposes that intermarriage between poor white people and Indians, and a removal of Native people from Native communities to a plantation culture, will be able to interrupt this system, recenter a heteropatriarchal family structure, and transform Native people into British subjects. While Lawson clearly argues that Native systems of gender and sexuality are savage, backward, and perverse, in order to make an argument for the desirability of assimilation instead of eradication, there appear moments when Lawson writes of gender and sexuality in a more favorable light. Beyond extolling what he sees as the virtues of Native cultures—if brought under the civilizing force of the British Empire—he uses these moments as a disciplining and pedagogical force to condemn and critique what he sees as the failings of Europeans. For instance, he writes that, if Native women "are provok'd, or affronted, by their Husbands, or some other, they resent the Indignity offer'd them in silent Tears, or by refusing their Meat."[81] This, he argues, is behavior that European women should strive for: "Would some of our *European* Daughters of Thunder set these *Indians* for a Pattern, there might be more quiet Families found amongst them, occasion'd by that unruly Member, the Tongue."[82] Native women, then, are constructed as the perfect subject for European male colonization—highly sexual, particularly desirous of white men, and, simultaneously, silent.

It is in one of these moments that an important *asegi* rupture appears in the text: "Although these People are call'd Savages, yet Sodomy is never heard of amongst them, and they are so far from the Practice of that beastly and loathsome Sin, that they have no Name for it in all their Language."[83] What is interesting to me about this passage is that Lawson was curious enough about "sodomy" among Native people to try to find out what word(s) existed for it. Lawson was, in general, curious about Native languages and documented some Tuscarora and Woccon (a Catawban language). His language documentation is fairly basic: numbers, animals, nouns, and verbs important for traders to know. None of them are about sexual acts. Did Lawson, then, attempt to find the word for "sodomy?" And if so, why? If he truly did, I think it was because of the obsessive nature of his writing to detail Indigenous sexual and gender practices. Since "sodomy" is a Christian European concept, category, and crime, there would—of course—not be a translation for "sodomy" in Indigenous languages. This moment also is written in a context that details Lawson's perception of Native customs around marriage and sex, including taboos around intermarriage within one's clan and Native men having multiple "wives." Native people may have savage customs around marriage, but it becomes important for Lawson to make it clear that they are not so "savage" as to undermine his arguments for conversion and assimilation through European marriage, family, and labor.

This *absent presence* of "sodomy" is significant within a text that characterizes Indigenous bodies as sexually perverse. Lawson's insistence on Indigenous women's sexual availability to white men, and his argument for a lack of resistance on the part of Native men to the claiming of women's bodies, are—we must remember—part of a strategy for colonizing Native lands and transforming Native people into British subjects. His representation of "whorish" Native women and "impotent," but also oversexed, Native men serves the colonial desires of white men in a colonial project that aims to move Native women and poor white men into a planter class that can produce offspring that would be placed into a firmly white, patriarchal culture as workers. The Spanish, as discussed earlier, had a history of killing "sodomites" en masse and using the presence of "sodomy" as an excuse for mass murder and the claiming of land. "Sodomy" was not a category restricted to the Spanish, of course, and within a context of ongoing British invasion and occupation of Indigenous lands in the Southeast, "sodomy" could indeed be used as evidence of "savagery" and as an excuse for mass murder. Lawson, however, worries that if the British were to follow Spanish methods of colonization it would create enemies who would then aid other European powers in the battles for control of the continent. Praising the Native people for particular attributes Lawson sees as virtuous, then, provides feasibility for his vision of a civilizing project. It simultaneously disciplines European bodies, genders, and sexualities. If the "savages" have no knowledge of "sodomy," the implication is that European "sodomy" is even more savage than the savages. If Lawson's plan is to civilize Indians through European intermarriage and setting an example, the sexualities of Indigenous people must lend themselves to such a project. That he writes in this absence rather than, for instance, not mentioning it at all signals a larger concern about "sodomy." If Native nations are spaces in which sexuality is unregulated, it must be a sexuality that serves a colonial project. A cultural tolerance for "sodomy" might, in fact, corrupt white men seeking Native nations as a space of unbridled sexuality. The instance of such an absence, then, helps to secure Lawson's vision of European patriarchal nuclear families and labor as redemptive for both Native people and poor white people.

In a similar *asegi* moment in the text, Lawson describes a Waxhaw women's dance in terms clearly meant to emphasize savage, and perhaps threatening, gender:

> Their way of Dancing, is nothing but a sort of stamping Motion, much like the treading upon Founders Bellows. This Female-Gang held their Dance for above six Hours, being all of them of a white Lather, like a Running Horse that has just come in from his Race. My Landlady was the Ringleader of the *Amazons*, who, when in her own House, behav'd herself very discreetly, and warily, in her Domestick Affairs; yet, Custom had so infatuated her, as to almost break her Heart with

Dancing amongst such a confused Rabble. . . . When the Dancing was ended, every Youth that was so disposed, catch'd hold of the Girl he liked best, and took her that Night for his Bed-Fellow.[84]

The dance form Lawson refers to is clearly a "stomp dance" style of dancing that is common in the ceremonial system of the Southeast. The women are characterized in both masculine and animalistic terms, at once dehumanizing Native women and representing them as gender nonconforming. The description of the dance as "like the treading upon Founders Bellows" invokes an image of masculine labor, which requires physical strength that would have been unbecoming to European women. Describing them as a "Female-Gang" likewise marks them as gender nonconforming. Lawson emphasizes this through describing them as a *female* gang, pointing to the masculine connotations of the word "gang," which, by the time of his writing, already carried an unfavorable and perhaps criminal edge, which is reinforced here by describing the woman Lawson is staying with as a "Ringleader." The women are not only dehumanized through a comparison to horses, but specifically *male* horses. The decision to describe the women as "Amazons" also clearly marks the women as outside of proper gender, and—together with a description of the women as a gang—specifically not only as an oddity, but as a potential threat to masculine colonial power. This threat, however, is mitigated through characterizing the "Ringleader" as conforming to proper femininity in the domestic sphere and, as is consistently mentioned by Lawson, sexually available for men.

Lawson was tortured and killed by Tuscaroras in 1711.

I would like to imagine that this dance was a group of Two-Spirit people. We can't tell from Lawson's text if this "gang of Amazons" was actually a group of warriors, and, even so, a group of women warriors does not mean they were people we would now think of as Two-Spirit. Even the fact that there was a women's dance is significant. But, still, there is something that delights me about imagining this gang of Amazons as Two-Spirit. Perhaps because the need to recover and continue cultural memories for our Southeastern Two-Spirit people is so necessary. Perhaps because I love the idea of a Two-Spirit gang making Lawson uneasy. Perhaps because I know a few of these gangs. There is no evidence that these women were people we would now call Two-Spirit. There is no evidence they were not. Like Cofitachequi, they disturb the gender expectations of the colonial gaze. Through an asegi retelling of this history we can clearly see the way Indigenous genders and sexualities were used to map colonial sexual and colonial fantasies.

ROUTE V: HENRY TIMBERLAKE

About sixty years after Lawson's writings about Southeastern Indians, Henry Timberlake, a British lieutenant, traveled into Cherokee territory and spent three months in the Overhill towns during a period in which the British were attempting to secure Cherokees as allies against the French.[85]

In 1730, a Cherokee delegation of seven Cherokee men to London resulted in Cherokees agreeing to a treaty of Friendship and Commerce in which the Cherokee delegation agreed that Cherokees would fight for the British in any battle and, further, that in the event "that any negroe slaves shall run away into ye woods from their English masters, the Cherokee Indians shall endeavour to apprehend them, and either bring them back to ye Plantation from whence they run away, or to ye Governor. And for every negroe so apprehended and brought back, the Indian who brings him, shall receive a gun and a matchcoat."[86] As is evidenced by the absence of women in the 1730 delegation, women were already seeing a major disruption of their traditional centrality to Cherokee governance.

The eighteenth century brought major challenges and brutal wars to Cherokee communities. Lawson's capture and execution took place within a larger attack launched against colonists by the Tuscarora, ushering in the Tuscarora War from 1711 to 1715, in which Cherokees fought on the side of the British.

Gendered politics were central to British colonial projects, and were at odds with Cherokee gender structures and understandings of the *duyuktv*. Still, in 1757, when Attakullakulla—a Beloved Man of the Cherokees and a respected leader who was the youngest man to travel to London in the 1730 delegation—appeared in South Carolina to negotiate with British settlers, he is quoted as saying, "Since the white man as well as the red was born of woman, did not the white man admit women to their councils?"[87] Cherokees had already learned that European diplomacy excluded women, and certainly Attakullakulla knew this, which makes his question to the British not one of surprise, but of challenge.

In the context of the Anglo-Cherokee War, which started after conflicts in the French and Indian War, Timberlake's interactions with Cherokees were not without an undercurrent of tension and danger. The British were often brutal in their dealings with Cherokees. In 1760, Colonel Archibald Montgomery, for instance, decimated the Cherokee Lower Towns, killing Native people with bayonets and burning people alive in their homes.[88]

rokee territory was to rebuild alliances
ther delegation to England, which took
l his observations of Cherokee culture.
gain, under particular scrutiny and sub-
headmen, likewise compose the assem-
arwomen are admitted. The reader will
ry of Amazons not so great a fable as we
being as famous in war, as powerful in
Women are again mentioned in order
mberlake, is outside of women's gender
women, who can no longer go to war, but
younger days, have the title of Beloved.
y; but it abundantly recompenses them,
is so great, that they can, by the wave of
nned by the council, and already tied to

ll Cherokee people, are rendered "queer"
n who are perceived as gender noncon-
of Southeastern women as a "gang of
n Timberlake describes his interest and
specially when the women played, who
all amusement of an European specta-
kee communities—much more exten-
or understood—is outside of the sphere
ed masculine. War, power, and rigorous
e sees as part of men's social role.
ligenous women's sexual autonomy as
ating, Timberlake's brief mentions of
opean gendered order onto Cherokees
n a heteropatriarchal framework. To
ly do Timberlake's "imperial eyes pas-
s and resources, they also objectify and
those with European ancestry.[93] "The
h is so long that it generally reaches to
to the ground, club'd, and ornamented
ept their eyebrows, pluck it from all of

While Timberlake's work in Ch
against the French and organize an
place in 1762, his memoirs also deta
Cherokee gender and sexuality are, a
jects of fascination: "These chiefs, or
blies of the nation, into which the v
not be a little surprised to find the sto
imagined, many of the Indian wome
council."[89] War Women and Beloved
to detail a cultural practice that, to T
roles.[90] "Old warriors likewise, or war-
have distinguished themselves in their
This is the only title females can enjo
by the power they acquire by it, which
a swan's wing, deliver a wretch conder
the stake."[91]

Cherokee gender, and by extension
through the bodies of Cherokee wome
forming, echoing Lawson's descriptior
Amazons." This echo appears again wh
amusement at watching a ball game, "e
pulled one another about, to the no sm
tor."[92] The power women had in Cher
sive, in fact, than Timberlake observed
of European femininity and thus rende
athletics are all domains that Timberlal

Just as previous colonists depict In
both gender nonconforming and titill
Cherokee women likewise reassert Eu
by eroticizing Cherokee women with
use Mary Louise Pratt's phrase, not on
sively look out to possess" Cherokee lan
eroticize Cherokee women, particularly
women wear the hair of their head, whi
the middle of their legs, and sometimes
with ribbons of various colours; but, exc

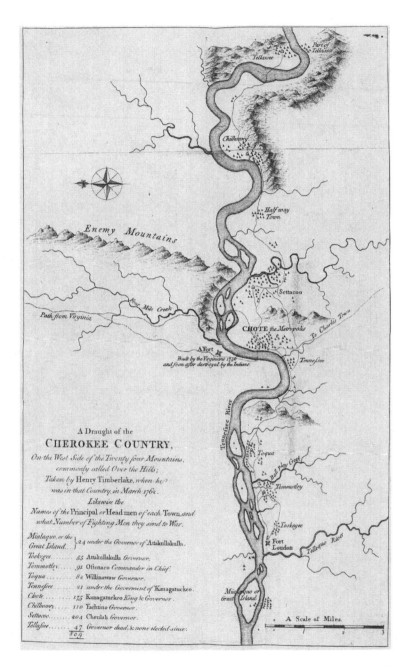

FIGURE 8. "A draught of the Cherokce Country: on the west side of the Twenty Four Mountains, commonly called Over the Hills," Henry Timberlake, 1765. Norman B. Leventhal Map Center at the Boston Public Library, http://maps.bpl.org/id/rb17634.

While Timberlake's work in Cherokee territory was to rebuild alliances against the French and organize another delegation to England, which took place in 1762, his memoirs also detail his observations of Cherokee culture. Cherokee gender and sexuality are, again, under particular scrutiny and subjects of fascination: "These chiefs, or headmen, likewise compose the assemblies of the nation, into which the warwomen are admitted. The reader will not be a little surprised to find the story of Amazons not so great a fable as we imagined, many of the Indian women being as famous in war, as powerful in council."[89] War Women and Beloved Women are again mentioned in order to detail a cultural practice that, to Timberlake, is outside of women's gender roles.[90] "Old warriors likewise, or war-women, who can no longer go to war, but have distinguished themselves in their younger days, have the title of Beloved. This is the only title females can enjoy; but it abundantly recompenses them, by the power they acquire by it, which is so great, that they can, by the wave of a swan's wing, deliver a wretch condemned by the council, and already tied to the stake."[91]

Cherokee gender, and by extension all Cherokee people, are rendered "queer" through the bodies of Cherokee women who are perceived as gender nonconforming, echoing Lawson's description of Southeastern women as a "gang of Amazons." This echo appears again when Timberlake describes his interest and amusement at watching a ball game, "especially when the women played, who pulled one another about, to the no small amusement of an European spectator."[92] The power women had in Cherokee communities—much more extensive, in fact, than Timberlake observed or understood—is outside of the sphere of European femininity and thus rendered masculine. War, power, and rigorous athletics are all domains that Timberlake sees as part of men's social role.

Just as previous colonists depict Indigenous women's sexual autonomy as both gender nonconforming and titillating, Timberlake's brief mentions of Cherokee women likewise reassert European gendered order onto Cherokees by eroticizing Cherokee women within a heteropatriarchal framework. To use Mary Louise Pratt's phrase, not only do Timberlake's "imperial eyes passively look out to possess" Cherokee lands and resources, they also objectify and eroticize Cherokee women, particularly those with European ancestry.[93] "The women wear the hair of their head, which is so long that it generally reaches to the middle of their legs, and sometimes to the ground, club'd, and ornamented with ribbons of various colours; but, except their eyebrows, pluck it from all of the other parts of the body, especially the looser part of the sex. . . . The women, particularly the half-breed, are remarkably well-featured."[94]

Here Timberlake's text repeats a pattern seen in Lawson through his attention to Indigenous genitals and through the sexualization of Indigenous women's bodies for the benefit of white men. While Timberlake is neither as explicit nor as focused on women's bodies and sexuality as Lawson, within a larger context of colonization of women's sexuality and bodies—and ongoing wars—these small moments signal a larger pattern of colonization through women's bodies. For Cherokees, these texts show how, in the words of Scott Lauria Morgensen, "the biopolitics of settler colonialism was constituted by the imposition of colonial heteropatriarchy and the hegemony of settler sexuality" through a process of charting Indigenous lands and bodies both for colonial regulation and for colonial use.[95]

An asegi *remembering of the moments in colonial texts pays attention to the ways Cherokee gender and sexuality becomes monitored through a colonial gaze. As Cherokee Two-Spirit people tactically remember these kinds of moments in historical records, we recognize that, even if people we would now recognize as Two-Spirit people were present, they also become rendered invisible through colonial heteropatriarchy's "reading" of all Cherokee bodies, genders, and sexualities as outside of proper gender and sexual norms.* Asegi *memories place gender and sexuality at the center of our memories as Cherokee people, recognizing the ways European constructions of gender and sexuality become mapped onto accounts of Cherokee people—and, thus, our genders and sexualities rendered "queer"—as part of a larger process of settler colonization. Colonial heteropatriarchy maps gender and sexuality onto Indigenous bodies in order to find routes into and through our homelands.*

ROUTE VI: WILLIAM BARTRAM

On the heels of Timberlake's expedition into the Southeast, another colonist documented his own explorations of Southeastern nations. As the son of a botanist, William Bartram's *Travels* take on a decidedly more "scientific" tone than is found in other accounts, and are part of what Linda Tuhiwai Smith points out is a "systematic colonization of indigenous peoples" in which "Indigenous peoples were classified alongside the flora and fauna; hierarchical typologies of humanity and systems of representation were fuelled by new discoveries; and

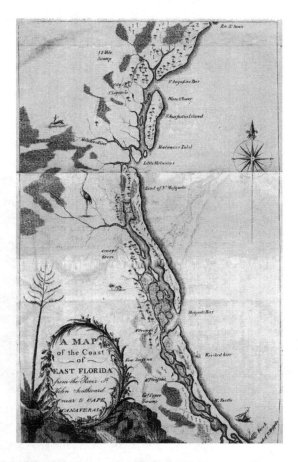

FIGURE 9. "A MAP of the Coast of EAST FLORIDA from the River St. John Southward near to CAPE CANAVERAL," William Bartram, 1791. William Bartram, *Travels Through North & South Carolina, Georgia, East & West Florida, the Cherokee Country, the Extensive Territories of the Muscogulges, or Creek Confederacy, and the Country of the Chactaws; Containing An Account of the Soil and Natural Productions of Those Regions, Together with Observations on the Manners of the Indians. Embellished with Copper-Plates*, Documenting the American South, University Library, University of North Carolina at Chapel Hill, http://docsouth.unc.edu/nc/bartram/ill1.html.

cultural maps were charted and territories claimed and contested by the major European powers."[96] Cherokee gender and sexuality are part of Bartram's cultural mapping in order to argue for the desirability—often in specifically sexual terms—of Cherokee bodies and land.

While Bartram's text is considered historically significant because of his descriptions of Southeastern Indigenous nations in the late eighteenth century (including a meeting with the Cherokee leader Attakullakulla), what I'm most interested in here is his eroticization of Cherokee women's bodies through continuing the trope of their attractiveness and sexual availability to white men. David Spurr points out a "rhetoric of surveillance," a colonial trope in which "[t]he eye treats the body as a landscape: it proceeds systematically from part to part, quantifying and specializing, noting color and texture, and finally passing an aesthetic judgment which stressed the body's role as object to be viewed,"[97] Bartram appears to illustrate this, as he begins by describing "a most enchanting view, a vast expanse of green meadows and strawberry fields; a meandering river gliding through, saluting in its various turnings the swelling, green, turfy knolls, embellished with parterres of flowers and fruitful strawberry beds."[98] Along with descriptions of frolicking wild animals, he then describes how

companies of young, innocent Cherokee virgins, some busily gathering the rich fragrant fruit, others having already filled their baskets, lay reclined under the shade of floriferous and fragrant native bowers of Magnolia, Azalea, Philadelphus, perfumed Calycanthus, sweet Yellow Jessamine and cerulian Glycine frutescens, disclosing their beauties to the fluttering breeze, and bathing their limbs in the cool fleeting streams; whilst other parties, more gay and libertine, were yet Collecting strawberries or wantonly chasing their companions, tantalising them, staining their lips and cheeks with the rich fruit.[99]

The description of "innocent Cherokee virgins" suggests that these are very young women, if not girls. They blend into the landscape and become classified along with the "native bowers of Magnolia, Azalea, Philadelphus, perfumed Calycanthus, sweet Yellow Jessamine and cerulian Glycine frutescens." They become indistinguishable from the flowers "disclosing their beauties to the fluttering breeze, " and an erotic scene is described in which strawberries stain their lips and cheeks as they wantonly tantalize each other.

Under this heteropatriarchal colonial gaze, young women's and girls' role in the story as the sexual objects of white masculine desire, and the suggestions of erotic desire among them, appear as a way of marking naïve and unbridled Indigenous sexuality that seduces colonial men. In fact, we are told that "[t]his sylvan scene of primitive innocence was enchanting, and perhaps too enticing for hearty young men long to continue idle spectators"—so enticing that Bartram and his fellow travelers, who "wished at least to have a more active part in their delicious sports," and "nature prevailing over reason," sneak up on the girls.[100]

While Bartram's tone seeks to transmit a feeling of sexual playfulness, an *asegi* reading of the text recognizes the threat of rape present in the account. Bartram says that the men "meant no other than an innocent frolic with this gay assembly of hamadryades, we shall leave it to the person of feeling and sensibility to form an idea to what lengths our passions might have hurried us . . . had it not been for the vigilance and care of some envious matrons who lay in ambush, and espying us gave the alarm."[101] Colonial heteropatriarchal violence is mapped into this story as part of claiming control over Cherokee women's bodies and land.

The Cherokee women here know the danger these white men pose and seek to protect the girls from sexual violence. Bartram and the men with him nevertheless chase down several of the "nymphs" who were not close to the women, who then hide from the men in a grove.[102] The entire scene is one in which sexual violence against Cherokee women and girls becomes a romanticized adventure to Bartram and the men with him, as well as the intended audience of his book. Tellingly, the older women who protect the girls from the sexual danger of white men are described as "envious matrons" who are jealous of the sexual attention the men are giving the girls. They, then, are suddenly described as outside of proper gender roles in warrior-like terms: "laying in ambush," spying, and "giving the alarm." The descriptions of the "matrons" repeat a trope of Cherokee and other Southeastern Indigenous women's "Amazonian" qualities, becoming obstacles to settler access of Indigenous women's bodies and lands. Just as De Soto's chroniclers described the Lady of Cofitachequi and other Indigenous peoples as feminine when seeming to comply with colonial desires and as masculine threats when opposing them, Cherokee women are described as feminine when characterizing a desire for colonization and as masculine when they become an obstacle to colonial violence.

Eventually, Bartram writes that the men gain the trust of the girls, who "confidently discovered themselves and decently advanced to meet us, half unveiling their blooming faces, incarnated with the modest maiden blush, and with native innocence and cheerfulness presented their little baskets, merrily telling us their fruit was ripe and sound."[103] Like the blending of Cherokee bodies with the flora, the strawberries become a symbol for Cherokee women's sexuality and bodies, one that is described as both sensual and innocent, and willingly "presented" for white men's use. The entire scene takes place in a field of strawberries, a metaphor that connects the land with Cherokee women's sexuality. Both the land and Cherokee women's bodies become available to white men, who freely give the strawberries to the white men. After leaving "these Elysian fields, we again mounted the hills, which we crossed, and traversing obliquely their flowery beds, arrived in town in the cool of the evening."[104] Cherokee lands, themselves, are described in highly sexualized terms as "flowery beds" that the men "mount" and traverse, rendering Cherokee gender, sexuality, and lands as "ripe" for creating a heteropatriarchal colonial paradise.

I would like to imagine that the older women were successful in protecting the younger women. It makes me wonder about other parts of the story that I don't know: was it common practice for older women to accompany girls in the gathering of strawberries, or were they there specifically to protect them within a context of war? Were any of them, in fact, warriors? Were any of them asegi *people? Juan Pardo encountered an* asegi *person gathering strawberries, and Bartram uses the strawberries as a way to eroticize Cherokee women. In our stories strawberries are a symbol of love. A fruit given by Unetlvnvhv to stop First Man and First Woman from quarrelling, a way of returning* duyuktv *to their relationship. A symbol of love, not violence. I like to imagine the spirit of that* asegi *person also present at this scene, joining the older women, who I also imagine as* asegi, *helping to protect the community.*

When I am focused on weaving baskets, wampum, fingerweaving, or engaged deeply in beadwork, I dream patterns. I dream how strands could interlock in ways I hadn't thought of while awake. I see the zigzag of lightning on a sash or how I can weave wampum beads into a turtle pattern.

This weaving is different. An un-weaving. Unraveling these threads of colonial history to find how a pattern emerges. I still dream patterns. I find them terrifying.

In my dreams I talk with the people who saw all of this happen. I visit with the Muskogee woman taken as a slave by De Soto and later used as an interpreter. Call it what you want: dreams, imaginings, trauma. I will call it asegi *memory. I listen to stories of each of these waves of invasion and know that for every story the colonists tell us, there are other stories that took place that colonists knew not to leave evidence of. The descriptions of uncivilized and often naïve children of the forest are deeply painful. Military reports. Treaties. Plans for stealing our land and our children.*

Baskets. Rivercane. Patterns. Strawberries.

My partner Michael tells me that while researching this chapter I've been waking up in the middle of the night from nightmares at least three times a week. I don't remember all of these nightmares, but I wake up exhausted.

The weight of all of these routes etched into my body.

ROUTE VII: JAMES ADAIR

On the edge of the American Revolution, a trader named James Adair recorded his observations of Cherokee and other Southeastern nations. Like other colonists, he hoped to serve his own ends.[105] And, like other routes through the Southeast, Adair marks Indigenous genders and sexualities as aberrant and perverse. This is particularly clear in the following statement:

> The Cheerake are an exception to all civilized or savage nations, in having no laws against adultery; they have been a considerable while under petticoat-government, and allow their women full liberty to plant their brows with horns as oft as they please, without fear of punishment. On this account their marriages are ill observed, and of a short continuance, like the Amazons, they divorce their fighting bed-fellows at their pleasure, and fail not to execute their authority, when their fancy directs them to a more agreeable choice.[106]

The trope of Cherokee women as "Amazons" reappears, signaling to his audience the sexual and gender nonconformity of Cherokee women. In order to argue for the colonization of Cherokee lands and bodies, however (and in order to provide evidence in his odd argument that Native people are descendants of "ancient Hebrews"), he provides a narrative after this passage that argues that "adulteresses" were punished with gang rape. He argues that this demonstrates that Cherokees (as well Southeastern Indigenous people) have a "patriarchal-like government" through a "misunderstanding" of Mosaic law because of a separation of time and space from Christendom.[107]

These contradictory moments create a chaotic, *asegi* space in the text that enables us to see the way colonial histories use gender and sexuality to mark larger colonial projects. On the one hand, Adair describes a nonmonogamous system of sexuality and "marriage" in which Cherokee women's sexual and social power is depicted as out of control and Cherokees as under "a petticoat government." On the other hand, Cherokee men's savage masculinity brutalizes Cherokee women. In his contradictory descriptions, there are both "no laws against adultery" and punishments for "adultery" that are too severe. In all cases, Cherokee gender and sexuality are volatile and dangerous and in need of Christian, colonial regulation.

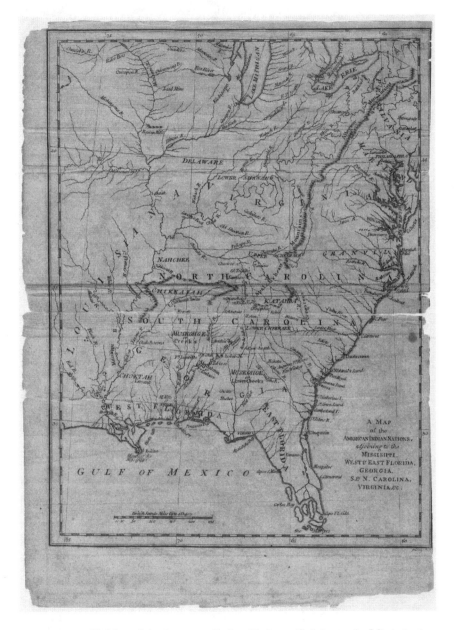

FIGURE 10. "A Map of the American Indian Nations, adjoining to the Mississippi, West & East Florida, Georgia, S. & N. Carolina, Virginia, &c," James Adair, 1775. North Carolina Maps Collection, University of North Carolina at Chapel Hill, http://dc.lib.unc.edu/cdm/ref/collection/ncmaps/id/2074.

Adair claims that such savage gender and sexuality is a devolution from the civilizing power of European Christianity, but that Native people have the potential to become "civilized" because, he argues, Native people are the descendants of ancient Jewish people who—separated from the rest of the world by time and space—were not given the benefit of Christian civilization.[108] He writes that, despite this, and despite negative cultural shifts brought on by the wrong kinds of Europeans, Native people are not "idolaters." As evidence, he relates the following story:

> I well remember, that, in the year 1746, one of the upper towns of the aforesaid Muskohge, was so exceedingly exasperated against some of our Chikkasah traders, for having, when in their cups, forcibly viewed the nakedness of one of their women, (who was reputed to be an hermaphrodite) that they were on the point of putting them to death, according to one of their old laws against crimes of that kind.—But several of us, assisted by some of the Koosah town, rescued them from their just demerit. Connecting together these particulars, we can scarcely desire a stronger proof, that they have not been idolaters, since they first came to America; much less, that they erected, and worshipped any such lascivious and obscene idols, as the heathens above recited.[109]

For years I misunderstood this passage, which I assumed was a story of a person thought to be Two-Spirit almost being killed. Perhaps because the larger context of violence against women and Two-Spirit people in colonial writings is often so severe that I begin to unconsciously assume that when an asegi *figure is mentioned, violence against them will follow.*

But no. This story is about Creeks almost killing Chickasaw traders who, while drunk, forcibly stripped a Creek person thought to be Two-Spirit in the Creeks' own town. Adair and other Creeks from Coosa saved the Chickasaw traders from being killed. I originally thought that Adair was saying there was an old law that would put Two-Spirit people to death, but instead he is saying that the "old law" was against the stripping and viewing of this person's body, which he uses to argue that there are "old laws" against idolatrous depictions of gender anomalies.

The rage of the Creeks in Coosa came from the violation of this person, Two-Spirit or not. I would like to imagine that this person was Two-Spirit, and that this moment points to a history in which the rage of the Creeks came from the violation and humiliation inflicted on this person's body. Obviously, the "old law" had nothing to do with the Second Commandment, despite Adair's strained logic. I would like to imagine that the "old law" was, instead, about the violation of the bodies of women and Two-Spirit people.[110]

ROUTE VIII: *ASEGI* MEMORIES

Our memory—as Cherokee people, as Two-Spirit people, as Indigenous LGBTQ people—is often limited by the exact colonial structures that dictate "knowledge" about our past. What if we looked at our past in ways that examine how all of our genders and sexualities as Cherokee people were "queered" by colonial powers to tell new stories, asegi stories, that rethink our cultural memories?

Within this network of routes, incursions into our bodies, attempted eradication of our lives and nations, our bodies survived. That there are even words for Two-Spirit people that are remembered in any language is a miracle. Asegi udanti. Nudale udanti.

Heteropatriarchy depends on a binary gender system in which men have power over women. As such, a feminine presence is both subject to, and constitutive of, heteropatriarchal violence. Within this logic, Spanish colonial Christian power is seen as a "proper" masculine force—a masculinity civilized through a marriage between the Church and the Crown and, thus, able to deploy this civilizing force onto Indigenous bodies. Indigenous people, then, are portrayed as either properly gendered—desirous of colonial power, and the bodies of colonists themselves, in a feminine submission to colonization—or rebellious to colonization, and thus displaying a savage masculinity that must be subdued through heteropatriarchal colonial control.

But Cofitachequi and other Native people, as well as Gómez and other Africans enslaved by De Soto, found ways to negotiate, resist, and subvert De Soto. We can remember Cofitachequi's story as a moment of resistance in an *asegi* story. It is not an uncomplicated story that imagines the pre-invasion landbase as a world without oppression. Cofitachequi, after all, was a leader of a powerful nation that had control over a huge area. The "chiefdoms" of this period in Southeastern history (what archaeologists call the "Mississippian Period"), in fact, had centralized power within large cities. This leader of Cofitachequi is spoken of as having slaves herself, and while the systems of Indigenous slavery may have been different than the racialized systems of slavery of European colonizers, and later the United States, there is no system of slavery that is not brutal.

Nevertheless, Cofitachequi's escape with Gómez, and perhaps others, can still be imagined as an *asegi* departure from a colonial agenda. Queer, in that Cofitachequi as an Indigenous woman who was a leader is queered by invaders, and queer in that her escape with Gómez is immediately sexualized by chroniclers, suggesting colonial anxiety about racialized castes. Though a sexual relationship is certainly not impossible, it is just as queer to imagine that Cofitachequi and Gómez (and, since we're imagining, why not imagine that the unnamed North African and Taíno slaves also escape, shall we?) and the other woman carrying the basket of pearls enter into other kinds of alliance. Gómez was fluent in Spanish and, of course, had inside knowledge of both De Soto's level of brutality and the direction they were traveling. Why not imagine, in fact, that this alliance contributed to the resistance from Indigenous people that De Soto met throughout the Southeast? Or, perhaps more to the point, what do we choose *not* to remember? Why do we employ memory in the ways we do, in ways that only consider the absence of Two-Spirit and queer people rather than our presence? Or forget that the absence of Two-Spirit people in the colonial record shows not only our absence, but our presence?

This is not to say that Cofitachequi *was* Two-Spirit, but to center an *asegi* critique of power to reimagine this as an *asegi* story that disrupts colonial sexual and gender power. However, why would we assume that Cofitachequi was *not* someone we would now call Two-Spirit? Knowing only that she was a powerful female Indigenous leader, the De Soto chroniclers would have had little to no understanding of the gender system Cofitachequi was living in. While she was certainly quite powerful, and there would be no reason for her to assume she couldn't serve as a negotiator with invading men, many Indigenous gender systems were (and are) not binary. She wouldn't have had to be presenting a male gender to be inhabiting a Two-Spirit space. Colonial and heteropatriarchal renderings of the past limit our imagination, dictate to us what of the past is remembered and how. An *asegi* approach to rereading these histories enables us to at least challenge the assumption that some kind of "lack of evidence" of Two-Spirit presence in the archive somehow proves a binary gender system. An *asegi* critique counters such an argument by pointing out that there is an equal "lack of evidence" that she was *not* someone we would now call Two-Spirit. Some approaches to reading this history might, in fact, argue that there is more "evidence" that she was someone we would now call Two-Spirit than "evidence" she was not. Additionally, Daniel Heath Justice reminds us that "we also have a lot of evidence of . . . things folks aren't thrilled about, like, oh, burning people alive at the stake in the 1700s, torturing them to death. I mean, I think having a bunch of queer folks running around in the Nation is a much nicer thing than burning people alive at the stake. I understand that there was a social role for that, whatever, but it doesn't necessarily fit my ethical protocols today. Kiss him, mustn't kill him."[111] Many contemporary Two-Spirit elders and teachers, for instance, often say that Two-Spirit people served as political mediators and negotiators during first waves of invasion, reflecting many Indigenous traditions in which Two-Spirit people often served.

Telling *asegi* stories about this very queer Lady of Cofitachequi enables us to create an *asegi* imaginary that examines how her queer presence disrupts colonial gendered and sexualized deployments of power. Re-membering Cofitachequi as inhabiting an *asegi* space offers us a vision of *asegi* identities as chaotic, not to Indigenous worldviews and communities, but to settler power. As Cherokee and other Indigenous Two-Spirit people engage in a process of remembering, continuing, and reimagining our histories, the Lady of Cofitachequi is significant not only because her interactions with De Soto can be seen as one of the origin stories about the ways colonial heteropatriarchy was used in the original invasions of Indigenous nations, but also because the Lady of Cofitachequi subverted colonial desires, formed alliances with others wanting to escape, and returned home.

An *asegi* return to home is not limited to a return to Cherokee homelands, but also includes a homecoming to who we are as human beings, regardless of our presence in colonial archives. Leslea, a participant in "On the Wings of *Wada-duga*," asserts that we must inhabit our identities in the present, refusing the idea that Cherokee Two-Spirit people need "evidence" of a precolonial past to exist.

> But really, at some point it has to stop being sharing about what we don't love about how we're treated, *being* the people we are. Taking on those roles. And so for me, that was learning how to play rivercane flute, it was fishing, it was helping Earl fix his ultralight plane, it was being out with the guys doing the cars. That sort of stuff. And just *being* who we are. And at *that* point we'll start . . . I feel *certain* that our mythology will start reemerging. Because *none* of this stuff is ever lost.[112]

We were never lost. While heteropatriarchal colonization attempts to claim land and bodies, *asegi* bodies remain unruly. We trick colonial powers. We escape. We survive. We re-create and re-member who we are. We come home.

Amid all of these bodies of our dead are also the bodies of the living. Our bodies. The bodies of those who survived in order to bring us here alive.

Our bodies protecting each other.

Our bodies holding each other.

Our bodies loving each other.

A kiss that burns their maps away.

3

UNWEAVING THE BASKET

Missionaries, Slavery, and the Regulation of
Gender and Sexuality

UNWEAVING

WITHIN THE CONTEXT OF over two hundred years of experience
with numerous forms of settler violence, but unsuccessful colonization of Cherokee territory, by the time the British began to
colonize the Southeast and establish trade and treaty relationships with
Cherokees, settler violence was well known. Cherokees had undergone major
social upheavals between the invasion of De Soto and the American Revolution. Between 1776 and the signing of the Treaty of New Echota in 1835,
"civilization" efforts continued to deploy gender and sexuality as integral to
colonization.[1]

In the previous chapter, I examined heteropatriarchal violence in colonial
discourse. This chapter will again look to settler-colonial discourse to examine the queering of Cherokee people and imagine *asegi* presence. Further, it
will examine how colonial concepts of gender and sexuality were internalized
by Cherokee communities as Cherokee forms of governance shifted from
autonomous, gender-egalitarian townships to a centralized, male-dominated
Cherokee Nation. It will trace these internalizations through both the efforts
of missionaries to "civilize" Cherokee bodies as well as the adoption of chattel
slavery and anti-Black laws that occurred in the nineteenth century before the
Removal.

My framework in this chapter is deeply informed by Tiya Miles's analysis in her pivotal book on the James Vann House, *The House on Diamond Hill: A Cherokee Plantation Story*, which details the connections between Cherokee adoption of chattel slavery and domestic violence. In remembering the experiences of Cherokee women and enslaved Black people at the Vann Plantation, Miles provides a deeper understanding of genealogies of gendered violence in Cherokee communities: "Shifting Cherokee attitudes toward women's role in politics and domestic spaces, often propelled by U.S. agents and white missionaries, profoundly affected . . . women's lives. Peggy Scott was among a first generation of Cherokee women to endure serial domestic violence at the hands of her husband, a cultural shift brought about by access to alcohol, and exacerbated, it can be argued, by the volatile context of a gendered and racialized plantation order."[2] Miles's analysis of these forms of violence within a context of white physical and cultural encroachments onto Cherokee lands and an increasing threat of forced removal enables us to look at how gendered and racialized legal and cultural shifts in the Cherokee Nation during this historical period are inseparable from the internalization of colonial heteropatriarchy.

This chapter is also indebted to the now long-established scholarship on Cherokee women's histories to help uncover *asegi* memories. Theda Perdue's work on Cherokee women is particularly significant in understanding Cherokee women's power and autonomy as well as colonial shifts in gendered power that served to disenfranchise Cherokee women, but also for her analysis of how Cherokee systems of gender held possibilities for "anomalous" genders outside of a strict binary. I revisit such historical work, as well as some of its primary documents, to imagine *asegi* stories that can disrupt erasures of *asegi* genders and sexualities. Colonial heteropatriarchal genders and sexualities become internalized and legally inscribed in Cherokee communities during the period between the late eighteenth century and the Removal. In order to understand how *asegi* stories, identities, and lives are erased or hidden in colonial records, and, in turn, the lives of contemporary *asegi* people, we have to unweave the strands of stories that have created the cultural memories we currently carry.

Marilou Awiakta writes, "Even a break in the cardinal balance may be restored to wholeness and harmony. Broken strands in the web of life may be repaired, as a basket out of kilter may be returned to balance if one unweaves it back to the original error, corrects it and reweaves from there."[3] The idea of needing to unweave a basket in order to find where the pattern was thrown off in order to begin the work of reweaving resonates with *asegi* stories. *Asegi* stories weave new patterns based on previous knowledge and memory, and part of this work is always an unweaving of splints, in order to understand where the pattern was thrown off so that we can *reweave* our futures. Through unweaving we find the stories hidden between the basket walls.

Such an unweaving is necessary because dominant cultural memories that erase *asegi* presence continue to disrupt *duyuktv*—the balance and justice that must be maintained among human beings and in relation to nature and spirit. The labor of unweaving the past is necessary for a reweaving of our present and future. In my conversation with Leslea, she offered:

> Some of the things that fall under the responsibilities that we would have had are some of the things going desperately wrong right now, and I have to say, I doubt if my generation and yours is going to correct it. There's work to do. So you need to gather your tools. There will be a time for the work. There's always time for the work. You need to take the moment to gather your tools, make sure you are emotionally stable enough to manage them, and do the work. And know when to stop and take a break. And do what you need to do.[4]

This chapter is part of a gathering of tools for engaging in the complex process of unweaving and reweaving cultural memories. In this story, the formation of "sexuality" takes a particular hold in the pre-Removal era of the late eighteenth and early nineteenth centuries through mutually reinforcing regulations of gender and sexuality through the "civilizing" projects of slavery and missionization. These two institutions give rise to formal regulations of Cherokee gender and sexuality through the passage of Cherokee laws that limit women's autonomy and regulate Black bodies. This period is an *asegi* space—a period of major transitions, disruptions, and chaos in Cherokee law, culture, and politics, as Cherokees officially dissolved town-based systems of governance based on war and peace structured by *duyuktv* among genders, and centralized the Cherokee Nation under a national constitution and an all-male governing body.

CHEROKEE GENDER AND SEXUALITY ON THE EDGE OF REMOVAL

While Spain was unsuccessful in establishing colonies in Cherokee territory, Spanish (and other European) incursions caused major disruptions of

Cherokee lives. Native communities throughout the Southeast experienced devastating losses due to smallpox as well as warfare. Swine brought by the Spanish spread smallpox and radically shifted ecosystems. Many "chiefdoms" throughout the Southeast collapsed. In Cherokee stories, a ruling class of priests, the *Ani Kutani*, were overthrown by a revolution. While it is not agreed upon when this revolution occurred, it is arguable that the fall of the "Mississippian chiefdoms" led to a radical and *intentional* restructuring of power that decentralized the authority of rulers in major cities and put in place the system of autonomous townships.

Townships operated through council-based systems in which women's authority was central. Cherokee townships had seven-sided council houses, one side to seat each of the seven matrilineal clans. Cherokee women held balance at the center of power in culture and governance. Women held authority and prestige, maintaining social order through matrifocal and matrilineal clan systems. Carolyn Ross Johnston explains the central role of women in Cherokee governance: "Cherokee women were . . . influential in political affairs, advising on war and peace. The women of each clan selected an elder woman to serve on the women's council, a highly influential body. One of these women, the beloved woman, who also represented her clan, presided over the council. Frequently beloved women who had distinguished themselves in battle could decide the fate of a prisoner."[5]

Women were able to gain the title of *Ghigau*, a title that Wilma Mankiller says probably translates as Red or War Woman, but is often translated as Beloved Woman.[6] Robert Conley points out that it is unknown whether titles such as Red or War Woman, Beloved Woman, and Pretty Woman were actually "different positions or different translations of the same position," but speculates they were separate positions.[7] Theda Perdue argues that "War Women probably became 'beloved' when they passed menopause."[8]

Even though separate women's councils existed, M. Amanda Moulder notes that in men's councils, women "would either transmit their concerns through the male members of their clans . . . or vocalize their concerns when the issue was relevant to an area of women's authority."[9] Michelene Pesantubbee explains further:

> [D]uring times of conflict or town- or nationwide decision making, a body of elders, or beloved people, operated as councils that cut across clans. . . . Thus,

seven war counselors called war, seven members of the national or a town council concurred with the order and declared war, and the Pretty Women, the women's council, determined the fate of captives and judged the conduct of war. The women also had a voice in the council's decisions regarding policy in war. Although the uku, or peace leader, stepped aside and the war leaders took over during time of conflict, the white and red were not completely separated. . . . Balance was thus maintained in a number of ways, including between elder (peace leaders) and younger (warriors), red and white, men and women.[10]

Duyuktv—balance and justice—was a structuring logic of Cherokee culture and governance at this time, particularly the balance between Red (War) and White (Peace). Cherokee literary scholar Daniel Heath Justice writes that "even when a formal warrior culture lost its emphasis in the nineteenth century, Cherokee resistance—physical and rhetorical—continued on unabated. Red and white, war and peace: linked by the enduring Cherokee spirit of defiance. I propose that this red/white structure, although officially discarded during the consolidation of the autonomous towns . . . has in fact persisted to the present day."[11]

"Marriage" (though even this word is misleading) before invasion was a very different institution than it was in European traditions. Clan—not marriage—was the central Cherokee social arrangement.[12] Women maintained jurisdiction over agriculture and their children. Women's brothers—not their husbands—were the central male figures to their children's lives. The idea that one would marry one person "until death do us part" was foreign to the Cherokee worldview, and women could separate from their husbands and remarry at will. Further, it was not uncommon for a man to marry two or more sisters, an arrangement that helped further maintain power within women's families. While there were certainly sexual taboos—for instance, having children with someone of your clan—Cherokee people enjoyed a great deal of sexual freedom.

The presence of same-gender loving people or same-gender erotic bonds is, unsurprisingly, mostly absent from colonial records. However, as Paula Gunn Allen argued in the 1980s, speaking generally of Indigenous cultures, "Young women were often separated from the larger groups for periods of months or years, as were young men. In such circumstances, lesbianism and homosexuality . . . may have been the norm for primary pair-bonding" even while people formed other household arrangements and had children with each other.[13] To assume same-gender bonds and sex didn't exist, or even that they were limited, is part of a very contemporary heteropatriarchal imaginary that constructs "sexuality" as a system of identity around a "heterosexual/homosexual" binary. In fact, as I discuss in the next chapter, there was even a ceremony that existed to mark "perpetual friendship" between two men or two women, suggesting that same-gender intimacies (sexual or not) were not only present but recognized as a specific kind of relationship by the community.

Cherokee people living outside of a European gender binary are also noted in colonial texts. In 1825, Cherokees told C. C. Trowbridge that "[t]here were among them formerly, men who assumed the dress & performed all the duties of women & who lived their whole lives in this manner, but they can give no reason of this singular fact."[14] This particular quotation is one of the few references to Cherokee people in Walter L. Williams's *The Spirit and the Flesh*, but it is quoted (and requoted by Perdue) without the final clause, "but they can give no reason of this singular fact."[15] The larger context in this part of Trowbridge's manuscript on Cherokee culture is family structure, courtship and marriage, and gender norms. No other mention is made of *asegi* people in the manuscript, but the final clause of the sentence indicates that Trowbridge was curious about this aspect of Cherokee culture. Trowbridge's "informants," it seems, want to distance themselves in time from "men who assumed the dress of women," making it clear to Trowbridge that the practice was in the past. That they "could give no reason" for this fact can be read as a form of resistance to Trowbridge's questioning. One possibility is that Cherokee informants simply could give no reason because the statement was already self-evident and was not seen as in need of explanation. Another possibility is that Cherokees were strategically hiding cultural information by refusing to relate "a reason" for the presence of *asegi* people. For Cherokees to tell a colonist that people living outside of Euro-American gender binaries was a continuing practice, or that there were particular cultural "reasons" for such people, would have placed *asegi* people, and all Cherokees, at a particular kind of risk of further colonial control. It also seems significant to me that Trowbridge doesn't relay any feelings of disdain that Cherokees had for males living as women. It is simply spoken of as a "singular fact" without further discussion. The relegating of *asegi* people to the past and without further explanation can be imagined as an act of resistance to settler gender norms and, perhaps, a way of protecting *asegi* people. However, even if male-embodied *asegi* people were not able to present themselves as women (or not men), their genders remained in living memory.

Within this same period, John Howard Payne was told, "Women in certain cases dressed in men's clothes and went to battle."[16] While War Women as well as Beloved Women were known of and written about, this particular description is significant because it says that War Women dressed in men's clothes in addition to going to battle. Such a description suggests that War Women inhabited, or could enter into, an *asegi* space. On the edge of removal, Cherokees still had a clear memory (if not a hidden current experience) of gender expressions outside of a European binary.

As detailed in the previous chapter, Indigenous gender and sexuality became central in settler-colonial projects, a key point in making arguments to justify European empire. In 1775, Bernard Romans published *A Concise Natural History of East and West-Florida*, in which he argues that Native people in the Southeast are "of different species from any in the other parts [of the globe]."[17] As evidence of this, he depicts Indigenous gender and sexuality as savage and backward, writing that, among the Choctaws, "Both sexes are wanton to the highest degree, and a certain fashionable disorder is very common among them. Sodomy is also practiced but not to the same excess as among the Creeks and Chickasaws, and the *Cinaedi* among the Chactaws are obliged to dress themselves in woman's attire, and are highly despised especially by the women."[18] Romans was not particularly concerned with the cultural specificities of Southeastern Indigenous people, but instead in characterizing all Southeastern Indigenous people as a "different species" than other humans as a part of justifying colonization. As evidence of a specific Southeastern Indigenous difference, gender and sexuality are depicted as a reversal of European civilization in need of colonial intervention and regulation. Whether or not "*Cinaedi*" were actually despised during this period (and even if they were—which I think we must question—this doesn't mean they were "despised" in earlier periods), Romans's point is that "sodomy" and gender transgression are behaviors and expressions that colonists could aid in eradicating. As part of this civilizing project, chattel slavery becomes a central logic seen as a force to transform and regulate Southeastern Indigenous gender and sexuality.

Because agricultural practices in the Southeast were tied to women, spiritually and through work, Europeans consistently characterized Native women as oppressed by Native men and forced to perform drudgery. A deep connection to heteropatriarchal gender binaries and enslavement appears in the text when Romans writes, "A savage has the most determined resolution against labouring or tilling the ground, the slave his wife must do that."[19] Implicit in this statement is the idea that "civilized" men would shelter "wives" from work outside the home and utilize slave labor instead. Speaking of the backward and savage gender roles of all Indigenous people in the Southeast, he continues, "A savage man discharges his urine in a sitting posture, and a savage woman standing. I need not tell how opposite this is to our common practice."[20] All Native people were seen as sexually deviant and gender nonconforming, and adopting chattel slavery was seen as key in obtaining gendered "civilization."

A restructuring of Cherokee gender and sexuality was central to the colonial project, not only through reshaping gendered labor but also through a restructuring of the entire matrilineal clan system, matrifocal family structures, and women's jurisdiction over land and children, replacing them with patrilineal traditions and patriarchal laws. Cherokee matrifocal and matrilineal culture posed major problems to the entire colonial enterprise.

Within such heteropatriarchal colonial logics in which all Cherokee people are gender and sexual deviants, Cherokee *asegi* people become unreadable. An *asegi* story, however, sees this absence as a hyper-presence in order to understand colonization and, in the words of Malea Powell, "how they did it" and "how we undo it."[21] An unweaving.

UNWEAVING SPLINT ꮔꮼ/*SOQUO*/ONE: SLAVERY

As the Cherokee Nation attempted to negotiate and resist violence from the United States and its citizens—which was already part of a larger history of settler violence—it began to adopt Euro-American laws and cultural practices. This was not a simple attempt at assimilation. In fact, it was an attempt to resist assimilation and—feasibly—genocide by the United States.

The United States government—and other European powers before it—had a particular investment in shifting Cherokee gender and sexual systems because these systems worked to resist colonial acquisition of land. Because women had control of land, property, and children and Cherokee law and custom held Cherokee land in common, the United States made concerted efforts to change Cherokee gender and sexual roles. The explicit thinking by the United States was that if the labor roles of Cherokee men shifted away from hunting—which requires use of large tracts of land—and began European-style farming on small plots of land, Cherokees couldn't argue that they needed as much of their traditional territory. In an 1803 letter from President Thomas Jefferson to William Henry Harrison (governor of the Indiana Territory), Jefferson makes the policy of the U.S. government clear:

> The decrease of game rendering their subsistence by hunting insufficient, we wish to draw them to agriculture, to spinning and weaving. The latter branches they take up with great readiness, because they fall to the women, who gain by quitting the labors of the field for those which are exercised within doors. When they withdraw themselves to the culture of a small piece of land, they will perceive how useless to them are their extensive forests, and will be willing to pare them off from time to time in exchange for necessaries for their farms and families.[22]

In the 1791 Treaty of Holston, "A Treaty of Peace and Friendship," the Cherokee Nation ceded lands for peace and "protection." As part of the exchange, the treaty states, "That the Cherokee nation may be led to a greater degree of civilization, and to become herdsmen and cultivators, instead of remaining in a state of hunters, the United States will from time to time furnish gratuitously the said nation with useful implements of husbandry."[23] The "exchange," of course, was designed not only to take land, but also to pursue the government's civilization project through a transformation of gender, labor, and land use. Haunting this "exchange" is the presence of chattel slavery, as the "herdsmen and cultivators" among the U.S. elite were, in fact, slaves.

The Civilization Fund Act of 1819 provided funding to "civilize" Native people:

> That for the purpose of providing against the further decline and final extinction of the Indian tribes, adjoining the frontier settlements of the United States, and for introducing among them the habits and arts of civilization, the President of the United States shall be, and he is hereby authorized, in every case where he shall judge improvement in the habits and condition of such Indians practicable, and that the means of instruction can be introduced with their own consent, to employ capable persons, of good moral character, to instruct them in the mode of agriculture suited to their situation; and for teaching their children in reading, writing, and arithmetic; and performing such other duties as may be enjoined, according to such instructions and rules as the President may give and prescribe for the regulation of their conduct in the discharge of their duties.[24]

As discussed in the previous chapter, John Lawson makes this suggestion to assimilate Native people and bring them under British jurisdiction nearly one hundred years earlier. Such a plan is repeated after the American Revolution through the "civilization project." Tiya Miles observes,

> In the view of federal officials, this lifestyle was backward and wasteful. They felt that Cherokee men were embarrassingly feminized, that Cherokee women were improperly masculinized, and that the vast, uncultivated Cherokee hunting grounds were underutilized. . . . So along with plows and looms, Cherokees were implicitly urged to acquire slaves. Benjamin Hawkins, the federal agent assigned to the southeastern tribes in this period, advised the tribes under his purview to take up slaveholding. . . . Progress and slavery were linked in Hawkins's view, so much so that he developed his own model plantation along the Flint River as an example for the Indians to follow.[*]

Within the context of European and U.S. slaveholding societies, adopting "civilization" meant adopting dominant Euro-American patriarchal family structures and gendered labor and relationship formations, and securing forced labor through slavery. Chattel slavery served as a pedagogy of violent control and as a means to transform Cherokee relationships with gender.

Even before colonists encouraged Cherokees to adopt chattel slavery, it had deeply impacted Cherokee life since the De Soto invasion. Cherokees already had a preexisting system of slavery, though it did not consider humans property, nor was it a system in which people were kept as slaves in perpetuity along with their descendants. Cherokee prisoners of war were often subjected to enslavement, though they often became members of families and communities. As discussed in the previous chapter, when De Soto invaded the Southeast he brought both African and Indigenous slaves with him and took numerous slaves with him along the way, including Cherokees, sometimes as *tamemes*, other times as sexual slaves for invading men, and probably—we can safely assume—as both. While Indigenous slaves may have escaped, other survivors would remain enslaved in Mexico or elsewhere within the Spanish slave trade.

Within the context of expanding European empires—including invading armies, genocide, land theft, and enslavement—Indigenous people of the Americas and diasporic African peoples do not occupy clearly separate categories of "enslaved" and "colonized." In fact, both Indigenous people of the

Americas and Indigenous African peoples, diasporic and not, historically share common struggles against colonial violence. Andrea Smith argues that "settler colonialism does not merely operate by racializing Native peoples, positioning them as racial minorities rather than as colonized nations, but also through domesticating Black struggle within the framework of anti-racist rather than anti-colonial struggle."[26] Current racial constructions of the United States cleave apart Native and Black struggles and histories in ways that obscure enslavement, settler colonialism, and genocide as facets of a larger, single-minded project. This cleaving erases more complicated histories of genocide and enslavement of African, Native, and Black Indian bodies.

One of these erasures is the memory that Native people in the Americas were enslaved up to, and past, emancipation. This erasure happens, in part, because Manifest Destiny structures dominant historical memories, transforming the history of the United States into a single project of westward expansion that begins with European and Euro-American colonization of the East Coast and marches steadily to the Pacific Ocean to create an American mythology of a unified country (and history) "from sea to shining sea."

Obviously, histories of settler colonialism do not follow such an easy narrative and trajectory. Numerous European powers colonized what is now the United States from different points of origin and in different ways. Too often we neglect to pay careful attention to the connections between histories we already know in ways that solidify the United States as a monolithic empire. While we know that the United States was only thirteen states at the beginning of independence, we still imagine the lower forty-eight states as well as Alaska and Hawai'i as part of "American history" at that moment.

The logic of U.S. empire forgets, or erases, the fact that the original thirteen states were in a precarious position between European and Indigenous powers and the newly formed United States was far from having a stronghold in North America. This logic also erases histories of enslavement by perpetuating the myth of enslavement becoming illegal after the Thirteenth Amendment in 1865. In addition to the fact that the convict leasing system essentially kept enslavement of Black people intact until the 1940s, Deborah A. Miranda notes that Indigenous people in California were commonly enslaved until at least 1866.[27]

The erasure of the enslavement of Indigenous people takes place because of another great American myth, of "the vanishing Indian," and the false assumption that Native people were merely victims of European-led genocide, seen as perhaps tragic, but inevitable. The enslavement of Indigenous people signals a particular type of Indigenous presence that is often unimaginable within dominant tellings of race and settler colonialism. Such a re-membering does not erase the fact that anti-Black racism became central to racial logics of enslavement. Indigenous people were often enslaved because of actual African ancestry or because anti-Black, pro-slavery laws and practices often racialized non-Black Native people as Black. As Arica L. Coleman details, "the overturning of Indian slave laws [in Virginia] did not lead to the mass emancipation of Indian slaves" and "[t]he criterion in determining who was White, Black or Indian was not applied with any consistency."[28] But, even before this, Indigenous people were targets of the slave trade by both white people and other Southeastern Native people (within a context of war and colonization) and used against each other and African diasporic peoples in the interests of European settler projects. Colonial fears of Red Black alliances and rebellions caused colonists to find ways to pit Africans and Indigenous people against each other, using Cherokees as slave catchers and Black people in military attacks on Cherokee communities.[29]

By the time Cherokees began enslaving Africans, many Cherokees had also survived (or been killed through) chattel slavery. By 1708, "the population of the colony of South Carolina totaled 9,850, including 2,900 African slaves and 1,400 Indian slaves."[30] Patrick Minges argues,

> In spite of a . . . tendency to differentiate the African slave from the Indian, the institution of African slavery was actually imposed on top of a preexisting system of Indian slavery. From the very first points of contact with Europeans, colonists used the term *Indian wars* as a justification for the enslavement of vast numbers of indigenous peoples. Even into the eighteenth century, Indian slavery was one of the primary sources of commerce for the colonies. . . . The colonists formed alliances with coastal native groups, armed them, and encouraged them to make war on weaker tribes deeper in the interior. Native Americans were seized and carried back to ports along the East Coast, where they were loaded on ships for the "middle passage" to the West Indies or to colonies farther north. Many of the Indian slaves were kept at home to work on the plantations.[31]

Generations of history with the slave trade, which took place on top of already existing systems of enslavement during war, combined with the influence of white male slave owners marrying into Cherokee families, helped to implement dominant Euro-American systems of power and control into Cherokee communities. By the time that Benjamin Hawkins established his model plantation for Cherokees, Cherokee people would have already been familiar with the risks enslavement posed to them. A 1693 delegation of Cherokees to Charleston, attempting to bring Cherokees captured by other Native people and sold into slavery back home, was told that they had already been sold into the West Indies and could not be returned.[32] Slavery became normalized in Cherokee communities through colonial violence, which, in turn, was reenacted through the adoption of chattel slavery.

UNWEAVING SPLINT W*P*/*TAL*/TWO: SLAVERY, BLACK BODIES, AND HETEROPATRIARCHY

The adoption of chattel slavery by Cherokees was entwined with an adoption of heteropatriarchal values and practices that fundamentally disrupted Cherokee gender and sexuality. Theda Perdue writes,

> Originally, slaves seem to have performed no real function in the Cherokees' economy, where the division of labor was sexual; in fact, the Cherokees' lack of regard for material wealth and the absence of a profit motive contrasted sharply with the capitalistic economy of the antebellum South in which black slaves played an essential role. Not until a well-developed commerce, an inequality of wealth, and a central government stimulated production did Cherokee society become able to support a large number of slaves and to utilize their labor effectively.[33]

As Tiya Miles illustrates, it is through the violence carried out on the bodies of enslaved Black people that violence against Cherokee women became entrenched. Speaking of the violence experienced by Margaret (Peggy) Scott Vann Crutchfield at the hands of her husband James Vann, Miles writes,

> Like his adoption of chattel slavery, the violence that James Vann perpetrated against his wife would prefigure a growing trend in some sectors of Cherokee society. . . . As early as 1805, Moravian missionaries began to chronicle spousal abuse on Diamond Hill. And certainly by the 1820s, when Cherokee women had

also lost political power through the ratification of a Cherokee constitution that denied them the right to vote, violence against women in the home had become amply documented.[34]

The incorporation of chattel slavery as a marker of "civilization" parallels the creation and refashioning of Cherokee systems of governance and sovereignty within the context of encroaching settler powers in the nineteenth century. Many of the cultural markers that colonists read as "proof" of Cherokees' "uncivilized" state begin to shift rapidly as Cherokees attempt to prove themselves as a "civilized" people who—it was hoped—would be spared forced removal or military attack from the United States. Cherokees began to internalize what Mark Rifkin calls "the bribe of straightness," in which

> marginalized persons and groups . . . play aspects of normality against each other as part of a counterhegemonic claim to legitimacy, distinguishing themselves from other, more stigmatized modes of deviance. This dynamic . . . includes arguing for the validity of indigenous kinship systems (native family formations, homemaking, and land tenure) in ways that make them more acceptable/respectable to whites, disavowing the presence of sexual and gender practices deemed perverse within Euramerican sexology.[35]

Not only did this play out through a concerted effort to minimize Cherokee women's centrality to Cherokee community and culture, and attempting to "normalize" Cherokee gender, sexuality, family, and marriage customs to correspond with dominant Euro-American models, but also by adopting chattel slavery and Euro-American styles of nationhood and governance. Cherokee gender systems were intentionally disrupted and reformed through "civilization projects," and the adoption of slavery further entrenched European gender formations. As Perdue explains,

> Gradually men began to take over more and more of the agricultural tasks traditionally reserved for women, and their sexual roles became blurred. Only when the identification of women with agriculture had ended was the introduction and utilization of slave labor for cultivation by even a minority of Cherokees possible. The modification of traditional sexual roles and the transformation of aboriginal definitions of male and female sexuality coincided with the sudden need for additional laborers as a result of the United States' "civilization" policy.[36]

It's important to understand that, even by the time of Removal, most Cherokees were not slave owners, Christian, or English speaking. And while the "civilization" project encouraged both slave owning and Christianity, the adoption of chattel slavery did not follow a Christian/"traditionalist" split. Slavery started to be adopted by Cherokees before the establishment of missionaries. Nevertheless, missionaries often supported slavery, tacitly or explicitly, and often taught Cherokees racist concepts and violent control of Black bodies through the missions.

UNWEAVING SPLINT
KT/*TSO'*/THREE: MISSIONARIES

In order to accomplish "civilizing" Native people, the U.S. government helped to fund Christian missionaries in the Cherokee Nation. These missions were often welcome in Cherokee territory, not because Cherokee leaders wanted Cherokees to be converted, but because missionaries promised to open schools for Cherokee children to teach them to speak, write, and read English, which was increasingly necessary in order to resist U.S. encroachment and land theft.

Histories of missionaries in the Cherokee Nation are not linear or consistent. John Marrant, a Black convert, claimed to have converted "the king of the Cherokees and his daughter" as early as 1769, and Moravians had preached to both Cherokees and Creeks in the 1760s.[37] The first major missionary effort to the Cherokees was made by the Moravians, a German-speaking congregation who were often outsiders because of their religious beliefs in Christian Europe as well as in Anglo-America. The Moravians began seeking permission from Cherokee leaders to establish a missionary presence in 1775, and in 1800 Cherokee leaders agreed to allow the mission in order to educate Cherokee children, particularly so they could acquire English. The Moravians founded Springplace Mission that year, on James Vann's plantation, and, later, a mission at Oothcaloga.

The Brainerd Mission was founded by the American Board of Commissioners for Foreign Missions (ABCFM) in 1817 on the Chickamauga Creek in what is now Chattanooga, Tennessee. ABCFM established missions at Toloney (later called Carmel), Creek Path, Willstown, Hightower, and Turnip Mountain (later called the Haweis Mission), and later in New Echota, Red Clay, Running Water, Amohee, and Candy's Creek.[38] Baptists founded the Valley

Towns Mission in 1818, the Hickory Log Mission, and a mission at Nottley in 1822 which moved to Coosawattee (Tinsawatta) in 1823.[39] Methodists began missionary work in the Cherokee Nation in 1822, establishing only temporary mission sites and instead focusing on circuit preaching.[40]

The presence of missionaries among Cherokees is complex, and my point here is not to characterize missionaries as "good" or "bad," but instead to examine how they hoped to regulate Cherokee gender and sexuality in a pivotal moment in Cherokee history. It is too simplistic to characterize missionaries as an "evil" among Cherokees (though, I do think that they were often a way of enforcing violent and genocidal logics of colonialists). They were allowed into Cherokee communities only under Cherokee terms. While missionaries had their own agendas to civilize and Christianize Cherokees, they often vocally opposed Cherokee removal and—once removal was enforced—often traveled with their congregations along the Trail of Tears or themselves removed ahead of the bulk of the nation to continue mission work in Indian Territory.

Methodist missionaries, for instance, issued a forceful argument against removal that was published in *The Christian Advocate*.[41] On December 22, 1830, the State of Georgia passed a law requiring white men living in the Cherokee Nation to receive a permit, and swear an oath of allegiance to the state. The law was designed to target white advocates against Cherokee removal. On December 29, 1830, Reverend Samuel Worcester of the ABCFM held an interdenominational meeting at his home in New Echota to write a joint resolution against removal, which was originally published in the *Cherokee Phoenix* and later in the *Missionary Herald*. Worcester and another missionary, Reverend Elihu Butler, refused to submit to Georgia's law and were arrested and imprisoned, resulting in the Supreme Court case *Worcester v. Georgia* in 1832. The court ruled that Georgia had violated the sovereignty of the Cherokee Nation, but neither the State of Georgia nor Andrew Jackson would enforce the ruling, and the two missionaries remained in prison until 1833.[42]

Even while missionaries were often vocal against removal—and clearly had honest and deep connections with Cherokee people (and, in fact, after conversion several missionaries *were* Cherokee people), they also worked to disrupt Cherokee values around gender and sexuality and replace them with dominant European Christian values. According to Perdue, "For women . . . the restrictions on sexuality further compromised their autonomy and, in practice, placed control of their sexuality in the hands of fathers before marriage and husbands afterward."[43]

In both the Moravian journals and the Brainerd Mission journals, anxiety about Cherokee gender and sexuality is constantly expressed. The cultural disjuncture between European patriarchal nuclear families and Cherokee matrifocal family and clan systems often became stark in the case of marriages between white men and Cherokee women. Within Cherokee tradition, all children born of Cherokee mothers were Cherokee. The father's ancestry made no difference, as children were part of their mother's family and clan. Missionaries expressed anxiety about the way Cherokee family formation, particularly Cherokee women's authority over their children, impeded their work to "civilize" Cherokees. Apparently, a similar concern existed for white men who married into the Cherokee Nation. The Moravian journal records the following:

> Mr Rogers, who lives about forty miles from here, came and asked if we would accept his daughter, a girl of twelve years, into our care. He said that it really concerned him that she, in addition to learning sewing and knitting, should learn reading, writing, and arithmetic. . . . Here she has the opportunity to practice *these skills* even more and to learn practical work. What most concerned him was that she develop her mind and her heart and learn to live in the way necessary to get along among well-mannered people. She would have to do without all of this if she stayed with her mother, who is an Indian.[44]

Clearly, Rogers hopes to have his daughter in the care of missionaries in order for her to learn European women's gender roles and to be outside of the cultural and familial influence of her mother.

Cherokee religious traditions were, not surprisingly, abhorred by the missionaries. In addition to the fact that these traditions were clearly not Christian, the Moravians were disturbed by the mixed-gender, intergenerational nakedness that accompanied events such as Cherokee stickball:

> Old grey-headed men and women as well as a considerable number of children came with great pomp from all corners and occupied our yard and house so that we were not able to hold our service until two o'clock. . . . Oh, how sincerely we would wish to experience the time when hundreds of these heathen, who are currently completely blind, might seek the word of salvation in Springplace with the same seriousness we observed today at their gather for play and come to our worship services in crowds!—No! Even on the most important festival days in the congregation, one does not see greater seriousness or zeal for the services than

we saw in these heathen today. . . . At twilight most of them came back. Many went past us quietly. Some of them had gambled away all their valuables, even the clothing off their backs.[45]

UNWEAVING SPLINT Ơ-Y/NVG'/FOUR: SLAVERY AND MISSIONARIES

The stance of missionaries on the issue of slavery was not uniform, though none of the missionaries in the Cherokee Nation were explicitly abolitionist. An insight into how missionaries through the ABCFM might justify not only missionizing Cherokees, but hiring Black slaves as laborers, is seen in an 1828 resolution adopted after discussion of the practice of missionaries hiring slaves within the Choctaw Nation: "*Resolved*, that the Committee do not see cause to prohibit the practice; but, on the contrary, they are of the opinion that it may be expedient, in some circumstances, to employ persons who sustain this relation, by contract with their masters and with their own consent; it being understood, that all the members of the mission family at each station, should feel the obligation of treating the persons thus hired with kindness, and laboring to promote their spiritual good."[46] The ABCFM also justified hiring slaves by saying it would contribute to slaves buying their freedom and their spiritual salvation. By 1836, however, the ABCFM passed a resolution to end the practice altogether.[47]

Both the Moravians and the Brainerd Mission saw the presence of Black slaves as yet another opportunity to save heathen souls. In 1818, for example, one of the writers of the Brainerd journal writes about slaves at Springplace:

There are many of this class of people in bondage to the Cherokees, & they all speak english. Their masters, so far as has come to our knowledge, are all willing to have them instructed, & generally very indulgent in giving them time to attend meeting. If the benefit of our mission could extend no farther than to these depressed sons of Africa, we should have no cause to regret our being sent to labor in this field, or to apprehend that our patrons who are contributing the temporal support of this mission will, in eternity, think their money lost.[48]

The Brainerd mission also justified slavery as a positive Christianizing and civilizing influence on both Cherokees and slaves, finding a justification for slavery through the opportunities of Black slaves to become Christian and, because many of the slaves spoke English, to aid missionary efforts to teach English to Cherokees. A Brainerd missionary records the following after a worship service in which there was a large Black attendance:

> The African part of our congregation was larger than usual. . . . One of these, who appears to be not more than 25, remembers when he was brought from Africa, & says he is very thankful that God caused him to be brought, though slave, into this land where he can hear of the Savior. He says he once thought it hard to be a slave, but now he cares nothing about it if he may be a christian. Another, on being asked if he thought he had been wicked, exclaimed, while his eyes filled with tears, "Wicked! O yes Massa. Wicked! nobody so wicked. Wy Massa, fore des people came here . . . we all wicked as could be—we do noting but bad bad all e time. An we know noting more an e cattle. O massa! you cant tink how bad we all den be. No sabbaday—no prayer—no tink u God at all—noting but drinken, froliken, fighten, O! every ting bad." . . . We are told their mistress (who is one of the late Cherokee converts,) is herself learning to read by their assistance & the occasional assistance of her little son; who is one of our schollars; & that she is making considerable progress.[49]

While it may be true that slaves found the mission to be a site of hope and resistance, the writer here (in addition to the racist depiction of Black language) clearly means to characterize slaves as both grateful for and spiritually redeemed through slavery. The only time in the Brainerd journals in which a writer explicitly critiques slavery is after an Osage boy living as a captive in the Cherokee Nation is sold into slavery and eventually apprehended and brought to the mission for care: "O when will this highly favored land, called the land of freedom, cease to traffic in human blood!"[50]

The Moravians, though often expressing horror at the level of violence to which James Vann subjected slaves, and welcoming Black converts, also often expressed racist attitudes and taught Cherokee converts that the violent disciplining of slaves was part of becoming Christian. In 1818, for example, the Moravian mission recorded ministering to Sally Scott McDonald (Peggy's sister):

> Another time she let us know of her concern that even if she dared to join the community of God's children, she still might not be able to treat her Negroes

in a friendly way all the time, which would after all be her duty. Indeed, it could even happen that she would err as much as punishing one or the other of them, because there were some of them who brought her much displeasure through their evil life. She was . . . calmed about this, since she otherwise is considered a person of very gentle character, and we explained that it was the Christian's duty to punish evil in her servants, as well as her children.[51]

Not only can we see in this passage a pedagogy of violent control through racial violence, but also a link between the discipline and control of slaves and the discipline and control of children. A genealogy of violence can be seen here that connects heteropatriarchal family violence and enslavement. Andrea Smith argues that "heteropatriarchy is the logic that makes social hierarchy seem natural. Just as the patriarchs rule the family, the elites of the nation-state rule their citizens."[52]

Such a religious mandate for violence was internalized by Moravian converts, as is evidenced in the 1824 interactions between Chulioa, a traditionalist leader at Etowah (Hightower) and Charles R. Hicks, a Moravian convert who was serving as Second Principal Chief. In reply to a letter and a messenger asking for the removal of the ABCFM mission at Etowah, Hicks sends the following reply: "[The messenger] stated . . . that Richard Howe's negroes will not obey him since he has joined the church and [he] himself had to turn in to ploughing his fields. . . . I stated to him . . . if any of my black people were disobedient to my orders I would assuredly correct them for it because the Gospell requires Servants to be Faithfull to their masters."[53] While non-Christian Cherokees certainly owned slaves, missionaries provided a theological underpinning to slavery and violence that taught Cherokees the violent control of Black bodies.

BETWEEN THE BASKET WALLS:
MISSIONARIES AND *ASEGI* RUPTURES

The Moravians were already thought of as outsiders in Anglo-America. A German-speaking Christian denomination, the Moravians' conceptions of gender and sexuality were not parallel with Anglo-American gender and sexuality. Derrick R. Miller writes that Moravians "believed all souls were female since all souls were similarly situated in marriage to Christ," so "earthly husbands were more truly heavenly brides." Gender and sexuality were conceived always as in relation to Christ. Miller continues, "[T]he gender of Moravian brothers was not quite the same as it was for non-Moravian men, and the distinction between brother and sister did not carry quite the same meaning as that between male and female. . . . Moravian identity was gendered and defined in relation to its desire for a gendered object: whether brother or sister, single or married, all Moravians were brides of Christ who desired Christ as a man and their husband."[54]

The Moravians structured their churches "into communal groups called choirs according to their age, sex, and marital status," which "ignored estate and other family relationships."[55] Even while the Moravians pushed Cherokees to enter into Christian marriages and worked to shift Cherokee gender to reflect Euro-American gender constructions, the choirs may have created spaces of intimacy (spiritual and erotic) between people of the same sex. Miller, for instance, draws attention not only to the Moravian choir system, but particular Moravian rituals (foot washing, the lovefest, and the kiss of peace) as creating particular same-sex intimacies. Further, the Moravian theological concept of female souls may have been recognizable to Cherokees as a space of *duyuktv*, resonating with matrifocal traditions and creating a space—within a context of a disruption of *duyuktv*—between genders, for women to claim power and authority, albeit one limited by Moravians' own gendered hierarchies.

Missionaries to the Cherokees had a large impact on Cherokee life and politics, through gaining Cherokee and Black converts and through restructuring Cherokee gender in order to have Cherokees mirror a dominant Euro-American gender structure. At the same time, however, the missions' concerns in the Cherokee Nation with Cherokee marriage and proper gendered relations (and separations) between men and women—and larger shifts of gendered labor—may have actually provided *asegi* spaces for same-sex love and erotics as well as for people who may have been continuing nonbinary gender systems.

While missionaries were gaining converts by the time that the Cherokee Nation created its constitution, most Cherokees were not Christian at this point and the concept of "sodomy" was probably not a major concern. "Sodomy" was not, in fact, a major concern of the missionaries in the Cherokee Nation, if it was a concern at all. "Sodomy," in the minds of missionaries, was connected to "idolatry," and a larger concern for missionaries in other parts of the world. Instead, opposite-sex gender and sexuality, naked (or near-naked) bodies, the commingling of men and women, gendered labor, matrifocal family structures, and polygamy were the targets of missionary efforts to control and civilize Cherokee bodies. Missionaries were quite concerned with polygamy, which was a common Cherokee arrangement, and hoped to instill Christian heteropatriarchal marriages and family structures into Cherokee communities: "A young man named Coody from Chicamauga came and asked if . . . Brother Wohlfahrt would come visit them in order to marry a young couple. As much as we dislike taking on such things, we did not see how we could refuse them because we do not know where else we should refer them; we really like to encourage Christian marriages as much as possible since things are generally so distressing here in these parts."[56]

The Brainerd Mission was similarly concerned with Cherokee marriage and family arrangements. Two Brainerd journal entries from 1818, which were subsequently struck out, are particularly telling. On February 2, a struck-out sentence reads, "It is pleasing to see the natives beginning to leave their old customs of taking & leaving their wives without ceremony, & in place of this adopting the christian form of marriage."[57] A few days later, another reference to the need for Christian marriages is struck out: "We hope the day is not far distant when all our Cherokee brothers will feel that 'marriage is honorable in all' & know that 'whore mongers & adulters God will judge.'"[58] The struck-out passages are particularly significant to an *asegi* reading, not only because of a literal editing out of the narrative elements of Cherokee life that, perhaps, the missionaries didn't want to overemphasize to the ABCFM and the organization's publications, but also because it points to additional possibilities of sexual and gendered behaviors that the missionaries wanted to omit altogether.

Against this backdrop of violence, control, major upheavals in Cherokee gender balance, and a growing threat of removal, where would asegi *people be? Would they be allowed, by the early nineteenth century, to live lives that looked similar to what they had always lived? While the record is stark, I think it is safe to imagine that the growing rigidity of Cherokee gender and sexuality, to conform to European norms, meant that* asegi *people would—at the very least—be unable to present themselves in many contexts. However, even with the reality of colonial violence—carried out by European and Euro-American powers as well as Cherokee powers—there still were numerous spaces in which Cherokees, while not untouched or unaffected by the laws coming out of New Echota, remained physically and mentally very separate from the attempts of missionaries and lawmakers to normalize Cherokee genders and sexualities.*

The fact is that, even now, there are asegi *people revitalizing our places within our communities. That revitalization is able to happen because those traditions remain in living memory. It would be easy—and tempting—to imagine that* asegi *expressions simply ended at this time. And while some of it may have gone underground, "traditional" communities often continued these lifeways openly until fairly recently. But our stories have been struck out of official histories.*

Even within this attempt to restructure Cherokee gender and sexuality (and, perhaps, *because of* this attempt), same-sex intimacy and love could have taken place. The missionaries' insistence, for example, on separating Cherokee students along a binary gender system opens up ruptures for radical imaginings of same-sex love and bonding. Further, Moravian theology may have actually encouraged such bonding as well as having been a space of spiritual gender fluidity for some Cherokees. In both Cherokee and Euro-American practices, men and women often inhabited separate social spheres. Intimate same-sex relationships (sexual, romantic, or not) would not have been uncommon among either colonists or Cherokees and probably not thought of as "sodomy." Same-sex friendships and social structures were created and encouraged by missionaries in order to control opposite-sex sexuality. In an attempt to regulate marriage and patriarchal family structure, the missions may have actually created intimate same-sex communities that would have been able to find spaces outside of the heteropatriarchal family structures the "civilization" project was encouraging.

It would be incorrect to assume that Cherokees involved with the missionaries, both converts and not, did not find these spaces of resistance or did not use the missions in ways that were subversive. Cherokee belief systems, for instance, survived in the missions through beadwork. Lois Sherr Dubin relates the following:

> An elder of the Eastern Band of the Cherokee relates that after contact, beadwork enabled cultural survival: "It was a visual language that kept beliefs alive." Attempting to suppress Native culture, colonists destroyed the Cherokee's wampum belts—the repositories of their sacred and historical knowledge. Cherokee teachings continued, however, though presented in acceptable Western forms. "When we worked with [images of] flowers, we made the missionaries happy.

But hidden in the flowers, as well as other images, the beliefs were kept alive. In the flowers were messages and telegrams. . . . One bead color touching another meant something. . . . The spiritual teachings still circulated."[59]

There is no reason to imagine that Cherokee concepts of gender and sexuality didn't also continue under the eyes of missionaries, even if not recognized as such by missionaries.

Even while the civilization project, and Cherokee law, sought to limit women's sexual and social autonomy, the missionaries (because of specific ideas of women's spiritual nature and racist notions of Cherokee male savagery) focused on Cherokee women and girls, and the first Christian converts were women. Cherokee women like Margaret (Peggy) Scott Vann Crutchfield, within a context of shifting gender roles for Cherokee women, found the missions to be places of empowerment and refuge from growing patriarchal violence. As Tiya Miles details, Springplace became a site of refuge for Peggy from her husband's violence. The Moravian journals record incidents such as the following:

> We heard horrible things about what he had done again last night, especially that he mistreated his wife so badly that it cannot be repeated. In the afternoon Sister Byhan visited Mrs. Vann because Mr. Vann was not at home. She took the opportunity to speak with her about her spiritual condition because now she is an especially troubled situation. . . . In the evening on the 19th, Mr. Vann came home again. However, he was so angry that he immediately knocked his wife to the floor. She then fled with Vann's mother and spent the night with us.[60]

Virginia Moore Carney points out that "education in [missionary] schools could indeed become a means of empowerment" and "a form of religious adaptability that enabled them to survive both personally and communally."[61] While the "civilization project" created the heteropatriarchal violence Peggy endured, spaces of rupture and resistance could be found within the missionary system for Cherokee women and, perhaps, *asegi* people.

I want to imagine a history in which Cherokee systems of gender and sexuality, with a concern with *duyuktv*, were able to persist despite efforts on the part of the United States to transform Cherokees into heteropatriarchal, gender-"normative," wealth-accumulating plantation farmers. It is important, then, to understand that the central goal of the "civilization project" was to transform Cherokee systems of gender in order for colonial powers to obtain land. Within the context of a colonial economic system in which slavery was central, encouraging Cherokees to adopt chattel slavery was a key element to colonization. While the federal government wasn't particularly concerned with Cherokees converting to Christianity, missionaries aided in shifting Cherokee gender, sexuality, and land use systems, all of which were central to colonization.

While the major shifts in Cherokee gendered labor and the creation of clear gender binaries were clearly disruptive, the shift of men's work from hunting to agriculture may not, in fact, have been as difficult for male-assigned *asegi* people and could have been a moment of continuation of other systems rather than a disruption.

UNWEAVING SPLINT ᏚᏬᎩ/*HISG'*: CHEROKEE LAW

As the Cherokee Nation began creating a centralized government—as opposed to the autonomous town system guided by clan and Red/White councils that existed previously—it began creating U.S.-style laws and documents. The laws passed during this period, shortly before the forced removal of Cherokees to Indian Territory, are clearly meant to protect Cherokee sovereignty and resist numerous forms of colonization, and to demonstrate to the United States that the Cherokee Nation was a valid nation capable of taking care of its own affairs through establishing U.S.-style laws and governance structures. However, through an *asegi* reading of these laws we also begin to see the legal creation of a discourse of gender and sexuality that hadn't existed previously, one that manifested the values of the "civilization project" brought about through missionaries and enslavement. If, as Michel Foucault argues, sexuality is a "proliferation of discourses," then formation of "sexuality" in Cherokee history takes place in part through shifts in law that regulate gender and sexuality. In 1808, a newly unified Cherokee Nation passed its first law, which established an all-male light horse force to police the Cherokee Nation. The law specifically mentions monetary compensation for the men,

> who shall be paid out of the national annuity, at the rates of fifty dollars to each Captain, forty to the Lieutenant, and thirty dollars to each of the privates; and to give their protection to children as heirs to their father's property, and to the widow's share whom he may have had children by or cohabitated with, as his

wife, at the time of his decease, and in case a father shall leave or will any property to a child at the time of his decease, which he may have had by another
woman, then, his present wife shall be entitled to receive any such property as
may be left by him or them, when substantiated by two or one disinterested
witnesses.[62]

Considering that, under Cherokee custom, property, land, and children were
all under jurisdiction of women, this law also reflects and further entrenches a
male head of household, even while ensuring his widow and children would receive the man's property. Further, it makes clear that while a man may have (or
have had) another wife and children by her—which was quite ordinary among
Cherokees—"his present wife shall be entitled to receive any such property as
maybe left by him or them."

One of the first major transformations of gender, and an undermining of
Cherokee women's traditional power, was through an "act of oblivion" passed
in 1810, in which the ancient law of blood or clan revenge was ended. The law
of clan revenge meant that any member of one of the Cherokee clans—or a
member of another tribe—could be killed to avenge a lost member of a clan.
It's important to remember that Cherokee clans are matrilineal and matrifocal,
and the principle of *duyuktv* guided Cherokee government and governance.
This was the subject of the second law passed under the new system of U.S.-
style governance:

> *Be it known*, That this day, the various clans or tribes which compose the Chero-
> kee Nation, have unanimously passed an act of oblivion for all lives for which
> they may have been indebted, one to the other, and have mutually agreed that
> after this evening the aforesaid act shall become binding upon every clan or tribe;
> and the aforesaid clans or tribes, have also agreed that if, in future, any life should
> be lost without malice intended, the innocent aggressor shall not be accounted
> guilty.
>
> *Be it known, also*, That should it happen that a brother, forgetting his natural
> affection, should raise his hand in anger and kill his brother, he shall be accounted
> guilty of murder and suffer accordingly, and if a man has a horse stolen, and over-
> takes the thief, and should his anger be so great as to cause him to kill him, let his
> blood remain on his own conscience, but no satisfaction shall be demanded for
> his life from his relatives or the clan he may belong to.[63]

On one hand, this may seem like a logical and just law—that someone not guilty of a crime should not have to pay for the crime. The formal dissolution of the practice of clan revenge also was meant to minimize possible retaliation from settlers: a Cherokee who practiced clan revenge on white people could feasibly trigger war. Further, such a practice made no sense to white Americans, who thought of it as evidence of lawlessness and savagery. It was important that Cherokees throughout the Cherokee Nation—regardless of town or clan affiliation—agree to the end of clan revenge for the safety of Cherokee people.

However, the ancient law of clan revenge *worked* in many ways. One was much less likely to commit a murder, for instance, if it meant someone from your family (and one's entire clan is considered your family) could be killed for your crime. It also was a system of law and punishment that kept power within the matriarchal clan system and maintained women's power as central to Cherokee justice.

Cherokee women's centrality to Cherokee politics and governance were eroded and transformed through both internal and external pressures for Cherokees to become "civilized." Cherokee women's power was severely disrupted and undermined through colonial invasions, missionization, and forced removal. Through this disruption, *hetero*patriarchy—not just patriarchy—became enforced and entrenched in Cherokee communities. The Cherokee Nation began passing laws to regulate and define marriage:

> *Resolved by the National Committee and Council,* That any white man who shall hereafter take a Cherokee woman to wife be required to marry her legally by a minister of the gospel or other authorized person, after procuring license from the National Clerk for that purpose, before he shall be entitled and admitted to the privilege of citizenship, and in order to avoid imposition on the part of any white man.
>
> *Resolved,* That any white man who shall marry a Cherokee woman, the property of the woman so marry [*sic*], shall not be subject to the disposal of her husband, contrary to her consent, and any white man so married and parting from his wife without just provication [*sic*], shall forfeit and pay to his wife such sum or sums, and may be adjudged to her by the National Committee and Council for said breach of marriage, and be deprived of citizenship, and it is also resolved, that it shall not be lawful for any white man to have more than one wife, and it is also recommended that all others should also have but one wife hereafter.[64]

Through this law we begin to see how Cherokee relationships are codified by law. On one hand, the resolution seems to be a clear way of protecting the Cherokee Nation from white encroachment and ensuring that women's power and autonomy over the home and her property stay intact when marrying a white man, whose heteropatriarchal cultural center influenced him to believe that he would be in charge of the property as well as his wife.

On the other hand, there is an undermining here of Cherokee forms of relationships/marriages in which men married more than one woman, often women who were each other's sisters. While a dominant white understanding of relationships and marriage might misinterpret the marriage of a man to more than one woman as an act that marginalizes and exploits women, in Cherokee social structure these relationships actually kept power within the matriarchal clan structures. While it becomes illegal for a white man to have more than one Cherokee wife—likely because white men did not understand matrilineal clan structure and saw this structure as a way of obtaining property—the fact that it becomes "recommended" but not legally enforced that Cherokee men also only have one wife shows an effort by the recently consolidated Cherokee government to create new norms of marriage and relationships. It's a move that begins to create and codify dominant white sexual norms through Cherokee law and policy and a demonstration to the ever-encroaching United States that the Cherokee Nation was encouraging "civilized" marriages between one man and one woman. In 1825, the law was revised, establishing marriage as an institution between one man and one woman.

While missionaries and slavery began to entrench heteropatriarchal forms of power in Cherokee communities, we can see an emergence of heteropatriarchy through the codification of laws created by a newly centralized Cherokee Nation. The "civilization project" that encouraged slavery and missionization is manifested through legal discourse that deeply transforms Cherokee gender and sexuality.

The establishment of a centralized Cherokee government and its accompanying laws and constitution was certainly an act of resistance against settler colonialism rather than an act of assimilation. I also think that these laws *simultaneously* replicated racial and gender hierarchies that were central to the logic of the dominant culture. Certainly, Cherokees who accommodated the "civilization project" did so to preserve and maintain Cherokee lives and the Cherokee Nation. Even the Cherokees who illegally signed the Treaty of New Echota were attempting to preserve the Cherokee Nation (even if it was in a way that was vehemently opposed by most Cherokees). An *asegi* approach to these laws holds these tensions: on one hand, they were an act of resistance against removal, land theft, and genocide; on the other, they also embedded gender and racial hierarchies into Cherokee law, thus perpetuating colonial logics.

Even while Cherokee women became officially disenfranchised by an all-male national council, Cherokee women continued to assert their authority (and, possibly, organized women's councils) through petitions written in 1817, 1818, and 1821. Beloved Woman Nancy Ward was one of the writers of the 1817 petition, and Peggy Scott Vann Crutchfield was one of the writers of the 1818 petition. Crutchfield also made an address to the council in 1818.[65] It is feasible, in fact, that the protections for Cherokee women and the firm laws against parting with land or agreeing to removal that appear in the Cherokee Nation's law and constitution during this period are present because of the women's petitions.

Nevertheless, with the adoption of U.S.-style laws in a process of arguing for Cherokee civilization and sovereignty, laws regulating sexuality and marriage appear, particularly targeting Black bodies, both free and enslaved, and undermining Cherokee women's traditional power and autonomy. The adoption of chattel slavery and anti-Black laws and the disenfranchisement of Cherokee women became central to the regulation of Cherokee bodies and sexuality in order to reflect a "civilized" Cherokee Nation that could retain its national boundaries and sovereignty and resist forced removal.

While the Cherokee Nation adopted laws to control marriage and sexuality between men and women, "sodomy" is not made a crime and does not appear in the laws. We can safely assume that Cherokees were well aware that "sodomy" was a punishable offense in the United States. During the eighteenth century and the pre-Removal nineteenth century, however, the crime of "sodomy" became less of a concern in the thirteen colonies and the newly formed United States than it had been under British law. After American independence, the death penalty as a punishment for sodomy was revoked, though laws criminalizing "sodomy" were passed throughout the thirteen states. As William N. Eskridge, Jr., explains, however, "[n]one of these new statutes defined precisely what conduct constituted this crime, but American courts and commentators uniformly followed the English buggery precedents in regarding it as the penetration of a man's penis inside the rectum of an animal, of a woman or girl, or of another man or boy. Nineteenth-century judges were usually unwilling to read sodomy laws expansively or to interpolate biblical admonitions into state criminal codes."[66] He also writes, "However ill-defined, the crime against nature was a cornerstone of the Anglo-American legal regime regulating sexuality. From the sixteenth to the twentieth century, the norm reflected in that regime was procreative marriage. Adultery and fornication laws insisted that sexual activities occur only within marriage; sodomy and seduction laws insisted that the sex be procreative."[67]

Anglo-America, however, was not just concerned with sex being procreative; it was also concerned that white "blood" remain "pure." Rachel F. Moran explains that the first "antimiscegenation" law was passed in Maryland in 1661, but that Virginia severely punished "interracial" sex before that:

> By punishing interracial sex severely, authorities in Maryland and Virginia sent a clear message that whites were not to adopt the sexual practiced of slaves. Slaves typically did not enjoy access to the formal institution of marriage, although they did conduct their own slave marriage rituals. Some slaves practiced polygamy or polygyny, and many did not condemn premarital intercourse. . . . Legislation prohibiting interracial intimacy clearly condemned these alternative sexual and marital practices as heathen and unfit for right-minded, white Christians.[68]

She explains, as well, that "[w]ith widespread interracial sex that threatened the color line, the Virginia legislature had to define and ultimately confine the relevance of the mulatto. A 1705 law classified a mulatto as 'the child of an Indian and the child, grandchild, or great grandchild of a negro.'"[69] Within a racialized context of the states bordering the Cherokee Nation and the white supremacist power structure of the United States, the Cherokee power structure found it imperative to clearly cleave apart Cherokee and Black people.

Within larger contexts of Anglo-American law, both before and after the American Revolution, Black bodies are a target for sexual regulation. "Sodomy" was a crime that was meant to regulate sexuality, marriage, and family structure, but, as Eskridge also points out, during the eighteenth century "the only notable capital case was the summary conviction of 'Mingo, alias Cocke Negro, for forcible Buggery' in Massachusetts on January 30, 1712."[70] Black bodies become sexually regulated both through violent control under enslavement and through laws meant to prevent "race mixing." While "sodomy" doesn't appear in the laws, Black bodies come to signify "sodomy" by being marked as sexually dangerous.[71]

Cherokees, before the colonial imposition of racialized and heteropatriarchal powers, had no such notion. Because Cherokee belonging was through matrilineal clans, any child born of a Cherokee mother was Cherokee. Even those without a clan—for instance, prisoners of war under a system of Cherokee slavery—could be adopted into the clan system and become Cherokee. After concerted efforts, however, on the part of both England and the United States, as well as the cultural influence of white intermarriage, Cherokee attitudes (at least on the part of Cherokees creating law and policy) began to shift. In order to prove that the Cherokee Nation was just as "civilized" as the newly formed United States, both the enslavement of Black people and anti-Black laws attempting to ensure a non-Black Cherokee Nation were put into law.

Both free and enslaved Africans within the Cherokee Nation inhabited an *asegi* space as people without a clan, and African bodies were monitored in order to ensure that African-Cherokees would not have clan affiliation. Thus, it is African bodies (and consensual sexual interactions with African bodies) that were specifically regulated before Removal. In the Euro-American imagination, as well as law, "civilization" was built on anti-Black laws and enslavement, and so Cherokees (and other Southeastern people) adopted similar laws and attitudes. The creation of "normative" genders and sexuality within Cherokee law, then, becomes codified through regulations of Black bodies, adoption of patriarchal and patrilineal laws, and a restructuring of Cherokee gendered practices. "Normative" Cherokee gender and sexuality becomes inseparable from anti-Black laws and the enslavement of Black bodies.

By 1824, we begin to see the regulation of Black bodies—free and enslaved—through Cherokee laws. One resolution forbids Cherokees from hiring "negro slaves belonging to citizens of the United States" without a permit.[72] While it is clear that this law is meant to ensure that Cherokee citizens do not employ noncitizens without a permit in order to help curtail the settling of non-Cherokees on Cherokee land, it is also an attempt to restrict Black presence in the Cherokee Nation outside of *Cherokee* enslavement.

A law addressing "free negroes" was passed on November 11, 1824, which reads, "*Resolved by the National Committee and Council*, That all free negroes coming into the Cherokee Nation, under any pretence whatsoever, shall be viewed and treated, in every respect, as intruders, and shall not be allowed to reside in the Cherokee Nation without a permit from the National Committee and Council."[73] *Free* Black bodies begin to be seen as a threat to the Cherokee nation here. Enslaved Africans were commonly owned by the Cherokee elite, but the fact that "free negroes" were written into law as "intruders" seems more than just a defense of Cherokee national boundaries and the legitimate concern of the Cherokee Nation about encroachment into Cherokee territories as a threat to Cherokee sovereignty and ability to resist removal. Rather, it seems a particular kind of performance to the United States government that Cherokees were "civilized," and, like the United States, would work to regulate and control the movements and lives of African diasporic people.

Shortly after this resolution, specific laws around sexual control through the bodies of slaves appear:

> *Resolved by the National Committee and Council*, That intermarriages between negro slaves and indians [*sic*], or whites, shall not be lawful, and any person or persons, permitting and approbating his, her or their negro slaves, to intermarry with Indians or whites, he, she or they, so offending, shall pay a fine of fifty dollars, one half for the benefit of the Cherokee nation; and
>
>   *Be it further resolved*, that any male Indian or white man marrying a negro woman slave, he or they shall be punished with fifty-nine stripes on the bare back, and any Indian or white woman, marrying a negro man slave, shall be punished with twenty-five stripes on her or their bare back.[74]

This law demonstrates the incorporation of heteropatriarchy through anti-Black and pro-slavery legislation. Such a law is meant to uphold the institution of slavery that had become central to the Cherokee economy by ensuring that marriages between slaves and non-slaves could not occur without punishment. But it also shows layers of sexuality being violently policed and regulated. "Proper" marriages could not take place between slaves and Native or white people and the punishment both for slave owners and for those who might marry an enslaved person was severe. Normative sexual relationships, then, become codified in Cherokee law through the violent racism of enslavement.

On this same day, the Committee and Council passed another resolution further restricting Black lives and further entrenching enslavement: "*Resolved by the National Committee and Council*, That it shall not be lawful for negro slaves to possess property in horses, cattle or hogs, and that those slaves now possessing property of that description, be required to dispose of the same in twelve months from this date, under the penalty of confiscation, and any property so confiscated, shall be sold for the benefit of the Cherokee Nation."[75] Such a restriction on property owned by slaves in the Cherokee Nation would, no doubt, make obtaining freedom and livelihood outside of slavery much more difficult, if not impossible.[76] Black bodies become clearly marked for slavery, and Cherokee slave owners begin working to ensure that slavery remains an institution within the Cherokee Nation.

The laws passed by the Cherokee Nation at this period also clarified punishments against rape. Older Cherokee laws and practices forbade rape, and perpetuators were often punished through cutting off their ears or parts of their noses or through execution. Women often carried out these punishments. These practices reflect the matrifocal system and the importance of women's sexual autonomy in Cherokee tradition. The new law around rape, however, puts power in the hands of men:

> *Resolved by the National Committee and Council,* That any person or persons, whatsoever, who shall lay violent hands upon any female, by forcibly attempting to ravish her chastity contrary to her consent, abusing her person and committing a rape upon such female, he or they, so offending, upon conviction before any of the district or circuit Judges, for the first offence, shall be punished with fifty lashes upon the bare back, and the left ear cropped off close to the head; for the second offence, one hundred lashes and the other ear cut off; for the third offence, death.
>
> *Be it further resolved,* That any woman or women, making evidence against any man, and falsely accusing him of having laid violent hands upon any woman, with intent of committing a rape upon her person, and sufficient proof having been adduced before any of the district or circuit Judges to refute the testimony of such woman or women, she or they, so offending, shall be punished with twenty-five stripes upon her or their bare back, to be inflicted by any of the Marshals, Sheriffs or Constables.[77]

While this law is based in older Cherokee punishments against rape, and it is certainly significant that such a law was put into place by the Cherokee Nation, the second part of the resolution should give us pause in thinking that such a law was a way of preserving Cherokee women's power or "protecting" Cherokee women from sexual violence. While previous systems of governance within the Cherokee Nation emphasized gender balance, the new version of Cherokee governance was all male. This would include circuit court systems that were, likewise, all male. It is not difficult to imagine that the fact that a woman who could not provide "sufficient proof" of rape or attempted rape would be whipped on her bare back by men in positions of authority would deter women from making any legal charges against men for rape.

By 1827, the Cherokee Nation adopted a constitution in order to protect its boundaries, assert its sovereignty, and resist forced removal. It also disenfranchised all women, Black, and Black Cherokee people. Article III, Section 4, reads:

> No person shall be eligible to a seat in the General Council, but a free Cherokee male citizen, who shall have attained to the age of twenty-five years. The descendants of Cherokee men by all free women, except the African race, whose parents may have been living together as man and wife, according to the customs and laws of this Nation, shall be entitled to all the rights and privileges of this Nation, as well as the posterity of Cherokee women by all free men. No person who is of negro or mulatto parentage, either by father or mother side, shall be eligible to hold any office of profit, honor or trust under this Government.[78]

Section 7 of the same article further disenfranchises Black Cherokees and Cherokee women: "All free male citizens (excepting negroes and descendants of white and Indian men by negro women who may have been set free) who shall have attained to the age of eighteen years, shall be equally entitled to vote at all public elections."[79] Within a relatively short amount of time Cherokees had moved from a diffuse power structure, in which women were central, to a centralized Cherokee Nation governed by a small group of men who supported slavery and continued the anti-Black legislation common to the government it was trying to resist. It was never imagined by the "civilization project" that Cherokees would use the features of "civilization" it hoped would assimilate Indigenous people to fight for sovereignty. But, perhaps, as well, before slavery and missionization Cherokees would never have imagined the Cherokee Nation would disenfranchise and decenter women, while undermining the clan system and township governance, or that Cherokees would consider human beings property and normalize violence and abuse.

REWEAVING THE BASKET

How do we, then, undo the colonization of Cherokee gender and sexuality? How do we honor the lives of those gender nonconforming and same-gender-loving people who have been rendered invisible in colonial discourse? Part of this is through a process of reviving and revising cultural memories, and through a practice of resistance that draws on our past not as nostalgic, but as a collection of complicated stories. A basket we unweave.

It is said that on the Trail of Tears people carried hot coals from the sacred fires to rekindle in Indian Territory. I like to imagine asegi *people carrying our older relationships with gender as hot coals of memory in their hearts during that horrific journey.*

Sometimes memory is uncomfortable and painful and frightening. Rivercane splits are sharp. Unweaving can cut open a finger, leave blood across the splints.

Our stories don't start or end here, though, in an unraveled basket. There has always been Cherokee resistance to slavery and missionization, there have always been people who remembered our asegi *stories. I think of the Keetoowah Society in Indian Territory after Removal, and their militant resistance against slave owners. I think of my own Black and Indigenous ancestors living during this period and the miracle of their survival. My body is evidence that there were Black/Cherokee alliances despite these regulations. Did Black and Cherokee* asegi *people build homes or communities with each other? Did African and Cherokee people outside of a European gender binary recognize each other's practices as familiar, as home? A call-and-response song that sounded like kin? Where are the stories of Cofitachequi and Gómez's* asegi *children? Perhaps they're right here, written across shining rivercane splints. Carried in the baskets of our bodies across every middle passage.*

Another Cherokee scholar told me once, during a conversation about the research I was doing on slavery and anti-Black racism in Cherokee history and communities, "You're just picking at a scab." The idea that these wounds have stopped bleeding is wishful thinking. Daniel Heath Justice, referencing the same-sex marriage controversy in the Cherokee Nation: "It hardly seems coincidental that other identity controversies have erupted at the same time, such as the disenfranchisement of the Cherokee Freedmen and the ongoing surveillance of non-federally recognized groups and non-enrolled Cherokees and Cherokee descendants."[80] *Regulations of sexuality and anti-Black racism in Cherokee history are inseparable.*

We undo and interrupt heteropatriarchal colonization through listening for asegi *stories that centralize Cherokee gender and sexuality as primary sites of both colonization and resistance. We confront those parts of our histories, and our present, which are often painful and frightening. These memories must be part of decolonial struggles. We must recognize the centrality of the colonization of our genders and sexualities within colonial history through larger systems of colonization and white supremacy.*

Our genders, sexualities, cultural practices, and language survived despite the "civilization project." Black and Red–Black people survived despite the violence inflicted on them from both white and Cherokee people. The township structure continued through the ceremonial grounds. I would like to imagine the asegi *people who escaped removal and remained near Giduwa, our mother mound, continuing* asegi *medicine and cultural practices, hiding them, if necessary—just as Cherokees hid from soldiers rounding up our families. I would like to imagine that* asegi *people loved, supported, and protected each other during the death march to Indian Territory.*

No doubt, this doesn't just have to be imagining. We survived. Look at our hands: we are reweaving.

4

BEAUTIFUL AS THE RED RAINBOW

Cherokee Two-Spirits Rebeautifying Erotic Memory

WITHIN "TRADITIONAL" CHEROKEE LOVE INCANTATIONS, there exists a set of formulas to "rebeautify" oneself. "Rebeautification" is a subset of formulas to "remake" oneself. Jack Frederick and Anna Gritts Kilpatrick explain the concepts of "rebeautifying" and "remaking" within Cherokee erotic incantations: "A person who has 'remade' himself has surrounded the ego with a spiritual aura through which the light of the old self is brilliantly refracted. It is obvious that in the popular mind the difference between 'to "remake" oneself' and 'to "rebeautify" oneself' lies in the greater emphasis that the latter lends to physical attractiveness as contrasted with spiritual attractiveness. The practical results of both are held to be very nearly identical."[1] *Asegi* stories engage a process of recovering histories of Cherokee erotic memory as a part of ongoing decolonial struggles: a *rebeautification* and *remaking* in which the light of our erotic pasts is "brilliantly refracted" through contemporary imaginings. *Asegi* stories rebeautify and remake the erotic for all Cherokees.

I am reading through the John Howard Payne papers while doing research for this chapter. Even though I have looked through this voluminous collection several times, I never looked closely at David S. Butrick's journal from the Brainerd Mission, which was located near one of the prison camps during the Trail of Tears. My previous focus stops as I read through the journal. It's horrific and painful. The Trail of Tears continues to be a deep slash in our cultural memory. It hasn't stopped bleeding.

As I read through the journal, I think of the stories in my family about the Removal. It wasn't that long ago. As a small child my grandmother heard stories of the Removal from her grandfather. When he remembered, he would sing songs to her in Cherokee and cry. She told me that there was blood from people's feet in the snow that hungry dogs ate. Fragments of stories embedded in our flesh. That close.

As an asegi *person, I can't help but try to imagine what the Removal was like for gender nonconforming and same-gender-loving people. Did lovers try to keep each other alive on the journey? Who did our* asegi *ancestors lose on the way? Were medicine songs and formulas whispered by* ani asegi didantvn*? How on earth did any of us survive?*

Butrick alludes to sexual violence in the journal. It's not surprising that sexual violence took place, but I've never seen it mentioned before: "The other day a gentleman informed me that he saw six soldiers about two Cherokee women. The women stood by a tree, and the soldiers with a bottle of liquor were endeavoring to entice them to drink, though the women, as yet were resisting them. He made this known to the commanding officer, but we presume no notice was taken of it, as it was reported that those soldiers had those women with them the whole night afterwards."[2]

This isn't the only mention of gendered violence. You should know these stories, dear reader, but I can't repeat them here. They cut too close.

Removal. Colonization. Missionization. Invasion. Slavery. Allotment. Boarding schools. Stolen children. Missing and murdered Indigenous women. These are our stories.

Against this backdrop of sexual violence and the stories of everything we lost, we sometimes forget that these aren't the only stories. Even now, colonization is only a tiny part of a much longer memory that stretches all the way back. Our stories are also of resistance, humor, love, sex, beauty. And that's why rebeautifying our erotic memory is so vitally important: we need to remember the stories that disrupt colonial violence. "I know there is something larger than the memory of a dispossessed people," writes Joy Harjo. "We have seen it."[3] *We need to rebeautify our erotic memory in order to remake our futures.*

This chapter extends my previous work arguing for a *sovereign erotic* that can resist settler-colonial sexual violence and heal the wounds of colonization. It also contributes to ongoing conversations in activist, academic, and artistic spaces that are working to transform Indigenous relationships with our bodies and sexualities through asserting sexuality and the erotic as central to decolonization. Daniel Heath Justice argues, "To ignore sex and embodied pleasure in the cause of Indigenous liberation is to ignore one of our greatest resources.

It is to deny us one of our most precious gifts. Every orgasm can be an act of decolonization."[4]

Erotic memory here includes sex, but draws on Deborah A. Miranda's concept of an "indigenous erotic" as more expansive: "the perpetual act of balanc*ing*—always working toward balance through one's actions, intent, and understanding of the world. Both love and the erotic are at odds with the violence and domination that structures any colonizing or patriarchal culture. . . . These oppressors are anyone seeking power in a patriarchal system—men *and* women—and the system, once the creative/erotic element is betrayed, perpetuates itself."[5]

Miranda's concept of an indigenous erotic resonates with the concept of *duyuktv*, and provides an important warning about the power of the erotic and rebeautifying as having a need to remain in balance. We know that colonization deploys sexuality and gender as weapons against us as Indigenous people, both through attacking Indigenous forms of gender and sexuality and through imposing (through both coercion and outright force) colonial, white supremacist systems of gender and sexuality onto our communities and into our bodies, imaginations, and behaviors. Most Cherokee love formulas use medicine in ways that aren't harmful or dangerous. But medicine can always be misused. History has already shown us that fusing radical politics with the erotic within movements that remain heteropatriarchal risks perpetuating male exploitation of women's bodies and perpetuates violence against queer and trans people, and we know that even within radical movements for social justice abuse takes place. Rebeautifying erotic memory is also a process of rebeautifying and remaking the erotic in our current lives and movements.

Rebeautifying erotic memory considers what Audre Lorde calls the "uses of the erotic" as a tool of decolonization and asserts what Lisa Tatonetti conceives of as a "Two-Spirit cosmology," which she defines as "a nonheterosexual desire that cannot be separated from understandings of indigeneity."[6] It interrupts heteropatriarchal exploitation of sex and bodies as well as heteropatriarchal claims to cultural memory within our communities.

While I believe that all straight Native folks have much to learn from their queer and Two-Spirit relatives, especially when it comes to the erotic—and I daresay queer and Two-Spirit Native people would like to think of ourselves as the original sexperts of Turtle Island—I want to specifically address *Cherokee* issues and erotic memory here. Especially with the strengthening of conservative Cherokee politics that are attempting to revision Cherokee sexuality and

gender in order to be in accordance with heteropatriarchal Christian supremacy, the voices of Cherokee Two-Spirit and queer people are needed not only to
recover queer and Two-Spirit memories, but to rebeautify and remake Cherokee erotic memory for all of our people.

The title of this chapter comes from a Cherokee love incantation for rebeautification that reads, *U-na-kv-la-ti gi-ga-ge-quu igv-wo-du-hi do-ti-qua-la-
svg gu-wa-du-hnv-v-hi igv-wo-duhi*, which is translated as, "From where my
feet stand, upward, then, I am as beautiful as the very blossoms themselves! /
I am as beautiful as the Red Rainbow."[7] Cherokee Two-Spirit and queer folks
are rebeautifying Cherokee erotic memory so that our present and futures can
become as "beautiful as the Red Rainbow."

Asegi people help us to both remember Cherokee erotic lives before missionization and critique how heteropatriarchal values continue to manifest in
Cherokee communities. The same-sex marriage bans within the Cherokee Nation and the Eastern Band—justified, in part, by arguing that Cherokee Two-
Spirit people are "not traditional"—are only one example of how some Cherokees are attempting to forget an erotic past. Part of what must happen in order
to heal colonial violence is to rebeautify Cherokee erotic memory through en-
gagement with our past in ways that can be used for the present and future.

A PECULIAR FONDNESS: *ASEGI* RUPTURES IN THE JOHN HOWARD PAYNE PAPERS

Early in my archival research, I stumbled across a reference to Cherokee same-
sex union ceremonies in John Howard Payne's manuscript on Cherokee life.
John Howard Payne was a Euro-American actor and playwright. In 1836 he
traveled to the Cherokee Nation in order to document Cherokee customs as
a guest of Chief John Ross. Extensive research had already been conducted by
the missionary Daniel S. Butrick, whose work was given to Payne in order to
write a history of the Cherokee Nation. Payne worked on editing and revising
Butrick's research for publication. While staying with Ross, Payne was apprehended by Georgia authorities and put under arrest in Vann's plantation at
Springplace.[8]

A ceremony is mentioned several times in the Payne manuscript, which
describes a particular ceremony to formalize "perpetual friendship." The description is a revision of Butrick's materials about the ceremony. In the spaces

between Butrick's and Payne's various revisions of this account, *asegi* ruptures appear that become an entrance to slip between the walls of constructed history in order to reimagine the past and rebeautify erotic memory.[9] The following description is the revision of Butrick's description that Payne intended to publish:

> To ascertain the precise signification of the Cherokee title for this festival, is by no means easy. It is derived from a peculiar bond between Indians of the same tribe, which is alluded to elsewhere in these pages. This can only be described in our language as a vow of eternal brotherhood. It sprang from a passionate friendship between young men, prompting them mutually to a solemn act of devotedness to each other. They plighted it publickly, at an appointed time and place, by the silent interchange of garment after garment, until each was clad in the other's dress; each, then considered that he had given himself to the other; they from that hour were one and indivisible.—The alliance embraced whatever is implied in peace, reconcilement, friendship, brotherly affection, and much more than either or all. When two were thus uniting, it was said of them *Ah,nah,tawh,hanoh,kah*,—they are about to make friendship,—and the union itself was called *Ah,tah,hoongh,nah*—friends made; whence the festival now under review takes its title.[10]

Payne's choice of words is particularly interesting. He seems slightly perplexed by the entire ceremony, perhaps in part because he can't make sense of it within the theory of Cherokees being the Lost Tribe of Israel that he and Butrick attempt to establish. What is also interesting here is the mistranslation of *Ah,tah,hoongh,nah* (*adahona*) and *Ah,nah,tawh,hanoh,kah* (*anadahanoga*). *Adahona* translates as "make wood" and *anadahanoga* seems to translate as "they make wood (with each other)."[11] This refers to a specific women's dance that Speck and Broom write about in connection to the Green Corn Festival, but which "may be detached from its ritual context and performed in other dance series."[12] They write that "the dance may express the functions of woman as a provider of wood for the dance fire, and woman's prestige as mistress of the hearth."[13] Payne did not speak Cherokee and was relying mostly on Butrick's research and translations for his information.[14]

Elsewhere in the manuscripts, this ceremony is called the "Cementation" or "Conciliation Festival." Cherokee Nation says that the "Cementation Festival" or "Friends Made" festival "renewed the Fire, and the people. It also brought friendship by ceremonially forgiving conflicts from the previous year. This was seen as a brand new start. There was also a cleansing ritual that was performed at the river in running water. This festival would last four days."[15] Knowing all of this, one must wonder if the mistranslation of these words was intentional on Butrick's part. If it was, perhaps an intentional mistranslation took place because "make wood" didn't seem to convey to Payne's imagined audience the ideas of "friendship" or "conciliation" that he felt were central to the ceremony. I suspect, however, that the same-sex intimacy and love conveyed by the ceremony confounded both Payne and Butrick, though it was probably clear, which is why it was "by no means easy" to explain to a white Christian audience.

Considering that *adahona* refers now to the "women-gathering-wood-dance," and has a connotation of wood gathered for a fire or hearth, it may (in part) have been about a particular kind of homemaking that struck him as "peculiar." The word "peculiar" in the nineteenth century would have the meaning of both "particular" as well as "strange, and perhaps Payne is indeed trying to clarify same-sex love and "romantic friendships" within his specific context. This ceremony is "peculiar" in both of its meanings *because* of the recognition of same-gendered love. In an attempt to erase or minimize same-gendered love by explaining it as friendship, his writing consistently points to an *asegi* presence.

I speculate that neither Payne nor Butrick were sure how to frame such information within a nineteenth-century white Christian male worldview. Furthermore, as people carrying a responsibility for a portrayal of Cherokee "antiquities" that wouldn't have negative ramifications for Cherokee people, and that could also support Butrick's theory that "ancient" Cherokee practices resembled ancient Jewish practices as evidence that Cherokees were one of the "Lost Tribes of Israel," formalized loving relationships—and, I imagine, homemaking—between two men undermined Payne and Butrick's larger arguments.

Perhaps James Adair, writing about fifty years earlier and attempting to advance this same "Lost Tribe of Israel" argument, found himself in a similar dilemma explaining loving relationships between men when he wrote, "The Cheerake do not marry their first or second cousins; and it is very observable, that the whole tribe reckon a friend in the same rank with a brother, both with regard to marriage, and any other affair in social life. This seems to evince that they copied from the stable and tender friendship between Jonathan and David; especially as the Hebrews had legal, or adopted, as well as natural brothers."[16] In both Adair and Payne, loving relationships between men are framed in terms of "brothers" or "tender friendship"—placing such relationships in a Christian framework, invoking what might now be called a "romantic friendship," a relationship between people of the same gender that would have been legible to many white Americans during this period.

However, the "passionate friendship" resulting in "a solemn act of devotedness to each other" resonates closely enough with Euro-American ideas of marriage that Payne uses the word "plighted" here, which during this period could mean a promise of loyalty, but also meant betrothed. Craig Womack's concept of "suspicioning" provides a way toward productive imagining within an Indigenous queer reading of texts.

> [S]uspicioning functions as an action, full of desire for a concrete resolution, a certainty it never achieves, an absence of closure that simply intensifies a hunger for verities. One suspicions when tackling subjects one feels unsure of, but risks a statement anyway. A suspicioner brings up taboos, secrets, impolite observations normally off-limits in states of self-assurance and control. Suspicioning takes advantage of doubt to go out on a limb and blurt out or whisper—a whooping ejaculation or a sotto voce aside. Suspicioning foregrounds subjectivity and intuition, those things least empirical.[17]

I *suspicion* that when Payne says the relationship was about "peace, reconcilement, friendship, brotherly affection, and much more than either or all" that he is well aware that this relationship is about same-sex love. Others appear to suspicion on this as well. In their annotations of Payne's papers, Anderson, Brown, and Rogers tell us, "The editors and one of our Cherokee language consultants were struck by the fact that this ceremony seems to reflect a tradition of homosexuality or alternative sexuality among the Cherokees, as such a tradition has been infrequently recorded."[18] Roy Hamilton, a Cherokee historian and teacher, agrees with such an assessment of this ceremony, and has pointed out that "oral history paints a picture of gay life among the Cherokee and that they viewed gay marriage as an autonomy right. . . . [Each] Cherokee lived his or her life as they liked and no one had a right to interfere in personal choice."[19]

While the ceremony could simply show friendship or clan adoption, I don't think this is what Payne is writing about here. Particularly considering his and Butrick's difficulty explaining the ceremony, I suspicion that Butrick and Payne understood the same-sex intimacy of the ceremony. Friendship or reconciliation would have provided easy explanations, but Payne qualifies their impact by placing them in a list: "The alliance embraced whatever is implied in peace, reconcilement, friendship, brotherly affection, and much more than either or all."

Butrick's earlier description of this ceremony offers further details which disrupt Payne's male-centered revision and places the ceremony in closer proximity to the concept of marriage:

> Among the Cherokees there used to be a custom of cementing perpetual friendship between individuals. Suppose two young men conceived a peculiar fondness for each other, and desired to enter into the strongest bonds of perpetual friendship. . . . Taking an opportunity sometime during that feast, when the people were seated in the council house, they arose, walked toward the fire, and then turned and commenced dancing around the fire, what is called the *A to hv na*, or friendship dance, each having on his best clothes. While dancing, in the presence of all the people, who looking, they exchanged one garment after another till each had given the other his entire dress, even to legings, mocasins etc. and thus each of them publicly received the other as himself, & became thus pledged to regard and treat him as himself while he lived. Sometimes two women, and sometimes a man and a woman contracted this friendship. Thus when a young man and woman fell in love with each other but were hindered from marrying, either by relation or by being of the same clan, they bound themselves in perpetual friendship. While dancing round the fire as above stated, the man threw his blanket over the woman, and the woman as soon as convenient threw hers to the man. The man also, having prepared a cane sieve, & hung it by a string over his shoulder, gave her that. He also presented her with a pestle to pound corn with. The mortar he had for her at home.[20]

Perhaps more shocking to a contemporary Cherokee audience than same-gendered love is the reference to a specific arrangement between a man and a woman who were in love, but of the same clan, in an arrangement accepted by the community. In Cherokee tradition, people in the same clan are considered brothers and sisters. Marrying or having children with someone of the same clan is considered incest and could mean death (a fact that Payne documents elsewhere).[21]

The reasoning behind this arrangement is clearer in a revision of this description: "After this she was to him as an own sister, and of course he could not think of marrying her any sooner than an own sister."[22] As mentioned in the previous chapter, clan was, traditionally, much more important to social arrangements than marriage. Before invasion, in fact, little to no ceremony took place to mark marriages. A man would simply move into the woman's home and, even if they had children, a man would continue to have primary responsibilities to his female relatives.

"Marriage" here, then, is a euphemism for having children. While, initially, a marked relationship for people of the same clan who fell in love seems incongruous with Cherokee practice, the ceremony actually helped to maintain the clan system and keep balance in the community. By sanctioning a relationship between people of the same clan, the ceremony may have actually *reemphasized* the clan relationship, publicly acknowledging love between the couple, but also making clear that the couple could not have children with each other. It would be a way for the community (and the couple) to make clear the terms and conditions of the relationship as specifically *outside* of having sexual relationships and children with each other. The potentially chaotic impact of opposite-sex relationships becomes rebalanced through the ceremony, and positions the couple as accountable to their clan as well as the entire community.

The gifting of the sieve, mortar, and pestle to the woman by the man was, perhaps, a way of reaffirming the clan structure by emphasizing women's relationship with corn as the mother of Cherokee people and emphasizing the relationship the couple had through matrilineal clan. The ceremony, then, was a way of structuring a potentially destructive relationship before it reached a point where it would be considered incest and clan relatives would be responsible for killing the couple. While contemporary homophobic discourse (both inside and outside of Cherokee communities) tries to argue that same-sex relationships and marriage pose a threat to family and society, this ceremony indicates that—at least in eighteenth-century Cherokee history—it is opposite-sex couples, not same-sex couples, that are potentially disruptive of the family and society, because of the risk that opposite-sex sexual relationships can pose to the clan system. The descriptions of the ceremony show that there may have been a protocol in place to mitigate the risks of such a relationship.

In the case of same-gender couples, the ceremony itself emphasizes a shared gender expression through the exchange of clothes. The trading of gender-specific clothing shows that members of same-gendered couples each "received the other as himself, & became thus pledged to regard and treat him as himself while he lived." Shared gender expression actually facilitates the joining together of two people.

Even here, Butrick's explanation (or, perhaps more accurately, Butrick's transmission of the cultural memories of elders) of opposite-sex couples in love, but not able to have children because of clan laws, indicates that Butrick understands that same-sex couples were also in love. In this version of his description, in fact, he says as much. Most of his description is verbatim from other versions, but here he writes, "Suppose two young men conceived into the strongest bonds of perpetual friendship, they mutually agreed to unite their hearts at the next medicine feast."[23] The choice to describe the ceremony as a way to unite hearts makes clear that a deep love between people of the same gender was the reason for the ceremony, and Payne's removal of this image may, in fact, point to Payne's understanding of this ceremony as beyond that of a close friendship.

Payne also removes references to two women entering into such an arrangement in his revision. Even though, earlier, Butrick clearly indicates that two women could also enter into this relationship, women are omitted in Payne's revision. I think this is because, in order to share this information with a white, Christian audience, the concept of "brotherly love" provides a context and explanation for same-sex intimacy that would be familiar, safe, and provide evidence for an argument meant to connect Cherokees with Biblical traditions.

In yet another version of this ceremony, Butrick's contextualization of this relationship within a Christian framework becomes even more clear, obscuring other, detailed descriptions of the ceremony in which a romantic implication seemed evident:

> When two were thus giving of themselves to each other, and entering into that closest connexion, it was said of them *A na to no ka*, and the relation thus formed was termed *A to ho no*. And may we not suppose that this word, whatever its precise meaning may be, is designed to express an idea something similar to expiation, reconciliation or atonement[?] When the two parties concerned, viz. God and his people, become reconciled, and, mutually, through the infinite condescension of God, give themselves to each other, and become one (in Christ).[24]

By looking into the ruptures that appear through different accounts of this ceremony, we can remember that our past is not "straight." Homophobia, sexism, and transphobia as part of racialized and colonial sexual violence have tried to erase other histories. I don't think that this is a "gay" ceremony according to the limited understandings of sexuality and gender in contemporary colonial culture. A rebeautification of these cultural memories, though, displaces the heterosexist bias that would want to render this history as "straight," and, thus, devoid of romantic and erotic implications. Rebeautifying this memory as an *asegi* story intentionally privileges same-gender love and desire. It reminds us that our communities acknowledged numerous kinds of relationships and that there was nothing unusual about people of the same gender building one fire, heart, and hearth together.

TOO JOYOUS TO BEAR TRANSLATION: REBEAUTIFYING CHEROKEE EROTICS

The colonization of our genders and sexualities hurts all of us, even if women, queer, trans, and Two-Spirit folks bear the brunt of that injury. The "straightening" of Cherokee gender and sexuality through colonial memories erases *asegi* memories of open sexualities without the fear of or shame about bodies and sex that were imposed through colonization. It also tends to flatten and sanitize our current practices as Cherokee people, perpetuating a stereotype of the noble, stoic, and humorless Indian. Our real lives, of course, say otherwise.

While English includes "swear" words—generally about bodies, sex, and gender—Cherokee doesn't have such a concept. The Cherokee language doesn't carry the sense of shock or shame around bodies that English carries. Colonial influences, however, often erase or minimize sex, bodies, and gender in our cultural memories in favor of a myth of "tradition." Justice critiques such moves, as evident in the Cherokee Nation's 2004 ban on same-sex marriage as "a decision accompanied by Cherokee politicians' often strident appeals to transparently dehistoricized 'traditional' gender roles and practices, and their insistence that oppressive and dehumanizing heteronormative and patriarchal values were supposedly also Cherokee values. An honest assessment of Cherokee history reveals a much more complicated, varied, and surprising picture of Cherokee gender and sexuality."[25]

Rebeautifying our erotic memory may be an *asegi* act, but through the chaos of counter-memories we can rebalance ourselves and our ancestors as complex, contradictory human beings. A brief anecdote from Payne's manuscript rehumanizes Major Ridge, who was one of the leaders of the Treaty Party that illegally signed the Treaty of New Echota, finalizing the process that led to the Trail of Tears: "At a party at Washington, Major Ridge was asked to give an idea of Indian Music & he sang a song, of too joyous a character to bear translation. He called on Capt. Taylor to assist. They were much amused at the

urgency of the Ladies to know its meaning. Ridge ended the pressing solici-
tations by saying 'Oh, you don't want to know. It's just like the white man's
song—all about Love & Whiskey.'"[26]

The story feels very contemporary: white romantic expectations about our
cultures don't assume that our songs would be about love and whiskey. Even
for a lot of Native folks, we don't expect that there were songs about sex. What
is particularly delightful to me about this story is Major Ridge's resistance in
this moment to colonial racism and its accompanying gender and sexual mores.
Ridge, in fact, critiques the entire colonial gendered and sexualized project, not
only through singing an erotic, "joyous" song, but also through a quip he gives
at the same party: "A Lady on that occasion remarked that [ms. mutilated]
Indian she would like to marry the man who had been to Washington & Philadelphia, for he would bring her a calico petticoat. 'O' was the reply, 'Washington Husbands are of no use to our women now, for they can weave their own
petticoats.'"[27]

Ridge subverts colonial gender and sexuality here, not only by asserting that
Cherokee women had no need of white men, but also by pointing out how
the "civilization program's" insistence that Cherokee women needed to learn
to weave meant that, by white standards, Cherokee women had become more
"civilized" than white women.

For me, this moment helps restore Major Ridge's full humanity. It is easy as
contemporary Cherokee people simply to remember Major Ridge and other
members of the Treaty Party as traitors who were part of enacting one of the
most traumatic events in Cherokee history, even if we understand—as Daniel
Heath Justice points out—that "the Treaty Party members sought to arrange as
beneficial a deal as possible, something that would protect both wealthy Cherokees . . . and those who were impoverished. The Beloved Path is a sometimes-
treacherous balance of Cherokee autonomy and adaptation to White assimila-
tive demands, and the story of the Treaty Party is an example of this delicate
negotiation."[28] While I continue to think of Major Ridge as a traitor, he was
also a real human being, not only a betrayer of Cherokee people. This brief
memory of Major Ridge—before he participated in the signing of the Treaty
of New Echota—helps to rebeautify our memories and relationships with our
ancestors. Some of them, indeed, did terrible things. They also were people who
lived, loved, and sang songs in Cherokee about sex and whiskey in the halls and
homes of colonial power.

FIGURE 12. Cherokee pipe, Seated Woman. Peabody Museum of Archaeology and Ethnology, Harvard University. Photograph by Qwo-Li Driskill.

Because there are often gaps in our cultural memories as Indigenous people in North America brought on through invasion, genocide, and concerted efforts to destroy our cultures through various "civilization projects" such as the boarding and residential schools, the idea of "tradition" can be a trap that uses a particular formation of cultural memory as a tool of power and control. Which "traditions" do we continue? Is Ridge's song, "too joyous to translate," "traditional?" When did these "traditions" begin? And why do we so often forget that sex, love, and the erotic are "traditions," too?

New practices, of course, can become "traditional," and that's part of the beauty of cultural resilience and survival. The Cherokee tear dress has become "traditional," even though it was designed in the 1970s. It's meant to remember the Removal era, and is based on a nineteenth-century design. That remembering of the Trail of Tears through regalia, though, is being transformed by the Eastern Band through the Warriors of AniKituhwa, who are readopting eighteenth-century-style regalia, pointing to cultural memories that predate the Trail of Tears. And, of course, when Europeans first started interacting with Cherokees, we often didn't wear very many clothes at all. But women only wearing a small wrap around their waist and covered with tattoos is not talked about as "traditional."

I don't necessarily have problems with "tradition" as an ongoing practice of continuance. I do worry that we often fall easily into ideas of "tradition" that erase bodies and sexuality. Our "traditions" sometimes get romanticized within the settler heteropatriarchal frameworks that we've internalized, and, because of this, entire cultural memories get erased. "Tradition," in this instance, becomes a tool of control rather than of continuance. And, as Leslea—a participant in "On the Wings of *Wadaduga*"—responded to another Native woman's critique that her artwork wasn't traditional enough, "I have some bad news for you. Everything you make is contemporary. 'Cause, you're now. (*Laughs.*) I hate to point this out, but you're now."[29] Our memory and practices are always *now*, even when we draw from older practices and memories.

There is an entire history of erotic pipes that enable us to rebeautify our erotic past. Adair makes specific mention of these pipes being made in the eighteenth century: "They make beautiful stone pipes; and the Cheerake the best of any of the Indians. . . . [O]n both sides of the bowl, lengthwise, they cut several pictures with a great deal of skill and labour; such as a buffalo and a panther on the opposite sides of the bowl; a rabbit and a fox; and, very often, a

FIGURE 11. Cherokee pipe depicting a couple having sex. Peabody Museum of Archaeology and Ethnology, Harvard University. Photograph by Qwo-Li Driskill.

man and a woman *puris naturalibus*. Their sculpture cannot much be commended for its modesty."[30]

An archaeologist in the 1940s described another Cherokee pipe he believes is from the nineteenth century: "The bowl is drilled between the shoulders of a kneeling figure, facing the smoker with head bowed. Although the wooden stem is missing, the stem portion of the pipe obviously represents the base of an exaggerated phallus clasped between the hands of the figure."[31] An *asegi* rebeautification of this pipe can't help make explicit that if the stem of the pipe was created to represent a penis, then the smoker of the pipe would have to have their mouth on the figure's penis to smoke the pipe. Another pipe depicts a naked female seated, legs open, her hands on her abdomen. She looks powerful and at peace. She wears a long braid that goes all the way down her back.

Because all genders used pipes, often for medicine, it would be a mistake to read heterosexist gender binaries onto the pipes. In fact, if pipe stems sometimes represented a penis, an *asegi* imagining could conceive of these pipes as

not only representing the erotic, but as possible *asegi* objects through the joining of gendered elements.

Regardless of whatever other uses the pipes may have had (recreational, medicinal, or both), they are clearly—and intentionally—erotic. We have an entire material history related to sexuality that gets ignored, where our bodies are present. In some cases (and, it seems likely, in many cases) it's been actively destroyed. John Haywood sends a report to Payne, for instance, that details several "phallic" sculptures, including one found in Smith County, Tennessee, of a male and a female in which the "male seemed to be a rude imitation of an ancient Priapus; he is more or less injured by the plough by which he was brought up, and which has broken a large *membrum genital virile in erectione. . . .* The person who ploughed it up mentioned that it possessed this member, but he considered it too indecent to be preserved."[32]

In my interview with Daniel Heath Justice for "On the Wings of *Wadaduga*," he challenges Cherokees to remember the role of the erotic in Cherokee traditions, histories, and lifeways in an act of rebeautification. He argues that a denial of the erotic disrupts Cherokee community, using the existence of erotic pipes as a touchstone:

> Cherokees were *incredibly* sexual people, though not nasty about it. At the Peabody Museum there's a pipe bowl from a Cherokee townsite, with a man and a woman fucking, in explicit detail, with their genitalia pointed right at the smoker. So, somebody's getting a little thrill looking at that. Early European accounts were horrified about how sexually free Cherokees were, that young Cherokee women had sex, out of wedlock, sometimes extra-wedlock. And young men. And, no mentions are—I haven't seen any mentions at all or hints at all of same-sex intimacies. But, people were very much sexual people. And frankly a lot of the fine upstanding folks who don't want to admit it . . . I'm sorry, but you can either deny your sexual desires and get in weird circumstances, or you can just admit the fact that we love sex, we're very sexual people, and that doesn't mean that we're crass about it. I think Cherokees would not have been crass, and I think that even very sexual Cherokees today have personal modesty, but it doesn't necessarily transfer always over to sexual prudery. But, it's depending on the context. It's depending on who's around, and I think that's okay. I think that's fair. I mean, walking around flashing your dick at everybody is not a nice thing to do. Not *everybody* wants to see that. So, I think part of it is also just a basic consideration for one another.[33]

Where are the pipes and effigies of asegi *people? Of same-gender sexuality? Of genders outside of a binary? What else was destroyed by colonist farmers, shocked not only to be reminded of the Indigenous presence in the land, but a sovereign erotic Indigenous presence? I would like to imagine those images existed. Maybe they still do, tucked into a box in a museum somewhere, or even surviving in people's families. Leslea expresses hope that an* un-covery *of historical and cultural memories of Cherokee Two-Spirit people is possible: "And I'm always dead curious, and hope at some point that more jars turn up with these stories in them, because we get them, a few a year, you know? Here's a prayer. In a jar. Here's a story. In a jar. Written on ledger paper. And I'm hoping to have more stories . . . that would address the issue of what we'd have to call 'Two-Spirit' Because the stories did exist, and the roles existed."*[34]

Perhaps as we rebeautify our erotic memories something will stir and more materials will come back to us. Or, perhaps, by approaching memory as an asegi *story, we'll be able to recognize older stories through the rebeautified refractions of our bodies.*

If decolonization on every level is the work of contemporary Native activists, artists, and scholars—and I believe it should be—our erotic histories cannot be ignored. And so, my hope is that our erotic memories can be rebeautified and remade, compelling us to employ our erotic lives as resistance and memory that can aid in decolonial struggles. Working against the internalization of dominant culture's values around sex and bodies entails a rebeautification of our cultural memory that honors our history and rebalances our present and future.

From where our feet stand, upward, then, we are as beautiful as the very blossoms themselves. We are as beautiful as the Red Rainbow.

5

D4Ꭹ DʃC (*ASEGI AYETL*)

Cherokee Two-Spirit People Reimagining Nation

N CHEROKEE, the word for "nation" is DʃC (*ayetl*). DʃC literally means "center," the seventh direction in Cherokee cosmology. Unlike dominant European views of the world, which understand only four fixed, flat directions, Cherokee traditions understand the world as multifaceted and in motion. "Center" is neither stable nor singular as a direction—the center is dependent upon one's perspective.

I want to hold both of these concepts—DʃC (*ayetl*, "nation/center," the seventh and moveable direction) and D4Ꭹ (*asegi*, "other")—to think about how contemporary Cherokee Two-Spirit people are telling stories that reimagine and re-story notions of nationhood and disrupt contemporary queer/transphobia within and outside of Cherokee communities. Listening to and for *asegi* stories helps us think about how they perform Two-Spirit critiques that potentially shift and re-create DʃC (*ayetl*).

Asegi stories, within a *third space*, perform Two-Spirit critiques that question reductive and autocolonial notions of "nation," and look at the ways that Native nationalisms are not exempt from falling into the same modes of conduct as other nationalisms.[1] *Asegi* stories are a rhetorical maneuver to intervene in heterosexist imaginings of Cherokee culture and histories. *Asegi* stories place Two-Spirit identities into a *repertoire* of cultural memories, employing Two-Spirit critiques in struggles for decolonization. Through our stories, Cherokee Two-Spirit people are challenging heteropatriarchy within Cherokee nation-building, exposing the ways oppression is replicated by narrow notions of "nation."

I would like to look to, and listen to, the *asegi* stories told to me by four participants in "On the Wings of *Wadaduga*" Robin Farris, Daniel Heath Justice, Chad Taber, and Corey Taber—to see how they perform *asegi* stories and re-story *ayetl*.[2]

During the interviews, I asked participants what terms they use for themselves to describe their gender-sexualities, and, not surprisingly, the answers point to the complexity and slipperiness of identity labels. While *Two-Spirit* is certainly used often as an umbrella term in contemporary Native Two-Spirit/LGBTQ communities, participants in this research have complex and conflicting relationships with the term. Daniel wasn't comfortable using the term *Two-Spirit* for himself because he felt the term was unnecessarily normalizing:

I actually don't use *Two-Spirit* very often. *Queer* works really well for me. I like its ambiguity, and I like that it kind of shakes things up a bit. For myself, I think *Two-Spirit* is a bit . . . I understand the reasons for connecting it to a spiritual tradition and I think that's important, but I think in some ways it normalizes in ways that I don't know if necessarily we need to be normalized. I like the idea that whatever roles we may have had in the past are roles today, that we could be really important in shaking up complacency and conservatism and reactionary convention, and reminding people that being Cherokee is about a lot more than blood and it's a lot more than breeding. There's a lot to being Cherokee that is really exciting and powerful and disruptive and beautifully quirky and weird and anomalous. So, I'm very happy with *Queer*. I probably identify myself much more as *Queer* than *Gay*. . . . *Queer* feels very much in keeping with being Cherokee to me. And *Gay* is weighted by a lot of representational burdens. Cherokees as a rule have always been . . . weird. For our neighbors. So, in the Southeast we were the only Iroquoian-speaking people. We were the people who lived in the mountains. Socially we were similar to the Muskogean peoples in a lot of ways, but we were also anomalous in a lot of ways. And anomalies are such a big part of our tradition. I mean, you have Uktena, you have Wild Boy, you have . . . even Thunder in some ways is anomalous.[3] These are figures who cross between worlds and represent a lot of different realities. That's been a Cherokee experience. Our history of intermarriage, our history of adaptation . . . we adapted pretty readily. Even traditionalists who didn't speak English adapted to changing circumstances. Not necessarily *gladly* all the time, but pretty practically, so, we've always been able to adapt and shift and . . . move ourselves as necessary, and I think *Queer* is a term that really gives us that as well.

Chad, Corey, and Robin all used *Two-Spirit* in specifically Native contexts, but also found it a difficult term to use outside of Native communities. Robin said that she uses the word *Gay* as more of a "universal" term, and also identifies as a Lesbian. On her use of the term *Two-Spirit* she says,

> *Two-Spirit* depends on where I'm at, 'cause so many people don't know what that is. . . . Obviously if I'm with Natives I would [use the term], if I thought they'd understand it. . . . I don't like the word *homosexual*, that's for sure. . . . [I]t sounds like a Christian sermon word to me. It's derogatory, it's meant to separate and define who's doing something they're not supposed to. I like what they said today, about the fact that *Two-Spirit* embraces more than just sexuality, that it embraces the whole spirit part of who we are as a person, honoring and being genuine to who we're born as.[4]

Chad and Corey—twin mixed-blood Cherokee/Creek/Osage brothers who are organizers in Oklahoma Two-Spirit communities—also spoke about their situational use of the term *Two-Spirit* and some of the challenges of using it outside of Native contexts:

CHAD: It depends probably I guess to whom I'm speaking. Usually I identify as Gay, but also because mainly where I live, it's very urban, there's not many opportunities for me to use the term *Two-Spirit* and be understood. So usually I just use the term *Gay* and I identify as Gay and Native American. (*To Corey*) How do you identify?

COREY: You know, I think that people that are not Native American have no idea what the word *Two-Spirit* means in almost every instance, and so I think it's kind of . . . it's a useless term in some scenarios. . . .

CHAD: Sometimes. . . .

COREY: Unfortunately. And I don't mean to take away from it, like, to say it's not worth having around, but just that in certain situations it's not applicable as . . . it's lost in translation, almost, you could say.

CHAD: Sometimes I use that as an opportunity to tell people a little bit about our history.

COREY: To educate.

CHAD: Mm-hmm. Especially in my day-to-day life, because I come in contact with a lot of people. I work as a stylist, and so I see a lot of people on a daily basis, and a lot of them . . . just because of the nature of the work, I develop a pretty close relationship with most of my clients, and so and a lot of them will ask me. And also, when I return from ceremony, like Green Corn Ceremony, where I have scratches on my body and people see that. Or my tattoos they see on my wrists and wonder what that's from or what it symbolizes.[5] And so that kind of gives me an opportunity to explain a little bit more about myself and maybe even identify with the term *Two-Spirit.*

Cherokee people, then, have a complicated and nuanced relationship with the term *Two-Spirit.* While Chad, Corey, and Robin all used the term for themselves, it was not the only term they used as an identity label. Daniel simultaneously questioned the rhetorical work of *Two-Spirit,* while also seeing its value in relationship to spiritual traditions. All four participants, then, are able to *disidentify* with the term as a tactic in constructing *asegi* and *ayetl.*[6]

Many Cherokee Two-Spirit people who are not fluent in Cherokee—including myself—struggle or have struggled with the absence and trauma caused by language-loss in relationship to our identities as Two-Spirit people. One of the first questions I had about my identity as a Two-Spirit Cherokee was, "What word or words exist in Cherokee to talk about who we are?" Just as there is no singular answer to this in English, there is no singular answer to this in Cherokee. The fact that most Cherokees are not fluent in Cherokee adds additional complexities to searching for these terms, as we often have to rely on other people—who may or may not be Two-Spirit and may have various relationships to and opinions about LGBTQ issues—to relay very specific cultural information. The conflation of sexuality and gender expression under umbrella terms like *Two-Spirit* and *queer* may further complicate this process. Asking a language speaker or elder if there is a word for *gay* in Cherokee, for instance, may cause the elder or speaker to say "no." However, asking elders or speakers if there are words for people who live as a gender other than that assigned at birth may bring different answers. Because the historical identities, roles, and expressions we are calling *Two-Spirit* are primarily about gender role and gender expression—*not* about what genders a person can fall in love with or are sexually involved with—there is no singular or simple answer to questions about Cherokee terms for our identities.

Cherokee Two-Spirit people are looking to language—or lack thereof—to make sense of our places in history, build our *practices* in the present, and transform the future through our stories. Because of the importance of language for contemporary Cherokee Two-Spirits, I asked participants if they knew terms in Cherokee for our identities. In answering a question about terms for Two-Spirit people in Cherokee, Robin responded:

Well, I liked finding out from another Cherokee . . . that there had been a word, because . . . I started out finding that among Native people—'cause I was finding out who I was as a Gay person at the same time I was trying to learn more about my culture as a Cherokee—and then I heard through a Cherokee that here amongst Native people, it's a non-issue. That we've always had them in our society, and I thought, "Oh, this is incredible." You know, I'd found this community that will accept me as a Gay person. And then, as I started investigating it, I found out—not the case. We've been so assimilated as a culture that a lot of them don't even know their history and don't even remember. And so, I was angry and disappointed and very sad. Then I found out from another Cherokee, of the Eastern Band, that, yes indeed, we were accepted and that there was a name for us, it was Two-Heart.[7] And I don't know how to pronounce that in Cherokee. He wrote it down, but I don't remember how to pronounce it.

In response to a similar question, Corey said he hadn't heard a specific positive term for Two-Spirit people in Cherokee contexts:

I would say that a lot of the words that you'll hear, they probably have some sort of negative connotation. Because I haven't ever experienced or haven't ever been informed of any position of reverence, we don't have a pretty word for it—you know what I mean?—like some tribes do. There just wasn't that. Not that I know of anyway. And a lot of the younger people now—well, younger people anyway are the ones who cause a lot of the issues or go out of their way to make people feel uncomfortable and that sort of thing, or harass all of the Two-Spirited people, that sort of thing. It's usually the younger people that do that. The older people have a quieter way. And so, younger people nowadays, a lot of them don't speak our language. And so for that reason *they* don't even know the words to use other than English words. So I've never really had any experiences or anything like that with being called negative or even positive words in the Cherokee language that reference GLBT status or anything like that.

Robin and Corey's responses here led to a core concept that all participants had about Cherokee Two-Spirit histories and present lives: that the gender role and/or sexuality of a Cherokee person is less relevant to their place in Cherokee communities than the *practices* of being in reciprocal and balanced relationship with—ᏚᏳᎪᏛ (*duyuk'ta*)—and productive cooperation with—ᎦᏚᎩ (*gadugi*)—those communities. Questions about the traditional place of Two-Spirit people within Cherokee lifeways and worldviews opened up discussions about larger obligations to community. When asked what he thought our traditional place was in Cherokee communities, Daniel said,

> I've asked a couple of elders this, both of whom said they don't think we had a special place, necessarily, or a culturally defined place, but they both said that was because it just didn't matter, that it wasn't so different as to require a distinctive role. Which surprised me . . . that wasn't the answer I was expecting. And I wonder about that, I think it's a real possibility that as long as you were still contributing to the community, whether you lived as a man or a woman or whatever, who you had sex with didn't matter. Are you having kids? Are you adding to the safety and security of the town? Are you fulfilling your obligations to your family? That mattered. On the whole, not everybody had to have children. Are you contributing to the welfare of the community? I think that's what mattered. That could very well have been it.

Corey had a very similar answer to this question:

> I haven't experienced a great difference between Cherokee and Creek communities, and what I've learned from my experiences with all of those people is that there wasn't necessarily a place of reverence for Two-Spirited people—*necessarily*. And there could have been, you know, I mean all of our people teach different things, but it was told to us that that's not how you're characterized. What's important is how you help out your family and how you take care of your people, whether it be your community, your family, your tribe—whatever circumstance. How you treat the people around you and what you do to give back. That essentially defines you as a person, and not who you choose for a partner.

Chad likewise emphasized the importance of community participation—ᎦᏚᎩ (*gadugi*)—to Cherokee identity rather than contemporary concepts of sexuality, gender, race, and blood-quantum: "Traditionally, we're told that you were

Cherokee based on your participation in the community and what you do for the community."

When I asked Robin what she thought our traditional place was within Cherokee communities, she replied,

> I have no idea. Like [Co-cké] was talking about—and that's what I found in my research—because it's an eastern tribe, so much of it was assimilated before people started getting it down on paper, that unless we do old manuscripts, that the people who wrote down certain things or know because it's been passed down orally or something like that. . . . I have no idea. I've heard that you were defined by your work role, so it could be that. I mean, I know there were warrior women. Whether that meant they were considered Two-Spirit or not, I don't know. I know there were Cherokee warrior women, because I've read about them. Like Nancy Ward was considered sort of a warrior woman—Beloved Women—I know there's that, but Beloved Women are not the same thing as warrior women or Two-Spirit. I guess you could be both, but not necessarily, so, I don't know. I'm still learning.

While Robin wasn't sure what place Two-Spirit people had within Cherokee communities in the past, she was sure that Two-Spirit people were "a part of the circle," a part of the larger whole of Cherokee community and lifeways: "Now I think we're struggling to get back in the circle. And then I think we were part of the circle, and it was accepted and it was just a different way of being, and unique to each individual, but all part of the whole community. I like what they say about, we didn't throw away people, we put them in their place.[8] I don't think that's true now. But I think we can get back there. I'm optimistic."

Not surprisingly, participants in "On the Wings of *Wadaduga*" both subtly and explicitly critiqued the Cherokee Nation's reaction to same-sex marriage, seeing its actions as a detriment to "the circle." Participants countered these politics with D4Ᏺ (*asegi*) stories, unsettling and disidentifying with notions of Cherokee DβC (*ayetl*) that are reductive and exclusive. Robin spoke fairly extensively about the same-sex marriage case and her own email exchanges with members of the tribal council. Robin challenges the Cherokee Nation's arguments and reasoning regarding same-sex marriage:

> Our history as a people is evolving, just like all people's history, so that was my big argument to the Nation council was (and is) that, I don't argue with your right to

say that you've decided at this point in time that—given how you view the world
or morality or whatever—that Gays shouldn't get married, but I do argue with
your denial of the fact the Two-Spirit were a part and accepted as a valuable part
of our people and our history. I mean, go ahead and say that it used to be okay
in the past but that you no longer find that being gay acceptable or whatever, but
don't pretend we didn't exist.

Daniel likewise found moves toward exclusion and normalcy contrary to
Cherokee lifeways, experiences, and traditions:

I'd be a little hesitant to say that to be Cherokee is to be Queer, but I think that we
are in an anomalous position in a lot of ways in broader Native America. I mean,
we're hated in Indian Country 'cause we're supposedly not Indian enough, but it's
been our transformative Indianness that has made us survive. And I find it really
troubling that there are so many people in the Nation who would want to take
away that transformability out of some sort of weird misguided fear about cultural purity, when we've always been inclusive, we've always been adaptive. Not
always *happily*. I think that's an important point, too, but, that would be Queer.
That's also about being Queer. That's survival. And not just surviving, but *thriving*.

Corey made explicit and confrontational reference to the erasure of Two-
Spirit people by the Cherokee Nation's tribal council during the same-sex mar-
riage case when I asked him what he would want to say to future generations of
Cherokee Two-Spirit people:

There's a lot, a lot, a lot of Gay Cherokees and a lot of Gay Creeks. And there
always have been and there always will be. And anybody on the tribal council that
tells you different is full of fuckin' shit. (*Laughter*). And I want you to *believe* that.
I want you to *know* that from us. . . . Just in case you didn't hear it anywhere else,
you heard it here. I mean that from the bottom of my heart, because that's what
our medicine people have taught us. You guys aren't something new, you aren't
some kind of spectacle we never seen. They treat us as if it's a non-issue, they treat
us like it's nothing out of the ordinary. Because it isn't to us. And I wanna make
sure that *that* gets in there. Aaayyeee . . .

Participants' re-storying Two-Spirit history is nested within larger work to
remember **D4Ʒ** (*asegi*) stories that have been marginalized by some aspects

of contemporary Cherokee nationalism. Daniel looked to history to disrupt moves to essentialize and simplify Cherokee "tradition" and "history." Part of Daniel's current scholarship, for instance, offers an **D4Ᏹ** (*asegi*) narrative to the history of Ada-gal'kala/Little Carpenter. He writes that "whatever orientation we might assume he would fit today, in his own time he was most decidedly *queer*, inhabiting and even embodying an anomalous space of influence that drew from many sources and was directed in service to Cherokee sovereignty and self-determination in a time of extraordinary cultural and political upheaval."[9] At the time of my interview with Daniel, he was in a process of re-storying Ada-gal'kala through a Cherokee-centered queer framework:

Little Carpenter is a really interesting figure to me. We have a lot of information on him, but he's . . . he's kinda quirky. He's honored, but it's clear that even in his own community of Chota he holds a somewhat ambivalent or ambiguous position. He's the father of Dragging Canoe, the great Chickamauga war chief. He's the uncle of Nancy Ward, Nan'yehi, the great Beloved Woman. He's a Beloved Man who is an advocate for peace. He was known as a very strong warrior before. But he disappeared for a long time, he was a captive of the Odawas, possibly. There's also some question that he might have been Odawa. He might have been of another nation who was adopted into the Cherokee Nation. He was renowned for his rhetorical skills, but he was also known to be very, very strategic. He was an amazing politician who worked very much for the benefit of Chota, but not necessarily for other Cherokee communities. He was very town-centered. He was one of the first Cherokee delegates that went to London, so he saw this force that was coming across the ocean, and he had a really unique perspective that a lot of other Cherokees at this time did not.

The pictures we have of him, and the descriptions we have of him, always that he was small, slight, and he's effeminized in a lot of these representations, even if it's just kind of by an aside. He had a *very* intimate relationship with a British military officer, I want to say John Stuart, but I don't remember exactly what his name was. Somewhere in memory they did the "brotherhood ceremony," which seems to me to be kind of a nice way of, or a very heteronormative way of, dismissing that intimacy. I guess when Little Carpenter died, Stuart or whoever this man was, was inconsolable with grief, which could be a brother situation, but just a lot of things lead me to wonder. No evidence, I have no evidence that he got it on with men. But just so many little things point to him being an anomalous figure and a figure who—yeah, he had a son, we know nothing, or very little, about his relationship with his wife. We do know he was estranged from his son, which would have made some sense, because the father would not have been any authority. But in their particular relationship, they were both Wolf Clan—not sure how that happened. They would have had a stronger relationship. And Little Carpenter's relationship with Nan'yehi—he was the uncle of Nan'yehi—he would have had a significant influence over her. And she had a very strong and contested relationship with Dragging Canoe. I also wonder—because we don't know a lot about the women's roles in the council, there's scattered bits and pieces. We know that there probably was a women's council. But we know in other Iroquoian and some Muskogean traditions, but particularly Iroquoian, the women's council has a male representative to men's council. And his relationship with the women seems to be very strong. So I wonder if there was something maybe similar to that. And who better than a queer boy to bridge that gap between the women and the men?

And, his nickname: Leaning Wood. It's really hard for me not to see that as a pun. I need to talk to a language speaker to have a sense of whether that would be the case, but things just point over and over to me that he was family. And so, he fathered a child. Yeah, and? That would not in any way preclude him from being queer. He's a Beloved Man at a younger age than a lot of other Beloved Men, if memory serves. So what does that mean? And just because he was a Beloved Man doesn't mean he wasn't also a warrior. But, he supported the British. I would love to know what was going on in England when those Cherokee boys were over there. Did they visit a molly house? Not likely, but they certainly stayed in the area of London where same-sex activities were notorious. I don't know. I have a lot of research to do on this, but . . . you know?

Just as Daniel brought an D4Ꮩ *(asegi)* interpretation to this part of Cherokee history, he also challenges Cherokees to remember the role of the erotic in Cherokee traditions, histories, and lifeways in an act of rebeautification.

Robin, Daniel, Corey, and Chad are pointing to an DᏰC *(ayetl,* nation/center) that asks Cherokee people, now and in the future, to remember other stories, other histories, that are inclusive, and in fact grounded in counter-stories—D4Ꮩ *(asegi)* stories—to versions of Cherokee history, sovereignty, and nationhood that seek heteronormativity.

Robin, Corey, and Chad all emphasized a past in which Two-Spirit people were "a part of the circle." Healing the circle—healing historical trauma—was a central part of the interviews with Corey and Chad. These conversations reflected the decolonial work in which Cherokee people and Two-Spirit people are currently involved. This revitalization work critiques the queer/transphobia internalized by Native communities and simultaneously positions Two-Spirit people as necessary to the well-being of both Native communities and the world:

> CHAD: I think that the basis of our work, fundamentally, is restoring what was lost. And that's a very general statement, but it means a lot of different things. Restoring what was lost as Two-Spirited people, restoring what was lost as Cherokee Two-Spirited people, meaning traditions and ceremonies. . . .
>
> COREY: Healing the part of the Cherokee circle that's been *gone* because these people have *ignored* us and cast us out.
>
> CHAD: Not just that, but, healing and restoring what is lost in the *world*. And I think our work is going to transition from regaining what we've lost in a smaller perspective to restoring what was lost as a whole.
>
> COREY: It's a part of a bigger healing that has to occur.

Corey and Chad's words here are reminiscent of other waves of Cherokee resistance that place *practice* at the center of maintaining SGA6ꞌ (*duyuk'ta*) and the continuance of the world. Like the Cherokee Ghost Dance movement that insisted on reclaiming particular dances in order to maintain the world, and like the Redbird Smith movement that worked to "get back what was lost" through both the *archive* and the *repertoire*, Cherokee Two-Spirit people are looking to both the archive and repertoire to "restore what was lost" and to imagine and create a present and future.

Because the goal of "On the Wings of *Wadaduga*" is to revise both the archive and the repertoire, and explicitly to bring our stories in the present to Cherokee Two-Spirit people in the future and to use our stories to imagine what we want our futures to look like, I asked participants about our future as Two-Spirit Cherokees. When asked what she would want our future to be, Robin replied, "That we'll get back into that place where we're accepted, protected, and allowed to add our spirit and gifts into the circle of our people and our community just like any other member of the tribe. I'd like to see all of us, in all tribes, model to the rest of the world that Native Americans see being Two-Spirit . . . as no big deal. It's just a different way of being, like having blond hair or blue eyes, being tall or short."

Daniel replied to a similar question by also speaking of having a place within what Robin, Chad, and Corey call "the circle":

> I want us to have a place on the grounds, with our partners, where we don't have to worry or feel like our partners aren't gonna be welcomed. I'm not a Baptist, but I don't imagine that one's partner would be welcome in the Baptist Church. There are some grounds where we're welcome, though not many. I want us to be healthy and happy and to not be seen as compromising our Cherokeeness by living honestly and loving honestly. I want that love and living to be seen as contributing to Cherokee nationhood, not drawing away from it.

While there are many ways that Cherokee Two-Spirits are regaining our places within "the circle," one way we are doing this work is through concentrated work in the archive in order to uncover *asegi* stories that have been forgotten or ignored. Through reweaving *asegi* stories, through our reimagining and retelling, Cherokee Two-Spirit and queer people are "regaining what we've lost."

EPILOGUE

DOUBLEWEAVE

An *Asegi* Manifesto

TO FINISH WEAVING A DOUBLE-WALL BASKET, you must carefully bring together the numerous splints from all four sides and weave them into each other at the bottom of the basket. This book is a basket woven from splints that, I hope, can carry imagination about our work as Two-Spirit people into our decolonized futures. All of us—Two-Spirit people and not—must be able to weave a future together in which colonial heteropatriarchy ceases to exist. Hopefully, this book is a small contribution to that much larger goal. Our Indigenous queer/Two-Spirit folks must be centralized in our numerous decolonial struggles because gender and sexuality are settler weapons that have been used to invade our lands and bodies, remove us from our homelands, steal our children, and erase us.

Paula Gunn Allen writes, "The root of oppression is loss of memory." [1] Reclaiming and continuing cultural memory and practice is central to decolonization, but we must ask critical questions about which stories get reclaimed, which stories get hidden, and which stories we hope our descendants tell. This book opens with words from Two-Spirit activist Corey Taber: "[I]f you can see that far into the past, you can see that far into the future." Our stories as *asegi* people are doublewoven: strands of the past and the future come together to create a new story that, like a rivercane basket, can withstand floods and fires, invasions and removals. A double-wall root-runner basket remembers its doublewoven rivercane ancestors. It tells the story of Water Spider's collaboration with Wadaduga (Dragonfly) to bring fire back to the world. Even though the materials have changed, a basket remembers the origin of fire at the beginning. Peggy Sanders Brennan, a Cherokee basket weaver, told me once as we were weaving together, "When you weave a basket, you create the world." The materials we use might change: we might use honeysuckle or brushbark instead of rivercane, Rit Dye to color our splints instead of bloodroot. We might imagine new designs to create even while we continue to weave our old designs. But we continue. Our hands remember stories each time a new creation is woven.

Asegi stories do the same: pull together the available materials—the stories we tell each other, the stories hidden in archives, the stories we learn from the people in our communities who remember our place around the fire—and weave something that is both ancient and entirely new. Through the double-weaving of *asegi* stories we *remake* the world.

SPLINT ꮤ/*SOQUO*/ONE: DECOLONIZING GENDER AND SEXUALITY

Colonization has always used our genders and sexualities as a reason to attack, enslave, or "civilize" us. The word *gender* itself is from the Latin word *genus*, a species/sort/kind, and related to the word *genre*. "Gender" is a logic, and a structural system of oppression, whose sole purpose is to categorize people in order to deploy systemic power and control. It is a wholly colonial imposition. This doesn't mean I think that our identities as men, as women, as Two-Spirit and trans people are some kind of false colonial consciousness. I do think, though, that "gender" is a weapon to force us into clear Eurocentric categories, keep us confined in there, ensure we monitor each other's behavior, and, then, while we are distracted, take our lands.

Similarly, the idea of "sexuality"—which is dependent on the idea of "gender"—is simply another way to sort people into "genres" of behavior, desire, and identity in order to exert power and control. The idea of "sexual orientation" too often hides the fact that most people experience desire and sex outside gender and sexual binaries. These colonial logics mean that when we look to our past, we "straighten" it: we make heterosexist and gender-binary assumptions about our ancestors and render a more complicated, erotic, and joyous history invisible.

While I'm certainly not the first to make such a call, and I have made this call before, I will make it again: we must dismantle the entire constructions of "gender" and "sexuality" as part of larger work to dismantle all forms of colonial heteropatriarchy. Decolonization is impossible without centralizing women, Two-Spirit people, and queer/trans folks, and memory sits at the center of how we imagine what is possible for our futures. If our lands and bodies are inseparable as Indigenous people, and I think they are, then it is impossible to reclaim our landbases and work for self-determination and decolonization while heteropatriarchal gender and sexual regimes continue to dictate our lives, lands, and imaginings of resistance. In the words of Métis artist and activist Erin Marie Konsmo, "our bodies are not *terra nullius*."[2]

SPLINT Wᴘ/*TAL*/TWO: THE SPIRIT OF COFITACHEQUI AND GÓMEZ

The regulation of Cherokee gender and sexuality and the creation of colonial gender and sexual binaries happen through the violent control of Black bodies. *Asegi* people must work to fight anti-Black racism inside and outside of our communities and recognize how anti-Black racism works to undermine our self-determination, destroy alliances, continue the occupation of our lands, and uphold white supremacy in our communities.

Indigenous people of the Americas and diasporic Indigenous people of Africa are part of each other's story in ways that both help us envision radical alliances of resistance and also remind us of how we use white supremacist colonial violence against each other. Our struggles—and, often, our identities as Red-Black people—have intentionally been separated in order for settler powers to have control of our lands, labor, and bodies. The connections between the control of our bodies, sexualities, genders, and landbases as Native people and the control of the bodies, sexualities, genders, and landbases of Black people are inseparable. We all bear the legacies of genocide, land theft, and slavery. We all have a responsibility to each other and to our decolonial imaginings to work in alliance.

SPLINT KT/*TSO'*/THREE: REBEAUTIFYING MEMORY

Decolonization is, in part, a process of continuing, or revitalizing, our lifeways, but we must ask which lifeways are being continued and which are being ignored. Decolonization requires a rebeautification of our memories and practices in order to restore the erotic as a site of *duyuktv*, balance and justice, to our lives. Even while I'm critically wary of how the idea of "tradition" can be used as a tool to control our behaviors, practices, and lives, I also think that continuing our lifeways, languages, songs, dances, and artistic practices is of vital importance to decolonization. In my interview with Adela, she says, "I think that the neatest thing that ever was told to me is that if my teacher knows a hundred songs, and I learn fifty of those songs, we just lost half of our culture. And so that's really what I think my job is, is to make sure we celebrate those people that came before us, that we celebrate the people who are working now, and that we pave the way for the little ones."

The problem is not the continuation of our lifeways—the problem happens when we ignore or erase the stories and practices that don't fit into our notions of what "traditional" is, in order to conform to colonial heteropatriarchal notions of who we are. There is nothing wrong with changing our practices— there are plenty of "traditional" practices that we have decided not to continue. We must ask, though, which practices or stories get abandoned, not because they cause harm, but because we have so internalized the sexual and gender norms of colonial culture that we cut off parts of our memories and decide to forget ancestors who make us uncomfortable in order to collude with an ongoing civilization project that wants its Indians subdued, normalized, complicit, and—ultimately—landless and dead.

There is beauty in cultural memories of loving our bodies, singing about sex, creating art that celebrates the erotic, and honoring love between people of the same gender. Why would we trade such luscious memories and practices for colonial notions of who we are? Where we have lost songs, we can create new ones. When our art is destroyed for being "indecent," we can remake it. Ancestors are tricky people, so who knows? Maybe creating something new is waking up what we think is lost. Maybe as we return to our memories, they return to us.

SPLINT ᏒᎩ/*NVG'*/FOUR: SEEING INTO THE FUTURE

Decolonization is an act of imagining. I envision a world in which all Two-Spirit people speak our languages, where we all practice our lifeways and teach those lifeways to our children on our own lands. Where the land is not poison, where our lives as humans aren't constantly at risk. I envision a world in which all Two-Spirit people have our places returned to the center of our communities,

one in which the colonial powers of the United States and Canada (and all settler regimes) no longer exist, and Indigenous people have created other forms
of governance outside of the nation-state. A world where our Red-Black selves
are celebrated and understood as part of our survival. Where women's leadership is centralized and respected. Where sexual violence is as unheard of as it
was in our past. Where our erotic lives are simply part of the larger reflection of
who we are.

Yes, I want it all back: our lives, our languages, our lands, our songs, our plants, our
children, our memories, our bodies. All of it. I want us to all remember who we are.

Two-Spirit people carry memories for our people. We must *remake* our past,
honor who we are in the present, and imagine the radical and gorgeous possibilities of our futures. Our work is to rebalance an unbalanced world. If we
are to survive as humans, we must. I am quite certain that part of that rebalancing is to dare to love ourselves and one another by telling *asegi* stories. We must
tell our stories, and reimagine our stories, in order to link arms together with
others to carry us out of the colonial present and into a decolonized future. Our
stories are waiting for us between the basket walls. Our stories reweave the
world.

NOTES

INTRODUCTION

The epigraph to the introduction is from Qwo-Li Driskill, interview with Corey Taber in "On the Wings of *Wadaduga*: Cherokee Two-Spirit Lives" (unpublished manuscript).

1. *Wado* to Robin McBride Scott and Tsi-ge-yu/Beloved Sharp for teaching me to weave baskets.

2. Casie C. Cobos, "An Other Chican@ Rhetoric from Scratch: (Re)Making Stories, (Un)Mapping the Lines, and Re membering Bodies" (PhD diss., Texas A&M University, 2012), 2.

3. Linda Tuhiwai Smith, *Decolonizing Methodologies: Research and Indigenous Peoples* (New York: Zed Books, 1999), 13.

4. Marilou Awiakta, *Selu: Seeking the Corn-Mother's Wisdom* (Fulcrum: Golden, CO, 1993).

5. Malea Powell, "Rhetorics of Survivance: How American Indians *Use* Writing," *College Composition and Communication* 53, no. 3 (2002): 399.

6. Malea Powell, "Down by the River, or How Susan La Flesche Picotte Can Teach Us About Alliance as a Practice of Survivance," *College English* 67, no. 1 (2004): 39.

7. Emma Pérez, *The Decolonial Imaginary: Writing Chicanas into History* (Bloomington: Indiana University Press, 1999), 6, 55.

8. Maylei Blackwell, *¡Chicana Power! Contested Histories of Feminism in the Chicano Movement* (Austin: University of Texas Press, 2011). Cobos, "An Other Chican@ Rhetoric from Scratch." Aydé Enríquez-Loya, "Crossing Borders and Building Alliances: Border Discourse Within Literatures and Rhetorics of Color" (PhD diss., Texas A&M University, 2012). Gabriela Raquel Ríos, "In Ixtli In Yollotl / A (Wise) Face a (Wise) Heart: (Re)Claiming Embodied Rhetorical Traditions of Anahuac and Tawantinsuyu" (PhD diss., Texas A&M University, 2011). Powell, "Down by the River"; Powell, "Listening to ghosts." Andrea Smith, *Native Americans and the Christian Right: The Gendered Politics of Unlikely Alliances* (Durham, NC: Duke University Press, 2008).

9. I put the term *postcolonial* in quotation marks here to remind us that, for Indigenous people in the United States, Canada, and other settler-colonial states, we are not postcolonial on any level.

10. For an in-depth discussion of the term "Two-Spirit," see Qwo-Li Driskill, Chris Finley, Brian Joseph Gilley, and Scott Lauria Morgensen, eds., *Queer Indigenous Studies: Critical Interventions in Theory, Politics, and Literature* (Tucson: University of Arizona Press, 2011).

11. Cherokee has two main dialects, the Giduwa dialect in North Carolina and the Overhill dialect in Oklahoma, as well as several dialects within each branch. Some of these words have different meanings across dialects. *Wado* to Wade Blevins, ᎬᏎ, ᎭᎠ ᎠᎾᏫ, and other friends for sharing these words and to Tim Nuttle for compiling them. Nuttle notes that they are descriptive, not classificatory. Tim Nuttle, "Cherokee Terms for GLB2S people," unpublished glossary, personal Facebook message to author, June 30, 2014.

12. Malea Powell, "Rhetorics of Survivance: How American Indians *Use* Writing," *College Composition and Communication* 53, no. 3 (2002): 399.

13. Christopher B. Teuton, *Cherokee Stories of the Turtle Island Liars' Club* (Chapel Hill: University of North Carolina Press, 2012), 2.

14. Ibid., 7.

15. Ibid., 8.

16. Patti Duncan, "history of disease," in *Q&A: Queer in Asian America*, ed. David L. Eng and Alice Y. Hom (Philadelphia: Temple University Press, 1998), 164.

17. Aurora Levins Morales, *Medicine Stories: History, Culture and the Politics of Integrity* (Cambridge, MA: South End Press, 1998), 24.

18. Joan Larkin and Carl Morse, eds., *Gay and Lesbian Poetry in Our Time: An Anthology* (New York: St. Martin's Press, 1988).

19. Will Roscoe, ed., *Living the Spirit: A Gay American Indian Anthology*, comp. Gay American Indians (San Francisco, CA) (New York: St. Martin's, 1988), 217–22.

20. Lester B. Brown, ed., *Two Spirit People: American Indian Lesbian Women and Gay Men* (New York: Haworth, 1997). Sue Ellen Jacobs, Wesley Thomas, and Sabine Lang, eds., *Two-Spirit People: Native American Gender Identity, Sexuality, and Spirituality* (Champaign: University of Illinois Press, 1997).

21. José Esteban Muñoz, *Cruising Utopia: The Then and There of Queer Futurity* (New York: New York University Press, 2009), 37.

22. After a long battle, the Cherokee Nation's Judicial Appeals Tribunal dismissed the injunction against the couple's marriage in February 2006.

23. Diana Taylor, *The Archive and the Repertoire: Performing Cultural Memory in the Americas* (Durham, NC: Duke University Press, 2003), 29.

24. Audra Simpson, *Mohawk Interruptus: Political Life Across the Borders of Settler States* (Durham, NC: Duke University Press, 2014), 34.

25. Blackwell, *Chicana Power*, 11.

26. Craig S. Womack, *Red on Red: Native American Literary Separatism* (Minneapolis: University of Minnesota Press, 1999); *Drowning in Fire* (Tucson: University of Arizona Press, 2001). For more in-depth history of Indigenous Two-Spirit and Queer literary production and scholarship, see Lisa Tatonetti's "The Emergence and Importance of Queer American Indian Literatures; or, 'Help and Stories' in Thirty Years of *SAIL*," *Studies in American Indian Literatures* 19, no. 4 (2007): 143–70; and Qwo-Li Driskill et al., "Introduction: Writing in the Present," in Qwo-Li Driskill, Daniel Heath Justice, Deborah A. Miranda, and Lisa Tatonetti, eds., *Sovereign Erotics: A Collection of Two-Spirit Literature* (Tucson: University of Arizona Press, 2011).

27. Deborah A. Miranda, *Bad Indians: A Tribal Memoir* (Berkeley, CA: Heyday, 2013), xiv.

28. Holly Kays, "Cherokee Affirms Gay Marriage Ban," *Smokey Mountain News*, January 14, 2015, http://www.smokymountainnews.com/news/item/14943-cherokee-affirms-gay-marriage-ban.

29. James Mooney, *History, Myths, and Sacred Formulas of the Cherokees* (Asheville, NC: Bright Mountain, 1992), 240–41.

30. Ibid., 241–42.

31. Ibid., 431.

32. Stickball is traditionally an important ceremonial and social event for Cherokees and many other eastern Native people. For an in-depth discussion of

stickball in Cherokee tradition and practice, see Michael J. Zogry's *Anetso, the Cherokee Ball Game: At the Center of Ceremony and Identity* (Chapel Hill: University of North Carolina Press, 2010).

33. Womack, *Drowning in Fire*, 200, 245; Daniel Heath Justice, *Our Fire Survives the Storm: A Cherokee Literary History* (Minneapolis: University of Minnesota Press, 2006).

34. Mooney, *History, Myths, and Sacred Formulas of the Cherokees*, 286–87.

35. Ibid., 287.

36. Ibid., 397.

37. Cat never identified herself to me as Two-Spirit. Her inclusion in the project was not because of her identification, or lack thereof, with any labels under a "Two-Spirit" umbrella. Rather, she was included in the project because she was willing to share a story that has important theoretical implications for Cherokee Two-Spirits and all Cherokees.

38. Qwo-Li Driskill, interview with Cat in "On the Wings of *Wadaduga*: Cherokee Two-Spirit Lives" (unpublished manuscript).

39. Previous to Cat's telling I had not heard anyone tell a version of this story with GꞭSꞬ (*Wadaduga*) involved. Mooney's brief references to GꞭSꞬ, however, helped me to imagine other versions of this story to theorize Cherokee Two-Spirit identities.

40. Thomas King, *The Truth About Stories: A Native Narrative* (Toronto: House of Anansi, 2003), 2.

41. "Dikaneisdi (Word List)," Cherokee Nation, http://www.cherokee.org/About TheNation/Language/Dikaneisdi%28WordList%29.aspx.

42. *Spirit of the Fire*, directed by Sam Jones (Tulsa, OK: KJRH-TV2, Scripps-Howard Broadcasting Co., 1984).

43. Raymond D. Fogelson and Paul Kutsche, "Cherokee Economic Cooperatives: The Gadugi," in *Symposium on Cherokee and Iroquois Culture*, ed. William Nelson Fenton and John Gulick, Smithsonian Institution, Bureau of American Ethnology Bulletin 180 (Washington, DC: Government Printing Office, 1961), 87.

44. Wilma Dunaway, "The Origin of Gadugi," Cherokee Nation, accessed August 15, 2014, http://www.cherokee.org/AboutTheNation/History/Facts/The OriginofGadugi.aspx.

45. Until the early nineteenth century, Cherokee politics were defined by these opposing—but complementary—political modes. Red (war) organizations led the people in times of war, while white (peace) organizations led the people in

times of peace. Daniel Heath Justice has used these political modes as a way of analyzing and interpreting Cherokee literature. Justice, *Our Fire Survives the Storm*.

46. Fogelson and Kutsche, "Cherokee Economic Cooperatives: The Gadugi," 88.

47. Robert K. Thomas, *The Origin and Development of the Redbird Smith Movement* (master's thesis, University of Arizona, 1954), 81.

48. Jason Baird Jackson, *Yuchi Ceremonial Life: Performance, Meaning, and Tradition in a Contemporary American Indian Community* (Lincoln: University of Nebraska Press, 2005), 30. While Jackson is speaking specifically of Creek and Yuchi ceremonial grounds, the same is true for Cherokee ceremonial grounds.

49. Thomas, "Origin and Development," 63. "Little captain," *usdi sgaigunst*, is a specific title from the Red Organization that was reinscribed as a title by the Keetoowah Society (62).

50. Charlotte Anne Wilson Heth, "The Stomp Dance Music of the Oklahoma Cherokee: A Study of Contemporary Practice with Special Reference to the Illinois District Council Ground" (PhD diss., University of California, 1975), 60.

51. Ibid., 124.

52. Womack, *Red on Red*, 226.

53. Smith, *Native Americans and the Christian Right*, xv.

54. Powell, "Down by the River," 57–58.

55. Qwo-Li Driskill, interview with Daniel Heath Justice in "On the Wings of *Wadaduga*: Cherokee Two-Spirit Lives" (unpublished manuscript).

56. Qwo-Li Driskill, interview with Corey Taber in "On the Wings of *Wadaduga*: Cherokee Two-Spirit Lives" (unpublished manuscript).

CHAPTER 1

1. Martin F. Manalansan IV, *Global Divas: Filipino Gay Men in the Diaspora* (Durham, NC: Duke University Press, 2003), 6. Malea Powell, "Down by the River, or How Susan La Flesche Picotte Can Teach Us About Alliance as a Practice of Survivance," *College English* 67, no. 1 (2004): 38–60.

2. *Wado* to both Angela Haas and Malea Powell for their ongoing work on material rhetorics.

3. Sarah H. Hill, *Weaving New Worlds: Southeastern Cherokee Women and Their Basketry* (Chapel Hill: University of North Carolina Press, 1997), 44. While

I understand Hill's description here, it is also a bit misleading. Doublewoven baskets are not two complete baskets with a common rim, though they might look that way. The process of doubleweaving—in brief—involves weaving the inside base and walls of the basket, then turning the same splints back down to weave the outside walls and base. Doublewoven baskets are one continuous weave.

4. Marilou Awiakta, *Selu: Seeking the Corn-Mother's Wisdom* (Golden, CO: Fulcrum, 1993), 34.

5. Daniel Heath Justice, "Beloved Woman Returns: The Doubleweaving of Homeland and Identity in the Poetry of Marilou Awiakta," in Dean Rader and Janice Gould, eds., *Speak to Me Words: Essays on Contemporary American Indian Poetry* (Tucson: University of Arizona Press, 2003), 74.

6. Daniel Heath Justice, *Our Fire Survives the Storm: A Cherokee Literary History* (Minneapolis: University of Minnesota Press, 2006), 18–31.

7. Ibid., 30.

8. Daniel Heath Justice, *Kynship: The Way of Thorn and Thunder, Book One* (Cape Croker Reserve, Ontario: Kegedonce, 2005); *Wyrwood: The Way of Thorn and Thunder, Book Two* (2006); *Dreyd: The Way of Thorn and Thunder, Book Three* (2007).

9. Kimberlé Crenshaw, "Demarginalizing the Intersection of Race and Sex: A Black Feminist Critique of Antidiscrimination Doctrine, Feminist Politics, and Antiracist Politics," *University of Chicago Legal Forum* 140 (1989): 149.

10. José Esteban Muñoz, *Disidentifications: Queers of Color and the Performance of Politics* (Minneapolis: University of Minnesota Press, 1999), 25.

11. Roderick A. Ferguson, *Aberrations in Black: Toward a Queer of Color Critique* (Minneapolis: University of Minnesota Press, 2003), 24.

12. De Certeau makes a distinction between strategies and tactics that are based in power differentials. He writes that a strategy is "the calculation (or manipulation) of power relationships that becomes possible as soon as a subject with will and power . . . can be isolated. . . . [I]t is an effort to delimit one's own place in the world bewitched by the invisible powers of the Other." A tactic, on the other hand, "is a calculated action determined by the absence of a proper locus. . . . The space of a tactic is the space of the other." Michel de Certeau, *The Practice of Everyday Life* (Berkeley: University of California Press, 2002), 35–36, 37.

13. Gayatri Gopinath, *Impossible Desires: Queer Diasporas and South Asian Public Cultures* (Durham, NC: Duke University Press, 2005), 11.

14. Ferguson, *Aberrations in Black*, 149n1.

15. Andrea Smith, "Queer Theory and Native Studies: The Heteronormativity of Settler Colonialism," *GLQ: A Journal of Lesbian and Gay Studies* 16, no. 1–2 (2010): 59.

16. Malea D. Powell, "Blood and Scholarship: One Mixed-Blood's Story," in *Race, Rhetoric, and Composition*, ed. Keith Gilyard (Portsmouth, NH: Boynton/Cook, 1999), 3.

17. For instance, see Muñoz, *Disidentifications*, 29; Ferguson, *Aberrations in Black*, 15, 17.

18. Gopinath, *Impossible Desires*, 19–20.

19. The quote is from ibid., 27–28.

20. Siobhan B. Somerville, *Queering the Color Line: Race and the Invention of Homosexuality in American Culture* (Durham, NC: Duke University Press, 2000), 13.

21. Chrystos, *Fire Power* (Vancouver, BC: Press Gang, 1995), 127.

22. Linda Tuhiwai Smith, *Decolonizing Methodologies: Research and Indigenous Peoples* (New York: Zed Books, 1999), 24.

23. Powell, "Blood and Scholarship," 4.

24. Scott Richard Lyons, "Rhetorical Sovereignty: What Do American Indians Want from Writing?" (*College Composition and Communication* 51, no. 3 (2000): 449. Emphasis in the original.

25. Robert Allen Warrior, *Tribal Secrets: Recovering American Indian Intellectual Traditions* (Minneapolis: University of Minnesota Press, 1995), 123.

26. It is important to note that this is not because Two-Spirit people are somehow more spiritual than non-Two-Spirit people, as the appropriation of the term by New Agers would try to suggest. Rather, spiritual and ceremonial traditions are part of a continuance of cultural memory that Two-Spirit people, like other members of Native communities, are often a part of. Beverly Little Thunder writes, "In the non-Native community of lesbians and gay people I have been told that being two-spirited means that I am a special being. It seems that they felt that my spirituality was the mystical answer to my sexuality. I do not believe this to be so. My spirituality would have been with me, regardless of my sexuality." Beverly Little Thunder, "I Am a Lakota Womyn," in *Two-Spirit People: Native American Gender Identity, Sexuality, and Spirituality*, ed. Sue-Ellen Jacobs, Wesley Thomas, and Sabine Lang (Urbana: University of Illinois Press, 1997), 207.

27. Chrystos, *Fire Power*, 128.

28. Andrea Smith, *Conquest: Sexual Violence and American Indian Genocide* (Cambridge, MA: South End Press, 2005), 12.

29. Lisa Tatonetti, *The Queerness of Native American Literature* (Minneapolis: University of Minnesota Press, 2014), 118, 175.

30. Scott Lauria Morgensen, *Spaces Between Us: Queer Settler Colonialism and Indigenous Decolonization* (Minneapolis: University of Minnesota Press, 2011), 55.

31. Gopinath, *Impossible Desires*, 11.

32. Craig S. Womack, *Red on Red: Native American Literary Separatism* (Minneapolis: University of Minnesota Press, 1999), 244.

33. Warrior, *Tribal Secrets*, 115–22.

34. Beth Brant, ed. *A Gathering of Spirit: A Collection by North American Indian Women* (Ithaca, NY: Firebrand, 1988). Will Roscoe, ed., *Living the Spirit: A Gay American Indian Anthology*, comp. by Gay American Indians (San Francisco, CA) (New York: St. Martin's, 1988).

35. Malea D. Powell, "Listening to Ghosts: An Alternative (Non)argument," in *Alt Dis: Alternative Discourses and the Academy*, ed. Christopher Schroeder, Helen Fox, and Patricia Bizzell (Portsmouth, NH: Boynton/Cook Heinemann, 2002), 15.

36. For an in-depth discussion of these movements, see Brian Joseph Gilley's *Becoming Two-Spirit: Gay Identity and Social Acceptance in Indian Country* (Lincoln: University of Nebraska Press, 2006).

37. Womack, *Red on Red*, 223.

38. Smith, *Conquest*, 178.

39. Gerald Vizenor, *Manifest Manners: Narratives on Postindian Survivance* (Lincoln: University of Nebraska Press, 1999), 15.

40. Powell, "Blood and Scholarship," 14n17.

41. Ibid., 13.

42. Womack, *Red on Red*, 301.

43. Ibid., 302. We should note that Womack also offers trickster strategies with a warning: "Celebrating tricksters, it seems to me, should be done with caution. It is important to remember that shape-shifting can also be a form of witchery and that tricksters can be oppressive assholes as often as liberators" (301).

44. Qwo-Li Driskill, "Call Me Brother: Two-Spiritness, the Erotic, and Mixedblood Identity as Sites of Sovereignty and Resistance in Gregory Scofield's Poetry," in *Speak to Me Words: Essays on Contemporary American Indian Poetry*, ed. Janice Gould and Dean Rader (Tucson: University of Arizona Press, 2003), 223–34. Qwo-Li Driskill, "Stolen from Our Bodies: First Nations

Two-Spirits/Queers and the Journey to a Sovereign Erotic," *Studies in American Indian Literatures* 16, no. 2 (2004): 50–64.

45. Anguksuar [Richard LaFortune], "A Postcolonial Colonial Perspective on Western [Mis]Conceptions of the Cosmos and the Restoration of Indigenous Taxonomies," in *Two-Spirit People: Native American Gender Identity, Sexuality, and Spirituality*, ed. Sue-Ellen Jacobs, Wesley Thomas, and Sabine Lang (Urbana: University of Illinois Press, 1997), 221.

46. David L. Eng, Judith Halberstam, and Jose Esteban Muñoz, eds., "What's Queer About Queer Studies Now?" special issue, *Social Text* 23, no. 3–4 84–85 (Fall–Winter 2005), 2.

47. Beth Brant, *Writing as Witness: Essay and Talk* (Toronto: Women's Press, 1994), 45.

48. The use of the term *making* here as an intellectual and rhetorical practice is specifically from Malea Powell's work on material rhetorics, and from conversations during and after visiting her Material Rhetorics graduate course at Michigan State University in the spring of 2008.

CHAPTER 2

1. See Sarah H. Hill, *Weaving New Worlds: Southeastern Cherokee Women and Their Basketry* (Chapel Hill: University of North Carolina Press, 1997), 90–91.

2. Cherríe Moraga and Gloria Anzaldúa, "Entering the Lives of Others: Theory in the Flesh," in *This Bridge Called My Back: Writings by Radical Women of Color*, ed. Cherríe Moraga and Gloria Anzaldúa (Watertown, MA: Persephone Press, 1981), 23.

3. Jacqueline Jones Royster, *Traces of a Stream: Literacy and Social Change Among African American Women* (Pittsburgh, PA: University of Pittsburgh Press, 2000), 280.

4. Walter D. Mignolo, *The Darker Side of the Renaissance: Literacy, Territoriality, and Colonization* (Ann Arbor: University of Michigan Press, 2003), 168.

5. Michelene E. Pesantubbee, *Choctaw Women in a Chaotic World* (Albuquerque: University of New Mexico Press, 2005), 3.

6. Mishuana Goeman, *Mark My Words: Native Women Mapping Our Nations* (Minneapolis: University of Minnesota Press, 2013), 19.

7. Jodi A. Byrd, *The Transit of Empire: Indigenous Critiques of Colonialism* (Minneapolis: University of Minnesota Press, 2011), xii–xiii.

8. Michel Foucault, *The History of Sexuality*, 2 vols., trans. Robert Hurley (New York: Vintage, 1990), 1:18. Eve Kosofsky Sedgwick, *Epistemology of the Closet* (Berkeley: University of California Press, 1990), 3.

9. Judith Butler, *Gender Trouble: Feminism and the Subversion of Identity* (New York: Routledge, 1990), 151.

10. Roxanne Dunbar-Ortiz, "The Grid of History: Cowboys and Indians," *Monthly Review* 55, no. 3 (2003): 83.

11. Hutcheson, Gregory S., and Josiah Blackmore, "Introduction," in *Queer Iberia: Sexualities, Cultures, and Crossings from the Middle Ages to the Renaissance*, ed. Josiah Blackmore and Gregory S. Hutcheson (Durham, NC: Duke University Press, 1999), 11–12.

12. Rowena McClinton, ed., *The Moravian Springplace Mission to the Cherokees*, vol. 1, *1805–1813* (Lincoln: University of Nebraska Press, 2007), 27.

13. Craig S. Womack, *Red on Red: Native American Literary Separatism* (Minneapolis: University of Minnesota Press, 1999), 200.

14. Daniel Heath Justice, "Notes Toward a Theory of Anomaly," *GLQ: A Journal of Lesbian and Gay Studies* 16, no. 1–2 (2010): 209.

15. Mary C. Churchill, "The Oppositional Paradigm of Purity versus Pollution in Charles Hudson's *The Southeastern Indians*," *American Indian Quarterly* 20, no. 3–4 (Fall 1996): 584.

16. Circe Sturm, *Blood Politics: Race, Culture, and Identity in the Cherokee Nation of Oklahoma* (Berkeley: University of California Press, 2002), 39.

17. Emma Pérez, *The Decolonial Imaginary: Writing Chicanas into History* (Bloomington: Indiana University Press, 1999).

18. Casie C. Cobos, "Embodied Storying, A Methodology for Chican@ Rhetorics: (Re)making Stories, (Un)mapping the Lines, and Re-membering Bodies" (PhD diss., Texas A&M University, 2012), 80.

19. Robert Allen Warrior, *The People and the Word: Reading Native Nonfiction* (Minneapolis: University of Minnesota Press, 2005), 182.

20. Mignolo, *Darker Side of the Renaissance*, 237.

21. For a thorough discussion of colonial cartography, including representations of bodies, see Mignolo's chapter, "Putting the Americas on the Map: Cartography and the Colonization of Space," ibid., 259–313.

22. Lawrence A. Clayton, Edward C. Moore, and Vernon James Knight, Jr., eds., *The De Soto Chronicles: The Expedition of Hernando De Soto to North America in 1539–1543* (Tuscaloosa: University of Alabama Press, 1995), 1:424.

23. Pietro Martire d'Anghiera, *De Orbe Novo, the Eight Decades of Peter Martyr d'Anghera*, trans. Francis Augustus MacNutt (New York: G. P. Putnam's Sons, 1912), 1:284.

24. Ibid., 1:285.

25. Deborah A. Miranda, "Extermination of the *Joyas*: Gendercide in Spanish California," *GLQ: A Journal of Lesbian and Gay Studies* 16, no. 1–2 (2010): 259.

26. Clayton, Moore, and Knight, eds., *The De Soto Chronicles*, 1:458.

27. Because she is not given a name aside from "the *cacica*," throughout this chapter I will refer to her as "Cofitachequi," using the spelling that is most common.

28. Chester B. DePratter, "The Chiefdom of Cofitachequi," in Charles M. Hudson, *The Forgotten Centuries: Indians and Europeans in the American South: 1521–1704*, ed. Charles M. Hudson and Carmen C. Tesser (Athens: University of Georgia Press, 1994), 207.

29. David L. Eng, *The Feeling of Kinship: Queer Liberalism and the Racialization of Intimacy* (Durham, NC: Duke University Press, 2010), 170.

30. I will refer to this chronicler simply as "Elvas" in this chapter.

31. Clayton, Moore, and Knight, eds., *The De Soto Chronicles*, 1:82.

32. Ibid., 278.

33. Robert A. Williams, Jr., *Linking Arms Together: American Indian Treaty Visions of Law and Peace, 1600–1800* (Routledge: New York, 1999), 76.

34. Clayton, Moore, and Knight, eds., *The De Soto Chronicles*, 1:314.

35. Clayton, Moore, and Knight, eds., *The De Soto Chronicles*, 1:85. *Tameme* is a word that comes from Nahuatl that means a human carrier. Within context of Spanish invasion and colonialism, it refers to Native people enslaved to carry loads.

36. Ibid., 281.

37. Ibid., 86–87. Xualla is thought to be either a Cheraw or Cherokee town. Pardo later refers to this town as Joara. Hudson argues that it sat on the border between Catawban-speaking and Cherokee-speaking peoples (*Knights of Spain* 188). Guaxule was a Cherokee town, also recorded as Guasuli.

38. Ibid., 281–82.

39. Ibid., 281.

40. Andrea Smith, *Conquest: Sexual Violence and American Indian Genocide* (Cambridge, MA: South End Press, 2005), 10.

41. Clayton, Moore, and Knight, eds., *The De Soto Chronicles*, 1:282–83.

42. Ibid., 8.

43. Ibid., 86.

44. Ibid., 280.

45. Ibid., 280–81.

46. Ibid., 282.

47. Ibid., 87.

48. Ibid., 77–78.

49. David Spurr, *The Rhetoric of Empire: Colonial Discourse in Journalism, Travel Writing, and Imperial Administration* (Durham, NC: Duke University Press, 1993), 170.

50. Charles Hudson, Marvin T. Smith, Chester B. DePratter, and Emilia Kelley, "The Tristán De Luna Expedition, 1559–1561," *Southeastern Archaeology* 8, no. 1 (1989): 32.

51. Herbert Ingram Priestley, *The Luna Papers, 1559–1561* (Tuscaloosa: University of Alabama Press, 2010), 121.

52. Ibid., 245.

53. Ibid., 237.

54. Ibid.

55. Ibid.

56. Ibid., 239.

57. Ibid., 239–41.

58. Ibid., 325–27.

59. Ibid., 327.

60. Charles M. Hudson and Paul E. Hoffman, *The Juan Pardo Expeditions: Explorations of the Carolinas and Tennessee, 1566–1568* (Tuscaloosa: University of Alabama Press, 2005), 267.

61. Ibid.

62. The Battle of Mabila was led by the Choctaw chief Tuscaloosa against De Soto's army in 1540. According to colonial records, twenty-five hundred Native people were killed. See Hudson, *Forgotten Centuries*, 264.

63. John Lawson, *A New Voyage to Carolina; Containing the Exact Description and Natural History of That Country: Together with the Present State thereof. And a Journal Of a Thousand Miles, Travel'd thro' several Nations of Indians. Giving a particular Account of their Customs, Manners &c.* (London: n.p., 1709), 236–38. Documenting the American South, University Library, The University of North Carolina at Chapel Hill. http://docsouth.unc.edu/nc/lawson/menu.html.

64. Ibid., 237–38.

65. Ibid., 238.

66. Ibid.

67. Ibid., 184–85.

68. Ibid., 51. Here Lawson is writing about a Congaree town.

69. Ibid., 188.

70. Spurr, *Rhetoric of Empire*, 170.

71. Lawson, *A New Voyage to Carolina*, 186. My emphasis.

72. Ibid., 29. My emphasis.

73. Ibid., 34–35. My emphasis.

74. Ibid., 35.

75. Ibid., 173. My emphasis.

76. Ibid., 186. My emphasis.

77. Ibid., 35–36.

78. Ibid., 36.

79. Ibid., 187.

80. Ibid., 185. My emphasis.

81. Ibid., 37.

82. Ibid. My emphasis.

83. Ibid., 186.

84. Ibid., 39–40. My emphasis.

85. Duane H. King, ed., *The Memoirs of Lieutenant Henry Timberlake: The Story of a Soldier, Adventurer, and Emissary to the Cherokees, 1756–1765* (Cherokee, NC: Museum of the Cherokee Indian Press, 2007), xiii.

86. William L. Saunders, ed., *The Colonial Records of North Carolina*, vol. 3, *1728–1734* (Raleigh, NC: P. M. Hale, Printer to the State, 1886), 131.

87. Carolyn Johnston, *Cherokee Women in Crisis: Trail of Tears, Civil War, and Allotment, 1838–1907* (Tuscaloosa: University of Alabama Press, 2003), 1.

88. King, ed., *Memoirs of Lieutenant Henry Timberlake*, 115–16.

89. Ibid., 36.

90. Timberlake also briefly mentions a Beloved Woman of Chota preparing medicine for a "physic-dance," or medicine dance. Ibid., 38–39.

91. Ibid., 37.

92. Ibid., 41.

93. Mary Louise Pratt, *Imperial Eyes: Travel Writing and Transculturation* (New York: Routledge, 1992), 7.

94. Ibid., 26–27.

95. Scott Lauria Morgensen, *Spaces Between Us: Queer Settler Colonialism and Indigenous Decolonization* (Minneapolis: University of Minnesota Press, 2011), 34.

96. Linda Tuhiwai Smith, *Decolonizing Methodologies: Research and Indigenous Peoples* (New York: Zed Books, 1999), 59–60.

97. Spurr, *Rhetoric of Empire*, 23

98. William Bartram, *Travels Through North & South Carolina, Georgia, East & West Florida, the Cherokee Country, the Extensive Territories of the Muscogulges, or Creek Confederacy, and the Country of the Chactaws; Containing An Account of the Soil and Natural Productions of Those Regions, Together with Observations on the Manners of the Indians. Embellished with Copper-Plates* (Philadelphia: James & Johnson, 1791), 356. Documenting the American South, University Library, The University of North Carolina at Chapel Hill. http://docsouth.unc.edu/nc/bartram/menu.html.

99. Ibid., 357.

100. Ibid.

101. Ibid.

102. Ibid.

103. Ibid., 358.

104. Ibid.

105. Adair's text is both odd and valuable. Odd in that he argues that Native people in the Southeast are descendants of "ancient Hebrews," and valuable because, in order to provide evidence for this argument, he detailed Southeastern Indigenous practices.

106. James Adair, *The History of the American Indians*, ed. Kathryn E. Holland Braund (Tuscaloosa: University of Alabama Press, 2005), 181–82.

107. Ibid., 182.

108. Adair's argument is, clearly, also anti-Jewish. He characterizes both Indians and Jewish people as uncivilized. "Whosoever attentively views the features of the Indian . . . and reflects on his fickle, obstinate, and cruel disposition, will naturally think on the Jews. English America, feelingly knows the parity of the temper of their neighbouring Indians, with that of the Hebrew nation." Ibid.

109. Ibid., 81–82. Kathryn E. Holland Braund makes a useful, but brief, annotation about this passage: "This drunken lark speaks to more than mere curiosity, for Europeans were very curious about the self-presentation, gender, and sexuality of native peoples, particularly when they spotted those who appeared to be biologically male or female dressed in clothing of the opposite sex or assuming

the opposite gender role" (483). The "Koosah town" referred to by Adair is the town of Coosa, mentioned earlier in the chapter. Originally a Creek town, it became a Cherokee town—Coosawattee—by the early eighteenth century.

110. Theda Perdue writes, mistakenly, that "James Adair reported an incident in which a young man whom the Cherokees considered too effeminate and suspected of homosexuality was scratched and ridiculed." Theda Perdue, *Cherokee Women: Gender and Culture Change, 1700–1835* (Lincoln: University of Nebraska Press, 1998), 37. The incident Perdue refers to concerns Chickasaws, not Cherokees. Adair reports that in 1766 he saw a Chickasaw "head man, called the *Dog-King*," inflict punishment on young people he saw as transgressing. "He began with a lusty young fellow, who was charged with being more effeminate than became a warrior; and with acting contrary to their old religious rites and customs, particularly, because he lived nearer than any of the rest to an opulent and helpless German, by whom they supposed he might have been corrupted." As punishment, the Dog-King "bastinadoed" (severely whipped the feet of) the "young sinner," and called him "*Chehakse Kanèha-He*," which Adair translates as "one who is wicked, and almost lost." Adair's argument is that this points to "the method the Hebrews used in correcting their criminals." Adair, *History of American Indians*, 190. If this incident did, indeed, occur, I am highly suspicious regarding the claim that it actually had anything to do with "effeminate" behavior or "sin." While this is not impossible—colonists had caused major cultural shifts in the Southeast—it is just as likely that the "lusty young fellow" was being punished for making an alliance with a German colonist in a context of war. Adair's forced connection between Indigenous practices and those of "the Hebrews" here should call the entire story into question. Regardless, this story does not have any connection to Cherokee understandings of gender and sexuality.

111. Qwo-Li Driskill, interview with Daniel Heath Justice in "On the Wings of *Wadaduga*: Cherokee Two-Spirit Lives" (unpublished manuscript).

112. Qwo-Li Driskill, interview with Leslea in "On the Wings of *Wadaduga*: Cherokee Two-Spirit Lives" (unpublished manuscript).

CHAPTER 3

1. The Treaty of New Echota was signed illegally (under both Cherokee and U.S. law) by the non-elected Treaty Party in December 1835. Despite the

efforts of Chief John Ross and the majority of Cherokees, the treaty was rati-fied in May 1836, setting into motion the Cherokee Removal.

2. Tiya Miles, *The House on Diamond Hill: A Cherokee Plantation Story* (Chapel Hill: University of North Carolina Press, 2010), 23.

3. Marilou Awiakta, *Selu: Seeking the Corn-Mother's Wisdom* (Golden, CO: Ful-crum, 1993), 26.

4. Qwo-Li Driskill, interview with Leslea in "On the Wings of *Wadaduga*: Cherokee Two-Spirit Lives" (unpublished manuscript).

5. Carolyn Ross Johnston, *Cherokee Women in Crisis: Trail of Tears, Civil War, and Allotment, 1838–1907* (Tuscaloosa: University of Alabama Press, 2003), 13.

6. Wilma Mankiller and Michael Wallis, *Mankiller: A Chief and Her People* (New York: Macmillan, 1993), 19.

7. Robert Conley, *A Cherokee Encyclopedia* (Albuquerque: University of New Mexico Press, 2007), 101.

8. Theda Perdue, *Cherokee Women: Gender and Culture Change, 1700–1835* (Lin-coln: University of Nebraska Press, 1998), 39.

9. M. Amanda Moulder, "'By Women, You Were Brought Forth into This World': Cherokee Women's Oratorical Education in the Late Eighteenth Century," in *Rhetoric, History, and Women's Oratorical Education: American Women Learn to Speak*, ed. David Gold and Catherine L. Hobbs (New York: Routledge, 2013), 28.

10. Michelene E. Pesantubbee, "Nancy Ward: American Patriot or Cherokee Na-tionalist?" *American Indian Quarterly* 38, no. 2 (Spring 2014): 189.

11. Daniel Heath Justice, *Our Fire Survives the Storm: A Cherokee Literary History* (Minneapolis: University of Minnesota Press, 2006), 30.

12. Sarah H. Hill, *Weaving New Worlds: Southeastern Cherokee Women and Their Basketry* (Chapel Hill: University of North Carolina Press, 1997), 30.

13. Paula Gunn Allen, *The Sacred Hoop: Recovering the Feminine in American In-dian Traditions* (Boston: Beacon Press, 1992), 256. While Allen's work has been critiqued by scholars in Native American and Indigenous Studies as some-times essentialist and too generalized, I agree with Lisa Tatonetti's assertion that Allen's scholarship is central to queer Indigenous critiques and Indigenous feminism. Lisa Tatonetti, *The Queerness of Native American Literature* (Minne-apolis: University of Minnesota Press, 2014), 25.

14. C. C. Trowbridge, Shea Collection, Georgetown University Library, 5. Im-mediately before this statement, Trowbridge writes, "Few, if any lived to an advanced age without being married. No old bachelors or maids was known."

15. Walter L. Williams, *The Spirit and the Flesh: Sexual Diversity in American Indian Culture* (Boston: Beacon Press, 1986), 4.

16. John Howard Payne, Transcripts of John Howard Payne Papers, The Newberry Library (Chicago, IL), Ayer MS 684, vol. 3, 24.

17. Bernard Romans, *A Concise Natural History of East and West Florida*, ed. Kathryn E. Holland Braund (Tuscaloosa: University of Alabama Press, 1999), 38.

18. Ibid., 82–83.

19. Ibid., 41.

20. Ibid., 42.

21. Malea Powell, "Dreaming Charles Eastman: Cultural Memory, Autobiography, and Geography in Indigenous Rhetorical Histories," in *Beyond the Archives: Research as a Lived Process* (Carbondale: Southern Illinois University Press, 2008), 118–19.

22. Francis Paul Prucha, *Documents of United States Indian Policy*, rev. ed. (Lincoln: University of Nebraska Press, 2000), 22.

23. Cherokee Nation, "Treaty of Holston, 1791," Cherokee Nation. http://www .cherokee.org/AboutTheNation/History/Facts/TreatyofHolston,1791.aspx.

24. Richard Peters, ed., *The Public Statutes at Large of the United States of America*, vol. 3 (Boston: Charles C. Little and James Brown, 1846), 516–17.

25. Tiya Miles, *Ties That Bind: The Story of an Afro-Cherokee Family in Slavery and Freedom* (Berkeley: University of California Press, 2005), 36.

26. Andrea Smith, "The Colonialism That Is Settled and the Colonialism That Never Happened," *Decolonization: Indigeneity, Education & Society* (blog), June 20, 2014, https://decolonization.wordpress.com/2014/06/20/the-colonialism -that-is-settled-and-the-colonialism-that-never-happened/.

27. Deborah A. Miranda, *Bad Indians: A Tribal Memoir* (Berkeley, CA: Heyday, 2012), 47.

28. Arica L. Coleman, *That the Blood Stay Pure: African Americans, Native Americans, and the Predicament of Race and Identity in Virginia* (Bloomington: Indiana University Press, 2013), 12–13.

29. Theda Perdue, *Slavery and the Evolution of Cherokee Society, 1540–1866* (Knoxville: University of Tennessee Press, 1979), 40–41.

30. Ibid., 28.

31. Patrick Minges, ed., *Black Indian Slave Narratives* (Winston-Salem, NC: John F. Blair, 2004), xvii–xviii.

32. Perdue, *Slavery and the Evolution*, 29. Charles C. Royce, *The Cherokee Nation of Indians* (Washington, DC: Smithsonian Institution Press, 1975), 139.

33. Theda Perdue, "Cherokee Planters: The Development of Plantation Slavery Before Removal," in *The Cherokee Indian Nation: A Troubled History*, ed. Duane H. King (Knoxville.: University of Tennessee Press, 1979),110–11.

34. Miles, *House on Diamond Hill*, 112–13.

35. Mark Rifkin, *When Did Indians Become Straight? Kinship, the History of Sexuality, and Native Sovereignty* (New York: Oxford University Press, 2011), 22–23.

36. Perdue, *Slavery and the Evolution*, 53.

37. John Marrant, *A Narrative of the Life of John Marrant, of New York, in North America* (London: C. J. Farncombe, 1815). Rowena McClinton, ed., *The Moravian Springplace Mission to the Cherokees* (Lincoln: University of Nebraska, 2007), 1:17.

38. Joyce B. Phillips and Paul Gary Phillips, eds., *The Brainerd Journal: A Mission to the Cherokees, 1817–1823* (Lincoln: University of Nebraska Press, 1988), 395–96, 398–99. American Board of Commissioners for Foreign Missions, "Report of the American Board of Commissioners for Foreign Missions; Compiled from Documents Laid Before this Committee at the Twelfth Annual Meeting, which was Held at Springfield, Mass. Sept. 19, & 20, 1821," vol. 12, parts 1821–1825, 53–69.

39. Vicki Rozema, *Footsteps of the Cherokees: A Guide to the Eastern Homelands to the Cherokee Nation*, 2nd ed. (Winston-Salem, NC: John F. Blair, 2007), 313. *The American Baptist Magazine, and Missionary Intelligencer* 3, no. 1 (1821): 185, 269, 465.

40. William Gerald McLoughlin, Walter H. Conser, Jr., and Virginia Duffy McLoughlin, *The Cherokee Ghost Dance: Essays on the Southeastern Indians, 1789–1861* (Macon, GA: Mercer University Press, 1984), 405.

41. Ashbel Green, ed., "The Rights of the Indians Ascertained," *The Christian Advocate* [Philadelphia, PA] 8 (February 1830): 73–78. https://books.google.com/books?id=w_wQAAAAIAAJ&pg=PP9#v=onepage&q&f=false.

42. See Jill Norgen, *The Cherokee Cases: Two Landmark Federal Decisions in the Fight for Sovereignty* (Norman: University of Oklahoma Press, 2004).

43. Perdue, *Cherokee Women: Gender and Culture Change*, 180–81.

44. McClinton, ed., *Moravian Springplace Mission*, 1:91–92. My emphasis.

45. Ibid., 74.

46. M. Spooner and H. J. Howland. *History of American Missions to the Heathen: From Their Commencement to the Present Time* (Worcester, MA: Spooner & Howland, 1840), 149.

47. Ibid., 267–68.

48. Phillips and Phillips, eds., *Brainerd Journal*, 56.

49. Ibid., 62–63.

50. Ibid., 133.

51. McClinton, ed., *Moravian Springplace Mission*, 1:227.

52. Andrea Smith, "American Studies Without America: Native Feminisms and the Nation-State," *American Quarterly* 60, no. 2 (2008): 312.

53. William G. McLoughlin, "Cherokee Anti-Mission Sentiment, 1824–1828," *Ethnohistory* 21, no. 4 (1974): 368. Chulioa was one of the leaders who approved of the Moravian mission station at Springplace on the condition that they start a school to teach Cherokee students English. His son, Tommy/Whirlwind, was a student at the Springplace mission from 1804 to 1810 (McClinton, ed., *Moravian Springplace Mission*, 2:445) and Chulioa (who the Moravians called "Gentleman Tom") was a frequent visitor to Springplace. Also significantly, one of the signers of the letter to remove the ABCFM's station at Etowah was Shoe Boots, whose relationship with Doll is detailed in Tiya Miles, *Ties That Bind*.

54. Derrick R. Miller, "Moravian Familiarities: Queer Community in the Moravian Church in Europe and North America in the Mid-Eighteenth Century," *Journal of Moravian History* 13, no. 1 (2013): 57.

55. Ibid., 54–55.

56. McClinton, ed., *Moravian Springplace Mission*, 1:55.

57. Phillips and Phillips, eds., *Brainerd Journal*, 46.

58. Ibid., 47.

59. Lois Sherr Dubin, *North American Indian Jewelry and Adornment: From Prehistory to the Present*, concise ed. (New York: Harry N. Abrams, 2003), 62.

60. Miles, *House on Diamond Hill*, 57.

61. Virginia Moore Carney, *Eastern Band Cherokee Women: Cultural Persistence in Their Letters and Speeches* (Knoxville: University of Tennessee Press, 2005), 48.

62. Cherokee Nation, *The Constitution and Laws of the Cherokee Nation Passed at Tahlequah, Cherokee Nation, 1839–51* (Tahlequah: Cherokee Nation, 1852), 3.

63. Ibid., 4.

64. Ibid., 10.

65. McClinton, ed., *Moravian Springplace Mission*, 2:527.

66. William N. Eskridge, Jr., *Dishonorable Passions: Sodomy Laws in America, 1861–2003* (New York: Viking, 2008), 19–20.

67. Ibid, 2.

68. Rachel F. Moran, *Interracial Intimacy: The Regulation of Race & Romance* (Chicago: University of Chicago Press, 2001), 19.

69. Ibid., 20.

70. Eskridge, *Dishonorable Passions*, 19.

71. Siobhan B. Somerville's *Queering the Color Line: Race and the Invention of Homosexuality in America* demonstrates that the later constructions of "homosexuality" took place "through a reliance on, and deployment of, racial ideologies, that is, the cultural assumptions and systems of representation about race through which individuals understood their relationships within the world." Siobhan B. Somerville, *Queering the Color Line: Race and the Invention of Homosexuality in American Culture* (Durham, NC: Duke University Press, 2000), 17.

72. Cherokee Nation, *Constitution and Laws of the Cherokee Nation*, 34.

73. Ibid., 37.

74. Ibid., 38.

75. Ibid., 39.

76. Tiya Miles points out that these acts were passed in the context of granting freedom to the children of Shoe Boots, a Cherokee, and Doll, his Black slave. "The statesmen seem to have used the occasion of Shoe Boots's petition as an opportunity to publicize its contempt for black and Cherokee 'race mixing' and to single out black womanhood as a lowly identity." Miles, *Ties That Bind*, 126.

77. Cherokee Nation, *Constitution and Laws of the Cherokee Nation*, 53–54.

78. Ibid., 120.

79. Ibid., 121.

80. Daniel Heath Justice, "A Queer Interlude, or, White Owl Abroad: Adagal'kala's Journey to London, 1730" (presentation, Native American and Indigenous Studies Association Meeting, Austin, TX, June 29, 2014).

CHAPTER 4

1. Jack Frederick Kilpatrick and Anna Gritts Kilpatrick, *Walk in Your Soul: Love Incantations of the Oklahoma Cherokees* (Dallas: Southern Methodist University Press, 1965), 12.

2. John Howard Payne, Transcripts of John Howard Payne Papers, The Newberry Library (Chicago, IL), Ayer MS 684, vol. 9, 81–82.

3. Joy Harjo, *In Mad Love and War* (Middletown, CT: Wesleyan University Press, 1990), 1.

4. Daniel Heath Justice, "Fear of a Changeling Moon: A Rather Queer Tale from a Cherokee Hillbilly," in *Me Sexy: An Exploration of Native Sex and Sexuality*, ed. Drew Hayden Taylor (Vancouver, BC: Douglas & McIntyre, 2008), 106.

5. Deborah A. Miranda, *The Zen of La Llorona* (Cambridge, UK: Salt Publishing, 2005), 4. Emphasis in original.

6. Lisa Tatonetti, "Visible Sexualities or Invisible Nations: Forced to Choose in *Big Eden, Johnny Greyeyes*, and *The Business of Fancydancing*," *GLQ: A Journal of Lesbian and Gay Studies* 16, no. 1–2 (2010): 164.

7. Kilpatrick and Kilpatrick, *Walk in Your Soul*, 82.

8. Lucian Lamar Knight, *A Standard History of Georgia and Georgians*, vol. 3 (Chicago: Lewis Publishing Company, 1917), 1297.

9. It's important to remember that Payne—writing shortly before (and during) Removal, is often revising material written by Butrick. Butrick's information was shared by elders, some of whom were very old. One of Butrick's informants about this ceremony was The Raven, who is described as "an old Cherokee supposed to be considerably over a hundred years old." Payne, Transcripts, Ayer MS 684, vol. 1, 17. The descriptions, then, are often about ceremonies that existed in the mid-eighteenth century.

10. Ibid., 56–57.

11. For *adahona*, see Frank G. Speck and Leonard Broom, *Cherokee Dance and Drama* (Norman: University of Oklahoma Press, 1983), 47, 80. *Wado* to Bo Taylor for pointing me to this reference. *Wado* to Tim Nuttle for his translation of *anadahanoga*. Another possible translation of Payne's "*Ah,tah,hoongh,nah*" is provided by Anderson, Brown, and Rogers, who write, "One language consultant says that today *ag-ta-hv-na* means "one has turned around." William L. Anderson, Jane L. Brown, and Anne F. Rogers, eds., *The Payne-Butrick Papers: Volumes One, Two, Three* (Lincoln: University of Nebraska Press, 2010), 345n82.

12. Speck and Broom, *Cherokee Dance and Drama*, 49.

13. Ibid., 80.

14. Another possibility is that the interpreter mistranslated these terms and instead attempted to describe the concept or feeling around them.

15. Cherokee Nation, "Cherokee Festivals." Cherokee Nation, http://www.cherokee.org/AboutTheNation/Culture/General/CherokeeFestivals.aspx.

16. James Adair, *The History of the American Indians*, ed. Katheryn E. Holland Braund (Tuscaloosa: University of Alabama Press, 2005), 218. Jonathan and David as well as Ruth and Naomi are now used by some queer people as examples of same-sex love in Jewish, Muslim, and Christian scriptures, and are sometimes invoked in contemporary same-gender unions and marriages.

17. Craig Womack, "Suspicioning: Imagining a Debate Between Those Who Get Confused and Those Who Don't, When They Read Critical Reponesses to the Poems of Joy Harjo, or What's an Old-Timey Gay Boy Like Me to Do?" *GLQ: A Journal of Lesbian and Gay Studies* 16, nos. 1–2 (2010): 133.

18. The authors also assert that *Oonah-weeh-sayh-nunghee*, which Payne records as the title given to the officiate of this ceremony, and which translates as One Who Renews Hearth and Body, "implies a feminine, or male-female, figure," but provide no further explanation. Anderson, Brown, and Rogers, eds., *Payne-Butrick Papers*, 345n81, n84.

19. Travis Snell, "Opinion: Equality Should Prevail," *Cherokee Phoenix*, October 31, 2014.

20. Payne, Transcripts, Ayer MS 684, vol. 3, 48–49. The description continues: "Friends among the Cherokees, must share with each other whatever they might have. They must also, if requested always reveal whatever secret they might know. To hide any thing from a friend was betraying a want of confidence inconsistent with the ties of that friendship by which they were bound. But friends must never reveal secrets thus made known to them."

21. Payne, Transcripts, Ayer MS 684, vol. 4, part 1, 22.

22. Ibid., vol. 4, part 1, 151.

23. Ibid., vol. 4, part 1, 149.

24. Ibid., vol. 4, part 2, 237.

25. Daniel Heath Justice, "A Queer Interlude, or, White Owl Abroad: Adagal'kala's Journey to London, 1730," presentation, Native American and Indigenous Studies Association Meeting, Austin, TX, June 29, 2014.

26. Payne, Transcripts, Ayer MS 684, vol. 2, 2–3.

27. Ibid., 3.

28. Daniel Heath Justice, *Our Fire Survives the Storm: A Cherokee Literary History* (Minneapolis: University of Minnesota Press, 2006), 85.

29. Qwo-Li Driskill, interview with Leslea in "On the Wings of *Wadaduga*: Cherokee Two-Spirit Lives" (unpublished manuscript).

30. Adair, *History of the American Indians*, 412.

31. John Witthoft, "Stone Pipes of the Historic Cherokee," *Southern Indian Studies* 1, no. 2 (1949): 48.

32. Payne, Transcripts, Ayer MS 684, vol. 10, 34–35.

33. Qwo-Li Driskill, interview with Daniel Heath Justice in "On the Wings of *Wadaduga*: Cherokee Two-Spirit Lives" (unpublished manuscript).

34. Qwo-Li Driskill, interview with Leslea in "On the Wings of *Wadaduga*: Cherokee Two-Spirit Lives" (unpublished manuscript).

CHAPTER 5

1. Emma Pérez, *The Decolonial Imaginary: Writing Chicanas into History* (Bloomington: Indian University Press, 1999), 55.
2. All quotes from interviews found below are from Qwo-Li Driskill, "On the Wings of *Wadaduga*: Cherokee Two-Spirit Lives" (unpublished manuscript). While all participants' identities are kept confidential as a matter of course, they also have the option of waiving their confidentiality. These four participants all wanted their real names to be used in this project.
3. ᎤᎩᏖᎾ (Uktena) is a giant winged, horned serpent that lives in mountains and waterways. Wild Boy, the son of ᏎᎷ (Selu, Corn) and ᎧᎾᏗ (Kanati, the Hunter), was unknowingly brought into existence when ᏎᎷ washed off blood in a river. Thunder is an important deity in traditional Cherokee cosmology, and is considered a protector of Cherokee people.
4. Robin is referring to a presentation and discussion led by John Hawk Cocké, an Osage Two-Spirit activist, at the 2008 Tulsa Two-Spirit Gathering.
5. Chad has tattoos of scratches on his wrists, symbolizing ceremonial scratches from Green Corn.
6. Jose Esteban Muñoz, *Disidentifications: Queers of Color and the Performance of Politics* (Minneapolis: University of Minnesota Press, 1999),4.
7. *Taliquo Didantvn.*
8. A reference to Co-cké's presentation at the Two-Spirit Gathering.
9. Daniel Heath Justice, "A Queer Interlude, or, White Owl Abroad: Adagal'kala's Journey to London, 1730," presentation, Native American and Indigenous Studies Association Meeting, Austin, TX, June 29, 2014.

EPILOGUE

1. Paula Gunn Allen, *The Sacred Hoop: Recovering the Feminine in American Indian Traditions* (Boston: Beacon Press, 1992), 213.
2. Erin Marie Konsmo, *Art Through a Birch Bark Heart* (blog), http://erinkonsmo.blogspot.com/2012/06/blog-post.html.

WORKS CITED

Adair, James. *The History of the American Indians*. Edited by Kathryn E. Holland Braund. Tuscaloosa: University of Alabama Press, 2005.

Allen, Paula Gunn. *The Sacred Hoop: Recovering the Feminine in American Indian Traditions*. Boston: Beacon Press, 1992.

Anderson, William L., Jane L. Brown, and Anne F. Rogers, eds. *The Payne-Butrick Papers: Volumes One, Two, Three*. Lincoln: University of Nebraska Press, 2010.

Anguksuar [Richard LaFortune]. "A Postcolonial Colonial Perspective on Western [Mis]Conceptions of the Cosmos and the Restoration of Indigenous Taxonomies." In *Two-Spirit People: Native American Gender Identity, Sexuality, and Spirituality*, edited by Sue-Ellen Jacobs, Wesley Thomas, and Sabine Lang, 217–22. Urbana: University of Illinois Press, 1997.

Awiakta, Marilou. *Selu: Seeking the Corn-Mother's Wisdom*. Golden, CO: Fulcrum, 1993.

Bartram, William. *Travels Through North & South Carolina, Georgia, East & West Florida, the Cherokee Country, the Extensive Territories of the Muscogulges, or Creek Confederacy, and the Country of the Chactaws; Containing An Account of the Soil and Natural Productions of Those Regions, Together with Observations on the Manners of the Indians. Embellished with Copper-Plates*. Philadelphia: James and Johnson, 1791. Documenting the American South, University Library, University of North Carolina at Chapel Hill. http://docsouth.unc.edu/nc/bartram/menu.html.

Blackwell, Maylei. ¡*Chicana Power! Contested Histories of Feminism in the Chicano Movement*. Austin: University of Texas Press, 2011.

Brant, Beth, ed. *A Gathering of Spirit: A Collection by North American Indian Women*. Ithaca, NY: Firebrand, 1988.

———. *Writing as Witness: Essay and Talk*. Toronto: Women's Press, 1994.

Brown, Lester B., ed. *Two Spirit People: American Indian Lesbian Women and Gay Men*. New York: Haworth, 1997.

Butler, Judith. *Gender Trouble: Feminism and the Subversion of Identity*. New York: Routledge, 1990.

Byrd, Jodi A. *The Transit of Empire: Indigenous Critiques of Colonialism*. Minneapolis: University of Minnesota Press, 2011.

Carney, Virginia Moore. *Eastern Band Cherokee Women: Cultural Persistence in Their Letters and Speeches*. Knoxville: University of Tennessee Press, 2005.

Cherokee Nation. "Cherokee Festivals." Cherokee Nation. http://www.cherokee.org/AboutTheNation/Culture/General/CherokeeFestivals.aspx.

———. *The Constitution and Laws of the Cherokee Nation Passed at Tahlequah, Cherokee Nation, 1839–51*. Tahlequah: Cherokee Nation, 1852.

———. "Dikaneisdi (Word List)." Cherokee Nation. http://www.cherokee.org/AboutTheNation/Language/Dikaneisdi%28WordList%29.aspx.

———. "Treaty of Holston, 1791." Cherokee Nation. http://www.cherokee.org/AboutTheNation/History/Facts/TreatyofHolston,1791.aspx.

Chrystos. *Fire Power*. Vancouver, BC: Press Gang, 1995.

Churchill, Mary C. "The Oppositional Paradigm of Purity versus Pollution in Charles Hudson's *The Southeastern Indians*." *American Indian Quarterly* 20, no. 3–4 (Fall 1996): 563–89.

Clayton, Lawrence A., Edward C. Moore, and Vernon James Knight, Jr., eds. *The De Soto Chronicles: The Expedition of Hernando De Soto to North America in 1539–1543*. Vol. 1. Tuscaloosa: University of Alabama Press, 1995.

Cobos, Casie C. "An Other Chican@ Rhetoric from Scratch: (Re)Making Stories, (Un)Mapping the Lines, and Re membering Bodies." PhD diss., Texas A&M University, 2012.

———. "Embodied Storying, A Methodology for Chican@ Rhetorics: (Re)making Stories, (Un)mapping the Lines, and Re-membering Bodies." PhD diss., Texas A&M University, 2012.

Coleman, Arica L. *That the Blood Stay Pure: African Americans, Native Americans, and the Predicament of Race and Identity in Virginia*. Bloomington: Indiana University Press, 2013.

Conley, Robert. *A Cherokee Encyclopedia*. Albuquerque: University of New Mexico Press, 2007.

Crenshaw, Kimberlé. "Demarginalizing the Intersection of Race and Sex: A Black Feminist Critique of Antidiscrimination Doctrine, Feminist Politics, and Antiracist Politics." *University of Chicago Legal Forum* 140 (1989): 139–67.

d'Anghiera, Pietro Martire. *De Orbe Novo, the Eight Decades of Peter Martyr D'Anghera*. 2 vols. Translated by Francis Augustus MacNutt. New York: G. P. Putnam's Sons, 1912.

de Certeau, Michel. *The Practice of Everyday Life*. Berkeley: University of California Press, 2002.

DePratter, Chester B. "The Chiefdom of Cofitachequi." In *The Forgotten Centuries: Indians and Europeans in the American South, 1521–1704*, edited by Charles M. Hudson and Carmen C. Tesser, 197–226. Athens: University of Georgia Press, 1994.

Driskill, Qwo-Li. "Call Me Brother: Two-Spiritness, the Erotic, and Mixedblood Identity as Sites of Sovereignty and Resistance in Gregory Scofield's Poetry." In *Speak to Me Words: Essays on Contemporary American Indian Poetry*, edited by Janice Gould and Dean Rader, 223–34. Tucson: University of Arizona Press, 2003.

———. "Stolen From Our Bodies: First Nations Two-Spirits/Queers and the Journey to a Sovereign Erotic." *Studies in American Indian Literatures* 16, no. 2 (2004): 50–64.

Driskill, Qwo-Li, Chris Finley, Brian Joseph Gilley, and Scott Lauria Morgensen, eds. *Queer Indigenous Studies: Critical Interventions in Theory, Politics, and Literature*. Tucson: University of Arizona Press, 2011.

Driskill, Qwo-Li, Daniel Heath Justice, Deborah A. Miranda, and Lisa Tatonetti, eds. *Sovereign Erotics: A Collection of Two-Spirit Literature*. Tucson: University of Arizona Press, 2011.

Dubin, Lois Sherr. *North American Indian Jewelry and Adornment: From Prehistory to the Present*. Concise ed. New York: Harry N. Abrams, 2003.

Dunaway, Wilma. "The Origin of Gadugi." Cherokee Nation. Accessed August 15, 2014. http://www.cherokee.org/AboutTheNation/History/Facts/TheOriginof Gadugi.aspx.

Dunbar-Ortiz, Roxanne. "The Grid of History: Cowboys and Indians." *Monthly Review* 55, no. 3 (2003): 83–92.

Duncan, Patti. "history of disease." In *Q&A: Queer in Asian America*, edited by David L. Eng and Alice Y. Hom, 157–65. Philadelphia: Temple University Press, 1998.

Eng, David L. *The Feeling of Kinship: Queer Liberalism and the Racialization of Intimacy*. Durham, NC: Duke University Press, 2010.

Eng, David L., Judith Halberstam, and Jose Esteban Muñoz, eds. "What's Queer About Queer Studies Now?" Special issue, *Social Text* 23, no. 3–4 84–85 (Fall–Winter 2005).

Enríquez-Loya, Aydé. "Crossing Borders and Building Alliances: Border Discourse Within Literatures and Rhetorics of Color." PhD diss., Texas A&M University, 2012.

Eskridge, William N., Jr. *Dishonorable Passions: Sodomy Laws in America, 1861–2003.* New York: Viking, 2008.

Ferguson, Roderick A. *Aberrations in Black: Toward a Queer of Color Critique.* Minneapolis: University of Minnesota Press, 2003.

Fogelson, Raymond D., and Paul Kutsche. "Cherokee Economic Cooperatives: The Gadugi." In *Symposium on Cherokee and Iroquois Culture,* edited by William Nelson Fenton and John Gulick, 87–123. Smithsonian Institution, Bureau of American Ethnology Bulletin 180. Washington, DC: Government Printing Office, 1961.

Foucault, Michel. *The History of Sexuality.* Trans. Robert Hurley. 2 vols. New York: Vintage, 1990.

Gilley, Brian Joseph. *Becoming Two-Spirit: Gay Identity and Social Acceptance in Indian Country.* Lincoln: University of Nebraska Press, 2006.

Goeman, Mishuana. *Mark My Words: Native Women Mapping Our Nations.* Minneapolis: University of Minnesota Press, 2013.

Gopinath, Gayatri. *Impossible Desires: Queer Diasporas and South Asian Public Cultures.* Durham, NC: Duke University Press, 2005.

Green, Ashbel, ed. "The Rights of the Indians Ascertained." *Christian Advocate* [Philadelphia, PA] 8 (February 1830): 73–78. https://books.google.com/books?id=w_wQAAAAIAAJ.

Heth, Charlotte Anne Wilson. "The Stomp Dance Music of the Oklahoma Cherokee: A Study of Contemporary Practice with Special Reference to the Illinois District Council Ground." PhD diss., University of California, 1975.

Hill, Sarah H. *Weaving New Worlds: Southeastern Cherokee Women and Their Basketry.* Chapel Hill: University of North Carolina Press, 1997.

Hudson, Charles M., and Paul E. Hoffman. *The Juan Pardo Expeditions: Explorations of the Carolinas and Tennessee, 1566–1568.* Tuscaloosa: University of Alabama Press, 2005.

Hudson, Charles, Marvin T. Smith, Chester B. DePratter, and Emilia Kelley. "The Tristán De Luna Expedition, 1559–1561," *Southeastern Archaeology* 8, no. 1 (1989): 31–45.

Hutcheson, Gregory S., and Josiah Blackmore. "Introduction." In *Queer Iberia: Sexualities, Cultures, and Crossings from the Middle Ages to the Renaissance*, edited by Josiah Blackmore and Gregory S. Hutcheson, 1–19. Durham, NC: Duke University Press, 1999.

Jackson, Jason Baird. *Yuchi Ceremonial Life: Performance, Meaning, and Tradition in a Contemporary American Indian Community*. Lincoln: University of Nebraska Press, 2005.

Jacobs, Sue Ellen, Wesley Thomas, and Sabine Lang, eds. *Two-Spirit People: Native American Gender Identity, Sexuality, and Spirituality*. Champaign: University of Illinois Press, 1997.

Johnston, Carolyn. *Cherokee Women in Crisis: Trail of Tears, Civil War, and Allotment, 1838–1907*. Tuscaloosa: University of Alabama Press, 2003.

Justice, Daniel Heath. "Beloved Woman Returns: The Doubleweaving of Homeland and Identity in the Poetry of Marilou Awiakta." In *Speak to Me Words: Essays on Contemporary American Indian Poetry*, edited by Dean Rader and Janice Gould, 71–81. Tucson: University of Arizona Press, 2003.

———. *Dreyd: The Way of Thorn and Thunder, Book Three*. Cape Croker Reserve, Ontario: Kegedonce, 2007.

———. "Fear of a Changeling Moon: A Rather Queer Tale from a Cherokee Hillbilly." In *Me Sexy: An Exploration of Native Sex and Sexuality*, edited by Drew Hayden Taylor, 87–108. Vancouver, BC: Douglas & McIntyre, 2008.

———. *Kynship: The Way of Thorn and Thunder, Book One*. Cape Croker Reserve, Ontario: Kegedonce, 2005.

———. "Notes Toward a Theory of Anomaly." *GLQ: A Journal of Lesbian and Gay Studies* 16, no. 1–2 (2010): 207–42.

———. *Our Fire Survives the Storm: A Cherokee Literary History*. Minneapolis: University of Minnesota Press, 2006.

———. "A Queer Interlude, or, White Owl Abroad: Ada-gal'kala's Journey to London, 1730." Presentation, Native American and Indigenous Studies Association Meeting, Austin, TX, June 29, 2014.

———. *Wyrwood: The Way of Thorn and Thunder, Book Two*. Cape Croker Reserve, Ontario: Kegedonce, 2006.

Kays, Holly. "Cherokee Affirms Gay Marriage Ban." *Smokey Mountain News*, January 14, 2015. http://www.smokymountainnews.com/news/item/14943-cherokee-affirms-gay-marriage-ban.

Kilpatrick, Jack F., and Anna G. Kilpatrick. *Walk in Your Soul: Love Incantations of the Oklahoma Cherokees*. Dallas: Southern Methodist University Press, 1965.

King, Duane H., ed. *The Memoirs of Lieutenant Henry Timberlake: The Story of a Soldier, Adventurer, and Emissary to the Cherokees, 1756–1765*. Cherokee, NC: Museum of the Cherokee Indian Press, 2007.

King, Thomas. *The Truth About Stories: A Native Narrative*. Toronto: House of Anansi, 2003.

Knight, Lucian Lamar. *A Standard History of Georgia and Georgians*. Vol. 3. Chicago: Lewis Publishing Company, 1917.

Larkin, Joan, and Carl Morse, eds. *Gay and Lesbian Poetry in Our Time: An Anthology*. New York: St. Martin's Press, 1988.

Lawson, John. *A New Voyage to Carolina; Containing the Exact Description and Natural History of That Country: Together with the Present State thereof. And a Journal Of a Thousand Miles, Travel'd thro' several Nations of Indians. Giving a particular Account of their Customs, Manners &c.* 1709. Documenting the American South, University Library, The University of North Carolina at Chapel Hill. http://docsouth.unc.edu/nc/lawson/menu.html.

Levins Morales, Aurora. *Medicine Stories: History, Culture and the Politics of Integrity*. Cambridge, MA: South End Press, 1998.

Little Thunder, Beverly. "I Am a Lakota Womyn." In *Two-Spirit People: Native American Gender Identity, Sexuality, and Spirituality*, edited by Sue-Ellen Jacobs, Wesley Thomas, and Sabine Lang, 203–9. Urbana: University of Illinois Press, 1997.

Lyons, Scott Richard. "Rhetorical Sovereignty: What Do American Indians Want from Writing?" *College Composition and Communication* 51, no. 3 (2000): 447–68.

Manalansan, Martin F., IV. *Global Divas: Filipino Gay Men in the Diaspora*. Durham, NC: Duke University Press, 2003.

Mankiller, Wilma, and Michael Wallis. *Mankiller: A Chief and Her People*. New York: Macmillan, 1993.

Marrant, John. *A Narrative of the Life of John Marrant, of New York, in North America*. London: C. J. Farncombe, 1815.

McClinton, Rowena, ed. *The Moravian Springplace Mission to the Cherokees*. 2 vols. Lincoln: University of Nebraska Press, 2007.

McLoughlin, William G. "Cherokee Anti-Mission Sentiment, 1824–1828," *Ethnohistory* 21, no. 4 (1974): 361–70.

McLoughlin, William Gerald, Walter H. Conser, Jr., and Virginia Duffy McLoughlin. *The Cherokee Ghost Dance: Essays on the Southeastern Indians, 1789–1861*. Macon, GA: Mercer University Press, 1984.

Mignolo, Walter D. *The Darker Side of the Renaissance: Literacy, Territoriality, and Colonization*. Ann Arbor: University of Michigan Press, 2003.

Miles, Tiya. *The House on Diamond Hill: A Cherokee Plantation Story*. Chapel Hill: University of North Carolina Press, 2010.

———. *Ties That Bind: The Story of an Afro-Cherokee Family in Slavery and Freedom*. Berkeley: University of California Press, 2005.

Miller, Derrick R. "Moravian Familiarities: Queer Community in the Moravian Church in Europe and North America in the Mid-Eighteenth Century." *Journal of Moravian History* 13, no. 1 (2013): 54–75.

Minges, Patrick, ed. *Black Indian Slave Narratives*. Winston-Salem, NC: John F. Blair, 2004.

Miranda, Deborah A. *Bad Indians: A Tribal Memoir*. Berkeley, CA: Heyday, 2012.

———. "Extermination of the *Joyas*: Gendercide in Spanish California." *GLQ: A Journal of Lesbian and Gay Studies* 16, no. 1–2 (2010): 253–84.

———. *The Zen of La Llorona*. Cambridge, UK: Salt, 2005.

Mooney, James. *History, Myths, and Sacred Formulas of the Cherokees*. Asheville, NC: Bright Mountain, 1992.

Moraga, Cherríe, and Gloria Anzaldúa. "Entering the Lives of Others: Theory in the Flesh." In *This Bridge Called My Back: Writings by Radical Women of Color*, edited by Cherríe Moraga and Gloria Anzaldúa, 23. Watertown, MA: Persephone Press, 1981.

Moran, Rachel F. *Interracial Intimacy: The Regulation of Race & Romance*. Chicago: University of Chicago Press, 2001.

Morgensen, Scott Lauria. *Spaces Between Us: Queer Settler Colonialism and Indigenous Decolonization*. Minneapolis: University of Minnesota Press, 2011.

Moulder, M. Amanda. "'By Women, You Were Brought Forth into This World': Cherokee Women's Oratorical Education in the Late Eighteenth Century." In *Rhetoric, History, and Women's Oratorical Education: American Women Learn to Speak*, edited by David Gold and Catherine L. Hobbs, 19–37. New York: Routledge, 2013.

Muñoz, José Esteban. *Cruising Utopia: The Then and There of Queer Futurity*. New York: New York University Press, 2009.

———. *Disidentifications: Queers of Color and the Performance of Politics*. Minneapolis: University of Minnesota Press, 1999.

Norgen, Jill. *The Cherokee Cases: Two Landmark Federal Decisions in the Fight for Sovereignty*. Norman: University of Oklahoma Press, 2004.

Perdue, Theda. "Cherokee Planters: The Development of Plantation Slavery Before Removal." In *The Cherokee Indian Nation: A Troubled History*, edited by Duane H. King, 110–15. Knoxville: University of Tennessee Press, 1979.

———. *Cherokee Women: Gender and Culture Change, 1700–1835*. Lincoln: University of Nebraska Press, 1998.

———. *Slavery and the Evolution of Cherokee Society, 1540–1866*. Knoxville: University of Tennessee Press, 1979.

Pérez, Emma. *The Decolonial Imaginary: Writing Chicanas into History*. Bloomington: Indiana University Press, 1999.

Pesantubbee, Michelene E. *Choctaw Women in a Chaotic World*. Albuquerque: University of New Mexico Press, 2005.

———. "Nancy Ward: American Patriot or Cherokee Nationalist?" *American Indian Quarterly* 38, no. 2 (Spring 2014): 177–206.

Peters, Richard, ed. *The Public Statutes at Large of the United States of America*. Vol. 3. Boston: Charles C. Little and James Brown, 1846.

Phillips, Joyce B., and Paul Gary Phillips, eds. *The Brainerd Journal: A Mission to the Cherokees, 1817–1823*. Lincoln: University of Nebraska Press, 1998.

Powell, Malea D. "Blood and Scholarship: One Mixed-Blood's Story." In *Race, Rhetoric, and Composition*, edited by Keith Gilyard. Portsmouth, NH: Boynton/Cook, 1999.

———. "Down by the River, or How Susan La Flesche Picotte Can Teach Us About Alliance as a Practice of Survivance." *College English* 67, no. 1 (2004): 38–60.

———. "Dreaming Charles Eastman: Cultural Memory, Autobiography, and Geography in Indigenous Rhetorical Histories." In *Beyond the Archives: Research as a Lived Process*, 115–27. Carbondale: Southern Illinois University Press, 2008.

———. "Listening to ghosts: An Alternative (Non)argument." In *Alt Dis: Alternative Discourses and the Academy*, edited by Christopher Schroeder, Helen Fox, and Patricia Bizzell. Portsmouth, NH: Boynton/Cook Heinemann, 2002.

———. "Rhetorics of Survivance: How American Indians *Use* Writing." *College Composition and Communication* 53, no. 3 (2002): 396–434.

Pratt, Mary Louise. *Imperial Eyes: Travel Writing and Transculturation*. New York: Routledge, 1992.

Priestley, Herbert Ingram. *The Luna Papers, 1559–1561*. 2 vols. Tuscaloosa: University of Alabama Press, 2010.

Prucha, Francis Paul. *Documents of United States Indian Policy*. Rev. ed. Lincoln: University of Nebraska Press, 2000.

Rader, Dean, and Janice Gould, eds. *Speak to Me Words: Essays on Contemporary American Indian Poetry*. Tucson: University of Arizona Press, 2003.

Rifkin, Mark. *When Did Indians Become Straight? Kinship, the History of Sexuality, and Native Sovereignty*. New York: Oxford University Press, 2011.

Ríos, Gabriela Raquel. "In Ixtli In Yollotl /A (Wise) Face a (Wise) Heart: (Re)Claiming Embodied Rhetorical Traditions of Anahuac and Tawantinsuyu." PhD diss., Texas A&M University, 2011.

Romans, Bernard. *A Concise Natural History of East and West Florida*. Edited by Kathryn E. Holland Braund. Tuscaloosa: University of Alabama Press, 1999.

Roscoe, Will, ed. *Living the Spirit: A Gay American Indian Anthology*. Compiled by Gay American Indians (San Francisco, CA). New York: St. Martin's, 1988.

Royce, Charles C. *The Cherokee Nation of Indians*. Washington, DC: Smithsonian Institution Press, 1975.

Royster, Jacqueline Jones. *Traces of a Stream: Literacy and Social Change Among African American Women*. Pittsburgh, PA: University of Pittsburgh Press, 2000.

Rozema, Vicki. *Footsteps of the Cherokees: A Guide to the Eastern Homelands to the Cherokee Nation*. 2nd ed. Winston-Salem, NC: John F. Blair, 2007.

Sedgwick, Eve Kosofsky. *Epistemology of the Closet*. Berkeley: University of California Press, 1990.

Simpson, Audra. *Mohawk Interruptus: Political Life Across the Borders of Settler States*. Durham, NC: Duke University Press, 2014.

Smith, Andrea. "American Studies Without America: Native Feminisms and the Nation-State." *American Quarterly* 60, no. 2 (2008): 309–15.

———. "The Colonialism That Is Settled and the Colonialism That Never Happened." *Decolonization: Indigeneity, Education & Society* (blog). June 20, 2014. https://decolonization.wordpress.com/2014/06/20/the-colonialism-that-is -settled-and-the- colonialism-that-never-happened/.

———. *Conquest: Sexual Violence and American Indian Genocide*. Cambridge, MA: South End Press, 2005.

———. *Native Americans and the Christian Right: The Gendered Politics of Unlikely Alliances*. Durham, NC: Duke University Press, 2008.

———. "Queer Theory and Native Studies: The Heteronormativity of Settler Colonialism," *GLQ: A Journal of Lesbian and Gay Studies* 16, no. 1–2 (2010): 41–68.

Smith, Linda Tuhiwai. *Decolonizing Methodologies: Research and Indigenous Peoples*. New York: Zed Books, 1999.

Snell, Travis. "Opinion: Equality Should Prevail." *Cherokee Phoenix*, October 31, 2014.

Somerville, Siobhan B. *Queering the Color Line: Race and the Invention of Homosexuality in American Culture*. Durham, NC: Duke University Press, 2000.

Speck, Frank G., and Leonard Broom. *Cherokee Dance and Drama*. Norman: University of Oklahoma Press, 1983.

Spooner, M., and H. J. Howland. *History of American Missions to the Heathen: From Their Commencement to the Present Time*. Worcester, MA: Spooner and Howland, 1840. https://ia600402.us.archive.org/2/items/cu31924029346875/cu31924029346875.pdf.

Spurr, David. *The Rhetoric of Empire: Colonial Discourse in Journalism, Travel Writing, and Imperial Administration*. Durham, NC: Duke University Press, 1993.

Sturm, Circe. *Blood Politics: Race, Culture, and Identity in the Cherokee Nation of Oklahoma*. Berkeley: University of California Press, 2002.

Tatonetti, Lisa. "The Emergence and Importance of Queer American Indian Literatures; or, 'Help and Stories' in Thirty Years of *SAIL*." *Studies in American Indian Literatures* 19, no. 4 (2007): 143–70.

———. *The Queerness of Native American Literature*. Minneapolis: University of Minnesota Press, 2014.

———. "Visible Sexualities or Invisible Nations: Forced to Choose in *Big Eden*, *Johnny Greyeyes*, and *The Business of Fancydancing*." *GLQ: A Journal of Lesbian and Gay Studies* 16, no. 1–2 (2010): 157–81.

Taylor, Diana. *The Archive and the Repertoire: Performing Cultural Memory in the Americas*. Durham, NC: Duke University Press, 2003.

Teuton, Christopher B. *Cherokee Stories of the Turtle Island Liars' Club*. Chapel Hill: University of North Carolina Press, 2012.

Thomas, Robert K. "The Origin and Development of the Redbird Smith Movement." Master's thesis, University of Arizona, 1954.

Vizenor, Gerald. *Manifest Manners: Narratives on Postindian Survivance*. Lincoln: University of Nebraska Press, 1999.

Warrior, Robert Allen. *The People and the Word: Reading Native Nonfiction*. Minneapolis: University of Minnesota Press, 2005.

———. *Tribal Secrets: Recovering American Indian Intellectual Traditions*. Minneapolis: University of Minnesota Press, 1995.

Williams, Robert A., Jr. *Linking Arms Together: American Indian Treaty Visions of Law and Peace, 1600–1800*. Routledge: New York, 1999.

Williams, Walter L. *The Spirit and the Flesh: Sexual Diversity in American Indian Culture*. Boston: Beacon Press, 1986.

Witthoft, John. "Stone Pipes of the Historic Cherokee." *Southern Indian Studies* 1, no. 2 (1949): 43–62.

Womack, Craig S. *Drowning in Fire*. Tucson: University of Arizona Press, 2001.

———. *Red on Red: Native American Literary Separatism*. Minneapolis: University of Minnesota Press, 1999.

———. "Suspicioning: Imagining a Debate Between Those Who Get Confused and Those Who Don't, When They Read Critical Reponses to the Poems of Joy Harjo, or What's an Old-Timey Gay Boy Like Me to Do?" *GLQ: A Journal of Lesbian and Gay Studies* 16, nos. 1–2 (2010): 133–55.

Zogry, Michael J. *Anetso, the Cherokee Ball Game: At the Center of Ceremony and Identity*. Chapel Hill: University of North Carolina Press, 2010.

INDEX